Lakshadweep Development Report

सत्यमेव जयते

Planning Commission
Government of India

Lakshadweep Development Report

सत्यमेव जयते

PLANNING COMMISSION
GOVERNMENT OF INDIA
NEW DELHI

Published by

ACADEMIC FOUNDATION
NEW DELHI

Cover photographs courtesy, Lakshadweep Administration

Front cover:

- Improving peoples' access to safe drinking water through a desalination plant.
- A day's catch of tuna, the primary source of income for the people of the Dweep.
- Myriad colours of undersea life, world's best diving spot.

Back cover:

- Runway at Agatti, gateway to Lakshadweep

First Published in 2007 by
Academic Foundation
4772-73 / 23 Bharat Ram Road, (23 Ansari Road), Darya Ganj, New Delhi - 110 002 (India).
Phones : 23245001 / 02 / 03 / 04. Fax : +91-11-23245005. E-mail : academic@vsnl.com
www.academicfoundation.com

Published under arrangement with :
Planning Commission,
Government of India,
New Delhi.

Cataloging in Publication Data--DK
Courtesy: D.K. Agencies (P) Ltd. <docinfo@dkagencies.com>

Lakshadweep development report / Planning Commission, Government of India.
p. cm.
ISBN 13: 9788171886234
ISBN 10: 817188623X

1. Human services--India--Lakshadweep. 2. Infrastructure (Economics)--India--Lakshadweep. 3. Lakshadweep (India)--Economic policy. 4. Lakshadweep (India)--Economic conditions. I. India. Planning Commission.

DDC 338.954 81 22

Designed and typeset by Italics India, New Delhi
Printed and bound in India.

The Core Committee

(i)	**Dr. (Mrs.) Syeda Hameed** *Member, Planning Commission*	**Chairperson**[1]
(ii)	**Administrator** *UT Administration of Lakshadweep*	**Member**
(iii)	**Principal Adviser (IDA/TRP/Edn/SP-UT)** *Planning Commission*	**Member**[2]
(iv)	**Director** *Institute of Applied Manpower, New Delhi*	**Member**
(v)	**Director (State Plans-IDA)** *Planning Commission*	**Convenor**

---

1. Dr. D.N. Tewari, Member Planning Commission was the Chairperson till 22nd May 2004.
2. Joint Secretary (State Plans) was Member till 21st February 2006.

एम. एस. आहलुवालिया
MONTEK SINGH AHLUWALIA

सत्यमेव जयते

उपाध्यक्ष
योजना आयोग
भारत
DEPUTY CHAIRMAN
PLANNING COMMISSION
INDIA

MESSAGE

The Lakshadweep Development Report is a result of the Planning Commission's initiative to sponsor State Development Reports, with much of the work in preparation of the Reports being done by reputed national level institutes. The endeavour is to produce quality reference documents on development profiles of individual States and UTs, and the possible strategies for accelerating growth and reducing poverty and inequality.

The problems and opportunities of our island territories vary from those of the mainland and the Lakshadweep Development Report reviews Lakshadweep's experience and highlights issues critical for its development in the years ahead. The Report has been prepared keeping in view the concerns of the people and I hope its publication will stimulate debate on the growth strategies appropriate for these islands. I am sure the road map indicated in the Report will lead to a broader awareness of the critical policy issues facing Lakshadweep, and will assist the islands to move to a higher growth path and to achieve all round human and economic development.

Montek S Ahluwalia

(M.S. AHLUWALIA)

योजना भवन, संसद मार्ग, नई दिल्ली – 110001 दूरभाष : 23096677, 23096688 फैक्स : 23096699
Yojana Bhawan, Parliament Street, New Delhi : 110001 Phones: 23096677, 23096688 Fax : 23096699 E-mail : dch@yojana.nic.in

डॉ. सईदा हमीद
Dr. Syeda Hameed

सत्यमेव जयते

सदस्य
योजना आयोग
योजना भवन
नई दिल्ली–110 001
MEMBER
PLANNING COMMISSION
YOJANA BHAWAN
NEW DELHI-110 001

FOREWORD

In the Tenth Plan, the Planning Commission had initiated the preparation of State Development Reports (SDRs) in coordination with and support of State Governments and Union Territory Administrations. These reports are prepared by reputed national level institutions, aimed at taking stock of the affairs in important sectors, identifying critical gaps and suggesting the road ahead.

The Lakshadweep Development Report is a well researched document which analyses the entire range of development issues faced by our island territory in the Arabian Sea. It has been prepared by the Institute of Applied Manpower Research (IAMR), Indian Council of Agricultural Research (ICAR) and Indian Council for Forestry Research & Education (ICFRE) after taking account of the views of the local people and experts at two seminars held in Kavaratti and Delhi.

The Report contains useful data on various sectors and issues which will be useful to policy planners, decision makers, NGOs and those who are concerned with achieving a better quality of life for the people of Lakshadweep.

I am grateful to Shri P.M. Sayeed, Hon'ble Minister of Power for his directions and guidance in the preparation of the SDR. I would like to place on record Planning Commission's appreciation for the services rendered towards the preparation of the Report by Dr. H. Ramachandran, Dr. Sudhir Krishna, Dr. K.D. Saxena and Ms. Madhu Srivastava of the IAMR; Shri R.P.S. Katwal and Shri Mudit Kumar Singh of ICFRE, Shri J.S. Samra of ICAR; Shri K.S. Mehra and Shri Parimal Rai, Administrators, Lakshadweep other serving and retired officials of Lakshadweep Administration. I also thank Dr. P.P. Koya, Hon'ble Member of Parliament, representatives of the District Panchayat and Dweep Panchayats and people of the Lakshadweep for their valuable inputs and suggestions.

Syeda Hameed

(SYEDA HAMEED)

दूरभाष : 23096570 फैक्स : 23096571
Telephone: 23096570 Fax : 23096571, E-mail: s.hameed@yojana.nic.in

Contents

...Contd. ...

List of Tables and Annexures

Tables

Annexures

Introduction

The social and economic development of small islands is beset with a set of challenges that are quite unique. The idyllic geography and climate of such islands have made many of these islands haven of tourism, some of the examples being the Seychelles, Mauritius, Fiji, Papua New Guinea, Maldives, Andamans, Lakshadweep and Singapore. However, these regions face serious threats as well from various sources. Their fragile ecology does not go smoothly with large influx of visitors. The smallness of these regions makes the cost of provision of administrative services and social-economic infrastructure too high, due to diseconomies of scale. These small island economies (or, SIEs) are also facing, in general, depletion of the natural resources. Tourism, which has been a mainstay for the economic sustenance of the SIEs, is vulnerable to the vagaries of natural climate as well as to the law and order situation prevailing in the neighbouring regions.

SIEs could be classified into sovereign independent countries such as Singapore, Mauritius, Maldives or Seychelles and into islands that are part of a mainland country, such as Hawaii, Tasmania, Lakshadweep, or Andamans. There is a case to examine if these two categories of SIEs face the same kind and level of vulnerability and, if so, do they respond to the situation differentially and with what results. While most of the independent island countries, notably Singapore, Seychelles, Maldives and Mauritius, have recorded tremendous growth, the islands attached to mainland countries have turned out to be a 'poorer cousin'. Therefore, on the face of it, one can draw some conclusion. But then, there are examples of the Hawaii or Tasmania that draw considerable strength from the economy of their parent country.

Seen in the global context as an SIE, Lakshadweep offers an interesting case study. It is neighbour to an independent but only relatively larger SIE country, Maldives, that comprises as many as 1,200 small and tiny coral islands, of which only one in six are inhabited, covering in all 298 square kilometres (sq km) of area and having a population of about 3,00,000. Thus, in terms of area and population, Maldives is six times as large as Lakshadweep. However, the difference in the economies appears to be fairly large and Maldives seems to offer hints for the growth and development of Lakshadweep.

Despite its smallness in terms of geographical landmass, Lakshadweep has a large territorial water (20,000 sq km) and Exclusive Economic Zone (4 lakh sq km), which makes it strategically very important for the country. The flora and fauna of Lakshadweep have survived the vagaries of times and nature including the tsunami of the 26th December, 2004.

While tourism appears to be a very important growth sector for Lakshadweep, there are certain critical in-house issues that need equal, if not greater, attention. These include public health, in terms of access to safe drinking water and disposal of sewage, medical care and employment opportunities. While agriculture remains the predominant land based economic activity for the island population and agriculture itself very largely means coconut cultivation. The yield in terms of nuts per tree and per hectare is very high, more than double the all-India average. Yet, coconut alone is unable to provide optimal returns from the land. The delicate ecology of these islands discourages large-scale use of chemical fertilisers. The strategy for enhancing the returns from agriculture, therefore, has to keep such constraints and expectations in view.

As the exploitable economic zone of Lakshadweep exceeds its landmass manifolds, the development strategy for it would necessarily need to focus on the marine aquatic resources. There are many marine aquatic resources, ranging from fishes to the sea-grass, available in large quantities awaiting potential to be exploited safely.

Analysis of the development prospects for Lakshadweep leads inevitably to the issue of nature and nature tourism. The richness and uniqueness of the flora and fauna of these islands offer a fascinating scope for nature tourism. However, while growth of tourism is desirable, but it needs to be coupled with preservation of the ecology and environment of this fragile zone.

The State Development Report on Lakshadweep has been prepared with the painstaking contributions from a set of carefully identified institutions and individuals. The institutions directly involved in preparing the initial draft chapters were the Central Marine Fisheries Research Institute, Kochi, Indian Council of Agricultural Research, New Delhi, Indian Council of Forestry Research and Education, Dehradun, Institute of Forest Genetics and Tree Breeding, Coimbatore, National Institute of Ocean Technology, Chennai, the Ministry of Non-Conventional Energy Sources and the Department of Ocean Development of the Government of India. The Lakshadweep Administration also contributed for specific chapters, besides providing valuable inputs and help to all other institutions. Their individual contributions were deliberated in a series of meetings with all the stakeholders, experts and other interested groups, which greatly helped in finalising the report. A lot of credit for the timely completion of this task would go also to the Planning Commission, in particular to Dr. Syeda Hameed, Member, Dr. Rajan Katoch, Joint Secretary and Shri Rajat Sachar, Director, who actively participated in this effort at various stages.

The State Development Report of Lakshadweep was launched by IAMR under Professor H. Ramachandran, the then Director IAMR, other study team members were Smt. Madhu Srivastava, Head (Employment and Unemployment Studies Unit), Shri Sant Lal Arora, Senior Research Officer, Shri I.C. Awasthi, Senior Research Officer, Shri U.S. Bhandari, Senior Research Officer, Shri S.K. Yadav, Senior Research Officer and Shri J.S. Chauhan, Research Associate. Excellent secretarial support was provided by Smt. Prem Maddan, Smt. Urmila Chakravarti and Shri Devendra P. Kohad. Credit also goes to Shri K.B. Saxena, Shri Sudhir Krishna and Shri S.R. Shukla, Consultants, IAMR for successfully completion of the project report.

The report consists of seven chapters, commencing with a review of the developmental framework for Lakshadweep. The subsequent chapters deal with economic issues, infrastructure, human development, biodiversity and environment protection, and governance issues.

Chapter 1

Development Paradigm

Introduction

A State Development Report is not a routine exercise of investments to be made and the achievements to be realised in terms of economic output and social attainments. Nor is it intended to be a narrative of sectoral schemes and programmes and their progressive expansion to cover the gaps. The report is essentially intended to be a vision of development goals which the society wishes to pursue and the direction in which various sectors of the economy should proceed to subserve them, anticipated externalities that may emerge in the process and the manner in which they would be dealt with. This vision is conceptually articulated in terms of what may be called the 'paradigm' of development. The strategy for development to be adopted for Lakshadweep Islands must, of necessity, spell out this paradigm before the sectoral components of the economy are discussed and their future growth outlined. Otherwise, the growth process in various parts may fall apart and/or work at cross purposes throwing up dissonance and even conflicts between what people had expected as its outcome and what it ended up achieving. This exercise needs to be squarely spelt out so that crucial decisions are taken on pursuable options with conscious realisation of the positive impact it will create along with the externalities to be faced. This is important in respect of Lakshadweep UT which is a group of small islands with a limited resource base and far removed from the mainland. The islands are inhabited by tradition bound and progressive minded people but having moderate standard of living and level of social amenities.

'Development' has become the most sought-after goal of all societies everywhere, influenced undoubtedly by the spread of ideas, shrinking of physical distances, breaking of cultural barriers, development of technology, and so on. Therefore, in all communities except those rare ones which have not come into contact with 'civilisation' at all, there is a groundswell of expectation in terms of how they wish their lives to be shaped, what they intend to preserve and what changes they are prepared to accept. The accommodation of this demand within the framework of the accepted overall goals available and mobilisable resources and social and cultural compatibility with the operational processes is what would constitute the essence of 'development'. But there is little unanimity in the development discourse on what really constitutes 'development'. This is because development is not a neutral, value free process with an easily acceptable consensus; it is a site of contested ideas and goals. It is, therefore, a politically driven effort with certain embedded values which determines not only what should be achieved but also how this is to be achieved. This is the reason why its various models have been articulated and practised.

A model of development for this reason cannot also be easily transplanted on any soil since it is so essentially conditioned not merely by the physical factors of production but also its social determinants—the organisation of society and polity, the superstructure of culture and values. Therefore, the dynamics of a development pattern may produce varied outcomes in different settings and even, within a single social entity, the development process may affect various social groups differently. This explains why a consensus is usually difficult to come by among people pursuing different and even conflicting interests. They are most likely to evaluate outcomes of a suggested pattern in terms of what they may possibly gain and what they may end up losing. Thus, a development process in any social setting may produce some unevenness, differentiation and even conflict. This outcome would be much sharper and deeper in societies which are already differentiated in terms of social, economic and political power. But even in a relatively more homogenous society, the process may end up by creating differentiation which may not have existed earlier. This aspect of change, therefore, may produce social stress and even tension which can ultimately affect the existing social stability and the direction of development itself. The capacity to manage/minimise these adverse impacts through appropriate trade-offs will, therefore, constitute an essential condition which will define the nature and process of development to be pursued.

Even where the goals of development are broadly accepted by all sections of society, their operationalisation may create *inter se* conflicts; the promotion of one goal may hurt the realisation of the other. This happens much too often in the development process, more sharply in some societies and less so in case of others. However, the capacity to harmonise this conflict so as to evolve an inclusive model is not uniform in all societies and, therefore, the overall impact it produces may be more painful in some than in others. The onus of deciding how much conflict can be absorbed and what degree of destabilisation can be tolerated will fall on the group which faces the brunt of adverse impact. Development, therefore, is a matter of choices. Sometimes, achievement of a particular goal may have to be sacrificed in order that the achievement of other goal/goals may be realised. This will depend on the relative weight placed on individual goals guided by the larger perception of what are considered to be the overriding imperatives. The exercise of choice in this matter will also be conditioned by the relative strength of different social groups in the power structure of the decision making process.

Development choices have to be made not only with reference to incompatibilities between the pursuit of different goals and the social structure, cultural values and overall ethos of the people but also externalities thrown up in relation to the local environment and ecology which also impinge upon the lives of the people vitally. Here the choices may be more difficult in some geographical locations where imbalances produced by the development process can potentially threaten the very survival of people. In such a situation the overriding prioritisation in respect of ecological protection would critically determine the nature and contours of development options and their processes and considerably limit their range.

Development is pursued with reference to the physical and human resource endowment of a territory. The physical resources in conventional economics are identified as land inclusive of water and vegetation, labour, capital and technology though in a highly developed economy, some of these factors can be transcended. While capital, labour and technology can be imported from outside, land remains a fixed factor and, therefore, the carrying capacity of the land both in terms of people inhabiting it and economic activities that can be pursued are limited to these factors. In the situation of an island territory, the sea and the marine resources subsisting on it are an additional resource and compensate for the lack of land to some extent. It also has the advantage that resources are replenishable unlike minerals or fossil fuels and if exploited with prudence can provide the much needed flexibility to accommodate a higher level of growth without undue worry about their exhaustion in the near future. But this nonetheless underlines a very important condition of development, namely, its sustainability. The notion of sustainability implies that limits needs to be drawn on the exploitation of resources in order that the survival of future generations is not threatened and development activities are intimately linked to and conditioned by the ecology. The adverse effect of development is visible in different islands from the lagoons getting polluted and losing its pristine beauty, loss of marine biodiversity, defacement of the beaches caused by the accumulation of sea weeds, etc. Needless to say, that this will also involve choices and at times hard decisions on what should be sacrificed and what can be pursued and within what limits.

Development substantially involves the pursuit of economic activities concerned with the creation of wealth. But it also has important social dimensions which influence the pattern of their distribution and utilisation. Even in respect of desired goals already agreed upon, the choices made from the available options can nowhere be pursued in an unrestrained manner because the resources required for this purpose are scarce. This consideration determines the pattern of allocating resources in a manner that maximises the gains among competing demands and satisfaction among the largest number of people. In this process of social accounting, some highly desirable options may have to be avoided, postponed or discarded because they involve a larger resource input with lesser output in terms of satisfaction. Therefore, the paradigm of development also requires a proper 'fit' between the cost of pursuing a measure, a programme or a facility and the quantum of social benefit that is likely to accrue from it. This calculus may also include a judgment on whether unfavourable equation between costs and benefits at the time of decision making can be turned into a favourable one in the foreseeable future so that, overall, the decision may be regarded as prudent and desirable. The decision making involved will no doubt be guided as much by the assessment of future costs and benefits but also by the evaluation of past experience of various programmes/investments or in other words, the efficiency of investment. However, this efficiency may not always constitute an overriding concern in allocation of resources. Distributive considerations may substantially redefine the efficiency factor. But even in such a situation benefits in terms of a more inclusive development model from investment should nonetheless be produced to justify taking recourse to this option.

The issues discussed in the preceding paragraphs have been brought out in some detail because these are relevant to the situation of Lakshadweep Islands and extremely germane to the articulation of the development paradigm that may be pursued for it. Since the decisions in respect of these complex matters may not be easy nor always based on social consensus, it is essential that they are taken by the affected community fully conscious of the various pros and cons of each measure. This will essentially imply involvement of the local community with widest participation in the decision making process. Such a democratic structure of decision making will, however, require the local community to be equipped with necessary information including the demystified substantive technical knowledge on the kind of choices available and how they could impact them. The finesse and the vigour with which this effort is pursued will alone determine the paradigm of development which is people-centred—a model where development is pursued for the people and not people for development.

Goals of Development

The opportunity available of interaction with local *panchayat* leaders, officials in administration, experts and others provided some indication of what kind of expectations people have from a development model to be pursued in Lakshadweep. The paradigm of development in their perception can perhaps focus on the following objectives:

- Raising the living standard of people: (i) through enhancement of income, and (ii) increasing employment opportunities for youth, particularly the educated youth.
- Enhancing the quality of life, particularly in respect of improving drinking water supply, primary and secondary healthcare, sanitation amenities and providing swift inter-island and islands-mainland connectivity.
- Promoting small family norm.
- Ecological protection.
- Preserving the existing social structure, vibrant community life and cultural values.
- Preventing migration from the mainland.
- Checking growth of social and economic inequalities, both inter-island and intra-island.
- Strengthening democratic decision making with widest level of participation.
- Taking up sustainable development programmes which are both efficient and generate largest satisfaction, do not create too much dependency and are within the capability of the community to manage.

While these development goals individually and together are unexceptionable, the pursuit of each individual goal may not be in harmony with others and may generate some degree of dissonance or conflict. Therefore, it will be necessary to assign some values and weight to each goal with a view to determining *inter se* prioritisation. This will determine which of them may take precedence over others and to what extent, where there are some externalities and conflicts involved. The idea is not to forgo the goal or to reduce its importance but to decide upon the mechanism of dealing with externalities. The issue obviously has never been placed before the people to take a view in this regard. But it is not merely desirable but also essential that people through widest participation should take a vital decision in the matter. The following prioritisation should be considered:

Ecological protection should constitute the top priority for the island people since it is the basic condition for their survival and growth. The ecology of the island is their greatest asset and the brand for any future growth and, therefore, it is something which should not be tampered with even for the sake of other goals. Similarly, the Island society also shares the happy situation of a relatively more egalitarian social structure with a great deal of harmony, community life and a social milieu of cooperation among people—something rarely seen in the mainland. This is their greatest strength which has enabled them to face life and many odds, both natural and man-made, with equanimity. The process of development should not tinker with this and destabilise their lives, create competition which strikes at the root of fellow-feeling. Checking migration should constitute a part of this design. The community is also very conscious of it and extremely zealous of protecting their culture and moral values which have been the bedrock of their existence. They are strong in their feeling that the pattern of development should not destroy it.

The people's representatives articulated that the development programmes should be conceived, designed and agreed upon only after widest possible consultation with them. This will help in ensuring that the local populace becomes active participants rather than passive recipients in the development process. Though several forums for people's participation in policy and programme formulation such as Home Minister's Advisory Council (HMAC), Administrator's Advisory Council (AAC), etc. have been existing even before the creation of two-tiered *panchayati* structure in 1996, there is ample scope for broad-basing and deepening it. This will help in better conceptualisation and implementation of many programmes, preventing wastage of large resources and adverse social effects. The development experience has shown that whenever community is taken into confidence before embarking upon anything new in the future helps in greater success and accountability. Even an 'authority' conscious bureaucracy should promote such a decision making process simply because the consequences of many decisions may hurt specific interests of some segments of the community. If decisions are taken in such matters by the community after achieving a consensus through transparent discussion, the bureaucracy would be absolved of any blame and greater cooperation will also be forthcoming. On the part of the community, such decisions will expose them to the externalities involved in various decisions and the kind of trade-offs in case of social costs and benefits. This pattern will also have the added advantage that the community would be deeply conscious of the extent to which it can possibly manage the consequences of certain development actions and what would not be acceptable to it.

The next priority should go to enhance the quality of life, particularly in two specific social sectors—supply of drinking water, sanitation (waste disposal) and arranging for convenient inter-island connectivity as well as reasonable connectivity between the islands and the mainland. The islanders have by all-India standards a reasonable though modest quality of life in other respects. They get subsidised food items, their housing stock assures reasonable safety and a healthy life. They have access to local productive resources for their livelihood and a reasonable level of subsistence. They also have free access to education and health and the available facilities are quite good. But drinking water is scarce as there are no durable underground water sources to tap. Rainwater is the only source of safe and potable water. Similarly, lack of transport between islands and with the mainland creates a feeling of helplessness in attending to emergency situations. A properly designed sanitation system with eco-friendly waste disposal arrangements given the terrain and topography is also extremely necessary to create a healthy life. With the provision of these three facilities, the people of the islands should boast of a much better quality of life than people anywhere else in India.

Most pressing though it is, the goal of raising the standard of living of people should be conceived in the above framework notwithstanding the fact that at 13.2 per cent the unemployment level is very high for such a small population. This will involve three segments of the population, one dealing with the local educated youth whose aspiration levels are soaring but with little opportunity for absorbing them in a gainful vocation in the islands. On the other hand, the level of their skills does not prepare them to compete for jobs outside the islands nor even to be engaged in ongoing development activities within them. Till recently, the expansion of opportunity in government employment provided for absorption but there is no scope for any incremental avenues here. The limited opportunities for creating skill-based employment in the islands will depend upon the kind of projects that are taken up either in the private sector or oriented towards self-employment. It is, therefore, an area of extreme concern and priority which has been articulated by the administration, the local people as well as by academics. The other aspect of this problem involves the segment of population which is already engaged in various vocations based on traditional skills or existing asset profile but whose levels of income are low while needs and aspirations are increasing. The development programme must focus on how this segment can be targeted for income enhancement through various inputs and by widening the opportunities for income generation. The third category involves people who are unskilled and would need avenues of employment. This is the group for whom it should be possible to generate livelihood opportunities on the islands through various programmes but it would be predominantly in the self-employment category.

None of these goals individually can be pursued as 'stand alone' since each of them in the process of operation would be riddled with conflicts with one or more other goals. This would limit the choices to be made between the goals and where conflicting goals have to be pursued, mechanisms will have to be put in place to neutralise the externalities.

Constraints and Strengths

Every unit of planning and development has its strong points and some constraining factors. Lakshadweep is no exception. In fact, it has far greater constraints than units of planning in the mainland. These constraints determine as well as limit the choices to be made for achieving the goals set upon. Foremost among these is the limited resource base though the islands are spread over a very large area surrounded by sea. Here, the landmass covers only 32 sq km of which the inhabited part is confined to 26.32 sq km. The area available for any agricultural activity is only 2,810 hectares, almost entirely consisting of coconut plantations. Even this area has dwindled owing to settlements, infrastructure and other development activities. Paucity of land, therefore, is a great limiting factor in taking up many activities which could generate resources, employment and build infrastructure. The nature of the land, soil profile and other features also preclude the possibility of cereal cultivation and even of horticulture of any significance which is most suited for coconut plantations. There are no forests either except for some bushes and even the local floral species are very few. Water scarcity is an even greater constraining factor along with lack of water retention capacity of the soil because it clearly constrains the possibility of growing any other crop. Fresh water resources of a durable nature are not available, thus affecting not only agricultural activity but also human life. Lack of safe drinking water all through the year is a source of several health related problems.

The pressure of population on the islands has been on the rise to the extent that average density per kilometre in many places is comparable to the Kerala coast. This is a matter of serious concern as it threatens the carrying capacity of the islands. This is one of the reasons why people from outside are not allowed to settle in the islands (under 1963 Regulation). Moreover, even visitors need entry permit to come to the Lakshadweep islands. Presently, the non-indigenous population coming from mainland includes government employees and labour force (who come on fixed work permit) only.

The island topography is generally flat, however there are few elevated patches in the islands of Minicoy, Kavaratti, Andrott, Amini, etc. Almost all the islands are located a few metres above the mean sea level. Their common features include a storm beach on the eastern rim, the coral sand plain to the west and wide boulder strewn inter-tidal space on the western side as also a shallow lagoon. This makes it particularly vulnerable to natural disasters, particularly during monsoons. The gales are a potential threat not only to life and property but also to the coral reef formation. The terrain also creates a drainage problem since no natural gravity is available. This causes severe problems with regard to sanitation and waste disposal. The existing sanitation practices using the sea fringe on the lagoon side constitute a threat to the health of the people as well as to the marine life.

Access to free education and fairly spread out educational infrastructure has created a high percentage of literacy in the islands. This has raised the level of aspirations of the youth in terms of the nature of job and the level of remuneration. The great constraining factor is that the potentialities of the educated youth are not fully utilised in cultivation or fishing or such other activities which involve manual work. They seek salaried white collared jobs. In the earlier years of development, expansion of government employment satisfied this urge. But this avenue is not available any more since the level of establishment expenditure in the island administration and the ratio of public servants to the population is pretty high. Within the islands, the avenues for providing high-end salaried jobs do not exist even outside government employment. Various other options for exploiting the growth potential of the island territory may not throw up job opportunities either. Due to limited opportunities and infrastructural support, youth are not able to take up self-employment activities, business or trade at a large-scale. Their level of skills by and large does not equip them for competing for jobs in the mainland.

People, in general, have been exposed to a relatively isolated life and a highly protected and dependent form of development. They have not been exposed to the vagaries of the market. Moreover due to small size of domestic market and geographical isolation, the population, in general, and youth, in particular, lack entrepreneurship and risk taking capacity. A slight exception in this regard may be people who are employed in the commercial merchant navy from Minicoy. Even in respect of these, while their tastes, needs and consumer behaviour may have been influenced by the larger exposure to the outside world, their engagement in salaried jobs does not prepare them for any entrepreneurial activity. Their life in the island also continues to be very traditional. The people, of course, have some traditional skills related entirely to their day-to-day existence, such as fishing, coconut cultivation, boat construction and value added activities from fishing and coconut produce, etc. The industrial activities have so far been confined to cottage industries, such as coir, rope making, handicrafts, shell work, carpentry, boat building and processing of coconut into various edible products. But the youth are not acquiring these skills either. Despite the limited resource base of land, water and forest, the islands share a favourable feature of huge territorial waters extending over 20,000 sq km and an exclusive economic zone stretching over 4,00,000 sq km, with a rich marine life. In fact, much of this area remains un-penetrated and unexploited owing to the low level of technology utilised by the local people in fishing and problems relating to disposal of produce. Similarly, for meeting scarcity of drinking water, seawater can be turned into sweet water after desalination. But, notwithstanding the availability of technology for this purpose, this option has other problems such as cost and sustainability. The technological options for extraction of natural resources, such as fish and other marine resources, also throw up problems of storage, transportation and marketing and the costs and benefits of new schemes. The lime rich coral base can be industrially exploited for cement making but would pose a severe threat to the existing marine ecology and cause irreparable damage to coral reefs as demonstrated in the mainland coast of North Saurashtra. Similar problems are associated with exploitation of other abiotic marine resources, such as low-grade phosphate and coral sands of the lagoon.

Connectivity poses a very severe problem, both for the quality of life and for marketing of local produce in the islands. Owing to the distance between the island and the mainland and even among the islands themselves, the cost of transportation is high, making it inviable for many commercial activities. Inter-island connectivity too is not without its share of difficulties, the foremost being lack of scope for berthing within the lagoons. This results in anchorage of vessels outside the reefs in the open. The building of jetties would involve deepening of navigable boats channel at the lagoon entrances. This would entail blasting of coral beds which would damage the living coral and the reefs. Even otherwise, during monsoons and tidal waves, it is problematic to keep the channel in the lagoon navigable. So, for the last few years no new construction of jetties, deepening of lagoons, widening of channels is being carried out in lagoon side (western coast). Instead administration is going for construction of jetties in the open seaside (eastern coast). Also, the traditional practices of community participation in reef/channel cleaning (called as *Narimagu Nalang* in Minicoy island) is being promoted.

Development activities taken up since Independence with considerable investment by the government not only highlighted some of the constraints referred to above but have also been exposed to several other constraints, such as small size of the market and inadequate economies of scale, small land area, lack of expertise, inadequate raw material base for any viable processing activity and ecological problems. To this are added problems of inadequate planning and lack of rigour in project appraisal. This is evident from the failure of several projects to attain their intended levels of output or the threshold of viability. The Desiccated Coconut Powder Unit at Kadmat with a capacity of producing 15 MT per month or 500 kg every day remains grossly underutilised with average production at 17 per cent of the installed capacity. Even when the market for this product is reasonably assured, the coconut oil produced from dried nuts is insufficient even to meet the local demand. Similar is the problem with coconut water extracted after breaking the coconut before it is desiccated. Its production of 20–25 litres per day is too low for any organised supply. The coconut water vinegar generation unit is also inviable owing to low quantity of water available to the factory. Insufficient raw material and low productivity level have also restricted the production of coconut powder in flake form. Most of the coconut available is marketed unprocessed because of the price support mechanism, leading to waste of established industrial infrastructure and investment. The coconut milk plant at Andrott for supplying coconut milk to Cochin has also run into difficulties because of high cost of transportation, lack of quality assurance and inviability in cost terms. This plant will remain underutilised owing to lack of raw material.

High cost of transportation for any produce to be marketed in the mainland or possibly to other countries poses the greatest problem. In fact, at present, a 90 per cent transport subsidy is provided for transportation of raw materials and finished products between the mainland and the islands. The low returns compel people to demand for maintaining the present subsidy level and for increasing it to 100 per cent. This also highlights the non-viability of any manufacturing processing and commercial activity.

The other constraint and more serious for the expansion of production and diversification lies in the potential threat to the environment. This has already been highlighted in various experiments taken up by the administration in this direction. For example, in the agricultural sector, banana cultivation initiated some time back had to be discontinued owing to the heavy evapo-transpiration rate and lack of sweet water for nurturing it; and livestock rearing for milk or meat is difficult because of non-availability of grass, fodder and water. The adverse environmental impact of livestock activities has also been affirmed by studies carried out by the Island Development Authority. Even poultry development is riddled with problems of waste disposal besides involving more serious ones relating to marketing support, development infrastructure, laboratory for certification of health of birds and products and cost and availability of feed. However, to meet the balanced essential dietary needs of the local populace stall-fed small units of cows and goats and poultry should be promoted by the government. In the industrial sector, the environmental constraints involved in jetty construction and construction of a cement plant have already been referred to which also apply to any attempt at construction of tourist huts on stilts in lagoons.

High cost of manufacturing, processing and value addition, in addition to transportation, makes any economic activity commercially inviable if it is meant for outside the islands. As it is, even the marketing of unprocessed *copra* is unremunerative to the local people without the huge transport subsidy and price support mechanism. This is also true of development infrastructure projects for improving the quality of life. For example, at present, electricity is supplied to the local people through diesel generation, the cost of which is Rs. 8.86 per unit while the recovery is only Rs. 3.50 per unit. The proposed alternative source of energy, the Biomass Gasifier Plant, has already suffered because of inadequate raw material supply. The desalination plant working in Agatti shows that the cost of processing is prohibitive and it is, therefore, not viable to replicate it. The desired alternative is to collect and store rainwater overground. But this possibility is also limited to the rainy season and further constrained owing to paucity of land for such storage.

Technology and marketing also pose severe constraints. This is nowhere reflected more sharply than in exploiting fishery resources. Fishing activity is largely confined to a single species—skipjack tuna. Its volume and productivity is restricted by the technology used in catching fish and its storage and transport. This activity is carried out by pole line-fishing. Even with the distribution of mechanised tuna pole and line-fishing boats of 25 ft. and 30 ft. size at subsidised cost, only 5,000 fishermen are directly involved. It would require much larger number of vessels and fishermen to achieve the fishing potential of the area through the present level of technology used by the poor local fisherman. The existing number of vessels is also too small. These cannot be increased as the fisheries sector faces an acute shortage of skilled manpower. The lack of shore-based infrastructure facility, such as ice plant, tunnel freezers, cold storages and means of transportation required for multi-day fishing constrains the possibility of using high technology, skilled manpower and extracting large volume of the catch. At present, fishermen go for fishing in the early hours and come back by the evening after they have exhausted their food, water and fuel stock. Yet, the already established ice plant in Agatti, two tunnel freezers in Chetlat and Agatti and five cold storages in Agatti, Kavaratti, Andrott and Chetlat are not being optimally used in view of the limited fish landing. The Tuna canning factory in Minicoy for producing high quality of tuna cans is not viable on account of the high cost of tin, heavy taxation on tin cans and stiff competition from cheap imported cans. Deep-sea fishing for yellow fin tuna for export requires capital-intensive technology, a huge working capital and large ships for storage and a larger fleet for operation. This obviously cannot be undertaken by individual fishermen. The experimental measure undertaken by the administration for overcoming these difficulties by borrowing monofilament technology from a Japanese company, modifying an existing vessel, and using Australian equipment for extracting fish stock for export purposes also faced a setback as a part of the catch could not be exported owing to non-availability of air space. There are other problems too associated with the use of this sophisticated technology. These problems relate to attracting private capital for investment and marketing which would produce several externalities. The processing of skipjack tuna into *masmeen* for export too has experienced marketing problems. Its demand has decreased owing to a changed life style where fresh fish is preferred over canned/dried. The low prices have affected the income levels of fishermen while the quality level of production has made this product unacceptable in the international niche market. The export of frozen skipjack tuna is also constrained by technology of infrastructure. The fishing grounds are far away from the homeland of fishermen. With their traditional small boats, they cannot return to their homes owing to inadequate food, drinking water and fuel. There is no landfall on the way. This restricts the number of active fishing days and raises the cost of collection. Even here, the proposal to build infrastructure for creating such a resting place in Beliyapani is fraught with environmental risk of damage to the coral reefs. At present, a huge subsidy is being provided by the Government of India for collecting the fish catch from a barge-mounted infrastructure with a fish storage system in Beliyapani for export purposes. The technology and marketing problems make it difficult to increase the size of vessels for fishing and for creating infrastructure for fish landing, berthing and outfitting of vessels. The bigger vessels, even if available, cannot operate in small islands. A more feasible option is to have a collector vessel which can provide food, drinking water and fuel to the boats as well as collect larger fish. Even if the economics and the operational feasibility of this arrangement turn out to be favourable, the augmentation of shore-based infrastructure facilities is difficult because of insufficient land near the jetties and the adverse impact on the livelihood of people if their lands are acquired.

The administration is also toying with the idea of exporting ornamental fish by setting up a hatchery to rear them. The broodstock of selected species will be caught from the sea, acclimatised in separate tanks and transferred to broodstock tanks for laying eggs. These eggs will then be removed to a hatching tank. Hatching larvae would be fed on the live feed. After growth, these will be packed in sterilised water and airlifted to various destinations. Such sophisticated proposals, though very attractive in the project documents, are seriously limited by several factors, not the least being skilled manpower, quality assurance, infrastructure, safe transportation, viability and management capacity. None of them at present are assured in respect of the island situation.

The other factor to be taken note of is with regard to the nature of skills available and the facilities created for skill development. As per the administration's own admission, the existing training infrastructure in the islands remains grossly underutilised. It suffers from lack of demand, the skilled manpower trained by it cannot be absorbed. The mismatch would be even sharper if high levels of technology are imported into various operations. The difficulty also lies in creating facilities for hi-tech skill development in the islands since the cost of providing such skills would be very high, base level education unsuited and utilisation would be inadequate. Quality would also suffer because of the reluctance of highly professional trainers to come to the island. In any case, even a revamped skill development infrastructure would not assure absorption of trained manpower in salaried employment in the islands and such persons would face stiff competition from better trained persons in the mainland.

Given the conditions of Lakshadweep, people lack avenues for generating adequate resources for their own development activities. However, concerted efforts need to be made to generate adequate resources for the purpose. By virtue of being a very strategic location and possessing a limited resource base for economic growth, the development of this territory has been entirely financed by budgetary support from the Central Government. Therefore, there has been no dearth of resources for investment. But this has led to a lot of inefficient investment with inadequate planning and lack of rigour in project appraisal. This is nowhere more evident than in the collapse of several high cost processing activities which suffer from inefficient feedstock and viability. This could have been easily foreseen. Therefore, availability of inadequate raw material, high cost of manufacturing/production, low levels of productivity, high levels of volatility in the market, infrastructure constraints, etc. severely circumscribe options for pursuing a path of development which can achieve the goals set out. When these factors are considered, in addition to the externalities involved in pursuing various options and conflicts *inter se* between various goals set out, it is evident that only a development path with very modest goals can be recommended and caution is advised in this regard, so as not to raise very high expectations.

While the island territory is lacking in many ways which, no doubt, are formidable given the resource development potential, the islands have some strong points as well. These strong points do not, however, neutralise the constraints. But they do help in working out a more consensual path of development with a least conflict-ridden trajectory. Among the strong points are the social determinants of development, foremost among which are a relatively egalitarian society which despite its differentiation, is reasonably homogeneous unlike most mainland societies. The level of awareness of people is high and they are very eager to be involved in the process of decision making. If all the necessary information is placed before them, they are confident of deciding, among available options, the one that suits them and would also be prepared to deal with the consequences emerging from its externalities, if any. This kind of social situation is not readily found in the mainland societies.

The island situation is also favourable because it is not vulnerable to food insecurity, malnutrition, acute poverty, severe exploitation and social disharmony. Nor does it have serious levels of inequality as regards assets, income, expenditure, social status and political power though there is a certain level of differentiation both intra-island and inter-island. This creates a better climate for initiating development programme with a consensus since the perception about their cost and benefits may not sharply vary or be coloured with serious apprehensions. Even where differences exist, amicable arrangement for trade-off may not be difficult to work out.

No studies are available about the distribution effects of various development programmes. It is, therefore, difficult to say whether the traditional inequalities emerging from the social and agrarian structure prior to Independence have been bridged or reinforced or even aggravated by the development process. The agrarian reforms have certainly sought to bridge some of these inequalities by empowering all the people with rights over productive assets. The various development programmes have favourably shaped social relations and the power structure. The experience in respect of mainland societies by and large has been that development programmes have been extremely skewed in conferring benefits, bypassing a large section of very poor people. In the islands, subsidised food and social amenities have ensured a much greater level of equality than would have been otherwise possible. This also makes for better participation in any development programme. It would also be possible to ensure that benefits are reasonably distributed amongst the population as per their needs if a proper mechanism is in place.

The interaction with people provides the assurance that the local community is not very ambitious in placing development demands since the externalities involved in pursuing various development programmes are of equal concern to them. This implies that if they are involved in the decision making, it should be possible to work out a more modest development model provided various pros and cons of each proposal are placed before them. This would, however, require that among other things, various technological options in exploiting resources and building up infrastructure are demystified for their understanding. This understanding is reinforced by the fact that people have been very critical about several investments in past development programmes which have failed to deliver.

The people are strongly committed to maintaining their social solidarity, culture and moral values. This provides great strength to decision makers because this concern will help limit the options to be pursued if the balance sheet of their possible impact is made known to them. While certain development proposals may involve quick economic growth and prosperity for some, they are likely to hurt the social solidarity as well as cultural values. This has been the experience with the development process elsewhere too. In any other society, given the sharp social divide, a consensus about options would be difficult to achieve. Here it may be possible to arrive at it without serious acrimony. This is a very positive factor.

The island society is crime free with virtually no law and order problem. There is a low level of indebtedness since people out of religious consideration do not borrow or lend money for usury. They do, however, help each other in need as a social gesture. In fact, such transactions of credit and financial help are carried out without any interest dimension though lately institutional finance has entered into the domain. People by and large also have the practice of settling issues among themselves rather than taking recourse to the law though litigation in respect of land etc., does take place. This indicates that the level of aspirations is also influenced by their societal ethos. Some change is, however, taking place particularly among the youth which is increasingly influenced by the entertainment culture flowing through the electronic media, with regard to their aspirations as well as the commitment to the social norms and cultural values. The community leaders also complain of their alienation and admit their loss of hold over them.

The status of women in the island society is a very positive aspect of development notwithstanding the relative conservatism usually associated with Islamic societies elsewhere. Women enjoy freedom from economic dependence on the husband as the *Tharwad* (ancestral) property under the personal law descends through the female line. The manager of the *Tharwad* property, the eldest male member of the family, has no right to alienate or sell any portion of it. This implies that the son, wife and children of the manager are not entitled to any share from it. The husband is also obliged to make annual payment towards maintenance of the wife which forms a part of the marriage contract under the personal law. The wife also enjoys freedom to demand a divorce from her husband on the ground of non-payment of customary dues. Divorce is easy but not a disqualification for seeking a fresh alliance. There is no stigma attached to the remarriage of a widow.

In Minicoy island women are particularly active in social life and enjoy a dominant position which is unique. All family affairs are handled by the female of the house. The pattern of occupation in Minicoy has also served to enhance the position of women since most males serve on international ships, leaving women behind to manage all household activities. In the village administration, women have an important role to play. The female chief is the head of the women's assembly who organises women labour for common purpose so women do not feel any inhibitions in participating in political fora, nor do they have any restrictions in social interactions. They communicate and articulate their problems with ease. They also exhibit a great deal of self-confidence in not only managing their domestic affairs but also in participating in public life whenever an opportunity arises. No information is available, however, on the level of their involvement in the development activities undertaken so far and the impact of these development programmes on them. But given their status and also the fact that they constitute nearly 50 per cent of the population, a development paradigm which involves them meaningfully would have a very positive influence in reaching benefits among households with a reasonable degree of equality and would further enhance the benefits to the women members.

The issues raised above will no doubt come in for elaborate scrutiny in the subsequent chapters where individual sectoral problems and situations are discussed and the future course of development options outlined. This will, hopefully, help in drawing up a more people-friendly conceptual frame and structure of development to be pursued for Lakshadweep islands.

Agrarian Structure[1]

There is considerable differentiation in the endowment of physical resources of the Lakshadweep islands which is reflected in the agrarian structure as well. The UT of Lakshadweep consists of 36 islands, of which only 11 islands are inhabited. These islands fall into three categories: (1) Laccadive group (2) Amindivi group and (3) Minicoy, together covering an area of 32 sq km The islands represent variety and differentiation in many respects. In respect of the physical size of their territories, Andrott has the largest land area (4.9 sq km) while Bitra is the smallest (01. sq km). Minicoy is the longest in terms of land (11 km) and Andrott is the widest (2.4 km). In terms of distance from the mainland, Andrott is the nearest (228 km) while Minicoy is the farthest (398 km).

The agrarian structure in the islands before Lakshadweep became a Union Territory was extremely skewed and complex and in many ways represented the acutely exploitative arrangements witnessed in the mainland *Zamindari* areas. Land tenure from the beginning of colonisation was intertwined with the caste system prevalent in Kerala society. The high caste group among the earlier settlers managed to appropriate all lands that could be brought under cultivation and became *Jenmis* (landlords) as per the prevailing practice in Kerala. They brought a number of labourers belonging to the lower castes who became *Kudiyans* (tenants) under them. The latter had to serve them in return for occupational and other rights. A typical feudal tenancy system was followed where the tenants were bound to the landlords socially and economically and had no scope for owning any land. The earliest pattern of land management consisted of a local headman, as the manager of all lands, called *Muthalal*, who worked as the representative of the king. During the rule of Ali Raja, the chief headmen captured uninhabited islands and uncultivated areas in the inhabited islands and that is how private ownership began. The *Karrnavans* (Chief Headmen) of the islands were incharge of the lands owned by Ali Raja which were known as *Pandaram* lands. These lands were converted into government lands by the British after they took over the islands and were given on long-term lease for cultivation to *Cowles*. A dual pattern of land ownership thus took root: (1) *Jenmom* land (private land) and (2) *Pandaram* land (government land). *Jenmom* land was under the absolute land ownership of the principal settler families, the high caste *Koyas*. The people who worked on these lands were the *Malmis* and *Melacheris* who were hired by the landlords and let out for short periods on rental basis. Under this *Jenmom* land system, three types of tenancy were operated in the past, namely, *Nadapu* tenancy, *Pattom* tenancy, and House Site tenancy.[2]

1. Abraham, 1987.

2. A Note on the different types of tenancy arrangements prevalent in Lakshadweep islands prior to the Britsh Rule may be seen at Annexure A-1.

Nadapu tenancy was prevalent in Agatti, Amini, Andrott and Kavaratti islands. Under this, in some islands there were two categories of tenants: one which enjoyed protection from eviction and another which could be evicted at will. Under this system, the tenant was bound to provide some customary services also, such as working as a part of the crew on the boats, thatching of the *Jenmi* boat sheds, repairing boats and rendering services on occasions of birth, marriage and death in the *Jenmi* households. In return, he was granted a certain number of coconut trees. *Pattom* tenancy represented a temporary arrangement in the form of a contract between the parties under which the tenant had to pay rent but did not render any mandatory service to the landlord. He was however obliged to carry out some customary functions, such as helping the landowner to thatch his house and provide services during social functions. The landlord, however, had the right to terminate such tenancy at will but was expected to give compensation for improvements made on the land. Under the House Site tenancy, a tenant could build a house on the plot which belonged to the landlord. No rent was charged from the tenant but he was required to render some customary services to the landlord. In case the house was dismantled, the site reverted to the landlord.

After the British took over the Laccadive group of islands in 1875 for Ali Raja's failure to pay annual rent, all *Pandaram* lands[3] were converted into full-fledged government lands. The British divided these lands into plots and leased them out to individuals for making improvements on them subject to payment of tree tax. This was known as the "*Cowle* system". This is how the land in Andrott and Kalpeni were cleared of the jungles and trees were planted. They were auctioned for five years on the specific condition that the lessee would plant a stipulated number of trees. After the land survey was carried out in 1976, a uniform rate for trees was fixed.

In Minicoy Island, the agrarian structure had a different character. This island had two types of lands, one occupied by villages and a small area near it and the other which consisted of *Pandaram* property. The small area near the occupied villages in the first category of land was owned by people belonging to the upper strata of society under an arrangement called "*Valiya Pattom*". The people also were permitted to cultivate the land on the seashore on payment of rent per tree. This was known as *"Athiri Pattom"*. The bigger chunk of the landowner was *pandaram* which was classified as 'common land' carrying communal rights.

The British divided the islands into nine blocks and granted *Cowles* for the village *Pandaram* land and lands held under *Valiya Pattom*. But the people strongly resisted any attempt to permit individualisation of their communal property and, therefore, the area of the south *Pandaram* lands was never leased out. Under a compromise arrangement, people agreed to the arrangement under which these lands were given to the local inhabitants as common property on payment of annual rent. In 1971, as a part of the land reforms programme, these south *Pandaram* lands were sub-divided and allotted to nine village chiefs for the collective enjoyment of the people belonging to each village as well as individual families who opted to have lands for themselves. Standardised *Pattas* were distributed to these village chiefs and individual families on payment of annual fees. However, new set of rules specifically for south *Pandaram* lands in Minicoy were enacted with the consent of all the villagers and the village chiefs of two villages where *Pandaram* lands set apart for these two villages were subdivided and allotted to individual families and a registered lease deed of allotment was given to them in 1979. These rules carried the stipulation that this arrangement could be replicated in case of other villages wherever individual families came forward to claim individual allotment.

The land reforms carried out by the administration during the 1960s consisted of a number of measures, namely, conferment of occupancy rights on *Kudiyans* and other persons in occupation of *Pandaram* lands, abolition of *Nadapu* tenancy, fixity of tenure to *Kudiyans* and tenants, etc. The Laccadive, Minicoy and Aminidivi Regulation, 1964, protects the landowners against transfer of their lands to outsiders. These measures conferred permanent inheritable and transferable rights on the occupants of the concerned lands. The land reforms also provided a statutory recognition to the voluntary agreements of 1963 made between the *Jenmis* and the tenants and terminated any obligation of customary service being rendered therein, thus freeing the tenants from all remnants of feudal bondage. The voluntary agreement was legitimised by the administration and in this manner a 'consensual' land reforms was carried out. The restructured agrarian relations also encouraged tenants to start building their own boats and to disengage themselves from *Jenmis* for

3. *Pandaram* lands consisted of uncultivated lands in the inhabited islands and the entire area of uninhabited islands considered by Ali Raja as their private property. These lands were managed by some inhabitants on their behalf. The cultivation was carried out by people of lower castes and there were different patterns of tenancy systems operating in various islands.

the duty of carrying their boats to the mainland. This measure acted as an instrument of empowerment and played a significant role instrumental in enhancing the social status of the lower castes. The tenants other than those operating under *Nadapu* tenancy also enjoyed fixity of tenure and had inheritable rights but could not transfer their lands except to a member of the family. This obviously was intended to protect tenants against wrongful eviction by the *Jenmis*. The tenants also had the option to acquire ownership of land either by paying a specified amount to the landowner or directly purchasing from him through a sale deed. Similarly, Home Site rights were conferred on the tenants by giving them fixity of tenure, known as *Kurdi* (the land and the home site). This right is inheritable but not transferable except to the wife/husband/unmarried minor child. The Scheduled Tribes Regulations prohibit alienation of land to non-tribes, thereby preventing the moneylenders from purchasing their land or attachment or sale of their land in execution of any decree of a civil or revenue court except where the dues of government, banks or cooperative societies are involved.

The tenant is now also entitled to create a simple mortgage on his interest in the trees in respect of any loan advanced to him but not on the land. No surrender of the land is allowed without the permission of the administration. The maximum rent has also been fixed as one-fourth of the produce by the administration. Further, land revenue has replaced the earlier system of tree tax through an arrangement of stage-by-stage implementation. The land reforms also carried out survey and settlement operations in respect of islands and have prepared a record of rights with a comprehensive land register.

Distribution of Holdings

As per the Agricultural Census data of 2000-01 (Provisional), Lakshadweep had a total operated area of 2,579 hectares, consisting of 10,209 operational holdings, of which nearly 87.35 per cent have an area of less than 0.5 hectare each, while another 8.16 per cent are in the size-class of 0.5 to 1.0 hectare group. The operational holdings in the size-class of up to 0.5 hectare, being 87.35 per cent of the total holding, possess only 46.23 per cent of the total operated area. At the other end of the spectrum of holdings, lie the larger holders. About 1.33 per cent of the total number of holdings was in the range of 2 hectares and above and these comprised around 19.82 per cent of the total operated area (See Annexure A-4.b for more details). The inequity regarding distribution of operational holdings is more significant in the case of total holdings. In both cases of distribution, there is considerable inequality in the Lakshadweep islands. However, a noteworthy factor is that everybody in Lakshadweep owns atleast some patch of land and as a result there are no landless labourers in Lakshadweep.

As the land reforms were carried out in the sixties, it is presumed that the 1971 agricultural census reflects the ground position regarding agrarian structure subsequent to the land reforms implementation. The situation may have undergone some change in the latest agricultural survey (perhaps of 2001) though the details are not readily available.

Social Structure[4]: Differentiation

There is considerable differentiation in the endowment of human resources and the impact of development benefits among islands as well as among social groups within them. These are brought out in respect of various norms as under:

Composition of Population—Social Divisions

The total population of the UT, according to the 2001 Census, is 60,650, out of which 95 per cent are local. The social character of the population now represents a unique mix of the Hindu tradition of the Kerala coast with an Islamic superstructure. Its Hindu tradition is reflected in the class cum caste divisions, among the *Koyas*, *Malmis* and *Melacheris*. In Minicoy also these social divisions exist but assume a different nomenclature such as *manikfans*, *thakrufans*, *thakrus* and *raveris*. All the islands have majority of the people belonging to the Shafi sect of Sunni Muslim. In terms of religious differentiation within Islamic society, Agatti also has a large number of Wahabis while Kalpeni has people following the Ahamadiya sect. The Islamic influence is reflected in the pursuit of the same religion by most of the population despite social differentiation. The Hindu-Muslim confluence is also characterised by the coexistence of the matriliny of Kerala Hindu society along with the patriliny structure of Islam, something which is not easily observed in a single social formation elsewhere. However, Minicoy stands apart from other groups of islands in this respect and shares greater affinity with the Maldives islands in the language spoken and the culture practiced.

The social structure in Lakshadweep UT, excluding Minicoy, distinctly represents a hierarchy of three classes: (1) *Koyas*, (2) *Malmis* and (3) *Melacheris*. The

4. Abraham, 1987.

upper end of this hierarchy are the Koyas who came from the principal families of the earlier colonisers and constitute the aristocratic class with ownership of land and large number of coconut trees. They also own *odams* (boats) for going to the mainland. *Koyas* were *Jenmis* (landlords) while the other two classes were *Kudiyans* (tenants) in the feudal set-up of the then social order. *Melacheris* were the lowest in the social scale whose occupation consisted of climbing coconut trees for plucking nuts and tapping sweet toddy. *Malmis* were the sailors who served on the *odams* owned by *Koyas* which plied on the trade route between the mainland and the islands. The relationship between these three groups was characterised by multi-faceted exploitation. The social divisions in Minicoy consist of four groups. The top layer corresponding to the *Koyas* of other islands is known here as *Manikfans* who owned the entire private lands earlier. The equivalent of the sailor class here are the *Thakrufans* and *Thakrus*. Of the two, *Thakrufans* had a higher position as they were the pilots of the *odams*. The lowest in the hierarchy are the *raveris* who did what the *Melacheris* did in other islands, namely, the coconut tree climbing and sweet toddy tapping. However, in the last three decades there is significant social mixing across social divisions and marriages between the high and low castes are quite common now.

Status of Economy

Resource Potential

Andrott and Minicoy have a larger land area, soil uniformly fertile and greater exposure to modernisation in resource exploitation. The Andrott *copra* produce is considered to be the best. Andrott is known for the high status but orthodox nature of its people. Kavaratti islanders are considered most progressive as women's education was first started here. Bangaram and Tinnakara are also very fertile islands with dense coconut trees. Minicoy is the most prosperous island. Chetlat, Kiltan and Amini are the most backward islands economically.

Skill Endowment, Agrarian Relations and Social Practices[5]

The islanders are also endowed with a variety of skills. Agatti islanders are expert sailors. Amini Island produces the best local craftsmen and stone engravers and can boast of boat songs as its folk tradition. Chetlat islanders make good quality utility articles from coconut leaves and are also good carpenters. But they are better known for their tradition of building *odams* (boats) for other islands. The people of Minicoy are good sailors and fishermen. '*Mas* making' is their speciality but they also share rich, artistic and aesthetic tradition as evident from their houses, household utensils and the range of cultural activities organised there.

Agrarian relations and social practices influenced significantly various aspects of the economy. In the context of Lakshadweep other than Minicoy, the ownership of sailing boats usually called *odam* and the labour practices built around it emerged as the crucial component of the agrarian relations, and is central to it even more than land. It is only through this productive asset that fishing and trading activities are carried out and articles of domestic consumption from the mainland are brought in for subsistence. The islands (other than Minicoy) had different systems of administration as different rulers held rights and interest in respect of them before British rule. Therefore, there was differentiation in the matter of ownership of boats/ships as in the case of land. The Amindivi group (Amini, Kadmat, Kiltan and Chetlat) was ruled by Tipu Sultan before being taken over by the British towards the end of 18th century. The other islands (Andrott, Kalpeni, Kavaratti, Agatti and Minicoy) were ruled by the Arackal kingdom before being colonised by the British in 1908. In the latter case, the ownership of *odams* tightly held by the upper echelons of the caste/class hierarchy in society prevented the lower castes from owning them. Minicoy and other islands represented a different type of economy and society. The distinctiveness of the two arrangements was reflected in the major produce of the two economies. The Laccadive and Amindivi islands had specialised in coconut cultivation which produced *copra* for export and various other articles based on them, such as, coir, vinegar and jaggery, partly for domestic consumption and partly for export. The Minicoy economy was dominated by the production primarily consisting of *mas* (dried tuna) and *rihakuru* (the blood and fat of the fish left over after processing) though coconut cultivation also features there. But, of all the islands, Minicoy was the most strategically placed on the trade route. This facilitated a large number of its men to work on the ships. Thus, remittances constituted a significant driving force of the economy. This may have led to a relative lack of interest in coconut cultivation despite a large land area available. The technology input also defines the

5. Chandra *et al.*, 1993; George, 1993.

typologies of the two economy sets and the cargo for export. In respect of Minicoy, this consisted of pole and line fishing in resource extraction and tuna processing in value addition though in recent times other islands have also taken up this activity. The trade route traversed and destination (ports) covered also brings out their different characteristics. The Lakshadweep sailing ships carried out trade with one or other of the Malabar Ports—Cannanore, Calicut, Kundapur or Mangalore. On the other hand, a larger reach and more diverse destinations marked the sailing activities of the Minicoy which touched Andaman and Nicobar Islands, Calcutta and Burma and, in some cases, even up to Bombay and Porbander. Minicoy's economy thus had a greater commercial character as it also engaged in trade between the above ports. On the other hand, Lakshadweep vessels mainly disposed of their internal produce in the mainland and thus experienced limited exposure of the impact of trade and cultural influence. The inter-port trade provided a substantial source of revenue to Minicoy Island and thus enhanced the social and economic status of boat owning classes. A mercantile class had grown around it. The nature of vessels used in trading activities was also different in the case of the two island sets. The vessels of Minicoy were known as *bandu otis*, nailed together by treenails. The boats of Lakshadweep called *odams*, used coir for sewing. The distinctiveness in the two arrangements was obviously dictated largely by the geographical position of Minicoy which facilitated its trading activity to distant ports. The location of Lakshadweep islands determined its profile of trade and led to the control of boat owners by middlemen of the mainland ports and prevented them from undertaking long distance navigation even if they could muster necessary spirit and boat construction technology. The Minicoy sailors were more independent, enterprising and engaged in trade of diverse commodities.

The cropping pattern of Lakshadweep islands' economy did not have any cereal cultivation which explains the absence generally of landless labourers. Coconut palms were leased out on tenancy arrangements and, in any case, did not require the degree of labour input as cereals do and, therefore, did not need a separate class exclusively to tend them. The soil, too, did not require much care. However, labour was required seasonally for collecting nuts, processing them into *copra*, vinegar, jaggery and coir on a small scale. The major labour demand came from operating the sailing boats during the limited period when trading activity with the mainland was to be carried out. The tenancy arrangements stipulating compulsory servicing of boat owners by intermediates/lower castes were an offshoot of this contingency. The loading and unloading of cargo, raising and lowering of sails, bailing out of water in case of leaks, repair and maintenance are very labour-intensive activities. These activities were carried out by the lower castes—the *malmis* and *melacheris* who were not permitted to own sailing boats or use them for trading with the mainland. They were also mandated to engage in trade with the mainland alone on the *odams* of their landlords. They received no wages for this work. But they had to pay freight for their goods being carried and also suffered exploitation in the pricing of products taken to and from the mainland.

Though the social stratification observed among Muslims in Kerala is based on presumed proximity to the lineage of the Prophet, the predominantly Muslim society in Lakshadweep has adopted the Hindu mode of hierarchical structure for exercising social and economic control over productive resources. Minicoy also reflects a fourfold social division with *Manikfans* landlords being on the top and *Tthakrufans*, *Thakrus* and *Raveris* occupying the remaining three positions respectively. *Thakrufans* and *Thakrus* rendered services on the sailing boats and also engaged in fishing. The labour-intensive coconut related work was assigned to *Raveris*. But, unlike Lakshadweep, the service providers on the boats in Minicoy received remuneration in kind. The social relations in Minicoy were also relatively more egalitarian as residents belonged largely to the intermediate and lower castes and fishing boats were mostly owned by the villages like land. Caste differentiation nonetheless existed in social intercourse, customary arrangements to engage labour, on social occasions, in the collection of firewood from common land, and restrictions in endogamy.

The differentiating features between the social structure in Minicoy and the other Lakshadweep islands were related to the main feature of their respective economies. In the former the economy was largely fishery based with the low cost technology of traditional fishing and communal ownership of land and boats. In the latter, land and boats were privately owned and the economy was primarily focused on coconut palms and their products. The communal ownership of the means of production in Minicoy had loosened the existing social relations to a limited extent and promoted sources of autonomous power for the subordinated social groups. On the other hand, private ownership of land and boats produced rigid control, social and economic, over labour and attempts at loosening it through struggles were frustrated. Though land reforms have now been carried out, this historical legacy may provide insights into and analytical leads for assessing how the development process has impacted social relations, namely, whether the erstwhile social stratifications have disappeared or still continue albeit in a different form and in particular whether new social stratifications are emerging through new avenues of economic power. This is an area which has not been looked into so far by any penetrating study.

Levels of Technology[6]

Although islanders everywhere are expert sailors, some degree of specialisation does get developed in certain groups. In northern and middle group of islands, the *Malmis* and in southern islands (Minicoy), *Thakrus* and *Thakrufans* are the groups which carried on this tradition. The people from these social groups were, therefore, sought out by boat owners as crew on board. This expertise over time gets naturally extended to the boat building technology as the isolated societies are forced into a culture of self-reliance for their survival. The expertise is still prevalent in the islands notwithstanding the increasing use of imported and motorised boats. Here too, the various islands represent different traditions as reflected in the type of boats, their size and workmanship. The boats built by northern and middle group of islands are small ones and do not exceed 70 tonnage capacity. These are used in lagoon-fishing as well as in live bait culture. The construction material for the body is derived from coconut palm produce, the planks from coconut timber, stitching is done with coir, caulking with coconut fibre and coating with fish oil. The southern islands use larger boats as they fish beyond the reefs for tuna. The material used is local timber of the coconut or the breadfruit tree. While the northern and middle group of island boats are built without keels and are not nailed, the southern island boats are nailed and keeled for windward sailing. The boats deployed for inter-island and open sea transshipping cargo carriers are built with teakwood, with some parts drawn from the wood of coconut, mango or breadfruit trees. These are also a nailed vessels. The nomenclature of the two types of sailing boats is also different. The larger sea going sailing vessel in southern island is known as *bandodi*, while sailing vessels in other islands are called *odams*. Minicoy also makes vessels larger than bandodi for cargo trade called *otis*. A race boat, known as *jehadoni*, is also built for use in the lagoon. This boat like the *odam* of Lakshadweep is made entirely of local coconut timber. Presently, only smaller boats are being built in the islands which are of three main categories: (1) lagoon boats, (2) reef boats and cargo carriers and (3) other sea vessels. Lakshadweep and Minicoy still carry two distinct traditions of boat building techniques though both have been affected by motorisation. The Lakshadweep vessels are coir-sewn, with limited use of wooden pins, but not nails. Minicoy boats are nailed. Minicoy boats are decked while others are not decked. Minicoy boats use square-rigged sails; Lakshadweep boats use lateen sails. Smaller boats in both places use local timber, primarily coconut, while the larger vessels use a variety of timber imported from the mainland. The locally built boats use the open beach under thatched sheds for construction activity while the larger vessels require more organised workshops. This distinction between two historical traditions of local boat building skills eloquently brings out that technology, and expertise were directly related to meeting the needs of the local economy as well as conditioned by the availability and access to the raw material. Thus, the non-availability of hard timber restricted the building of larger sized vessels in Lakshadweep islands. Importing it from the mainland would not have been economically viable. The environmental conditions, such as shore site topography and the tide profile in the lagoons along with the steep slopes of the coral reefs militate against the construction of large boats. The beaches in the reef ridges are very shallow. Large boats cannot enter the lagoon and island shores. The depth of the lagoons as well as the entrance into them, thus, effectively restrict the size of the boats and along with the tidal range limit the mobility within the lagoons and therefore can create difficulties in launching internally built boats into navigable water. In some places however, the administration has widened and deepened them for building jetties. Large vessels cannot be built on the beaches nor navigated in shallow lagoons owing to a prolonged monsoon season and high waves and rough water. Minicoy alone provides deep lagoons for such purposes but even there the underwater topography near the shore is not suited for building large sized vessels on the beach and pushing them into deep waters. The size of the cargo from different islands is also a factor determining the size of boat construction. This explains why minimum size sea-going vessels were jointly owned by persons from different islands. This analysis brings out how the local ecology and economy limit the development of the ship-building technology in the two categories of islands.

6. Karanim and Arunachalam (ed.), 1993.

Poverty and Income Distribution

The poverty profile like other profiles also differs from island to island. Based on a 1987 study it appears that[7] Minicoy has the lowest percentage of population below the poverty line while at Kiltan and Chetlat it accounts for more than 50 per cent (The poverty level used in this study is the consumer expenditure of Rs. 15 per person for a month at 1960-61 rural prices). The corresponding current figures are not contained in the handbook issued by the Lakshadweep Administration nor are they available in a comparable recent study. But it may be reasonable to presume that this number may be much smaller now considering that food items are available at subsidised rates. The current island-wise position is not available though the overall poverty level in Lakshadweep in 2000 was 15.60 per cent while the all-India average was 26.10 per cent. The per capita consumption expenditure in Lakshadweep is Rs. 967 per month as against the all-India average of Rs. 591. While the data may provide a rough indication of the economic condition of UT residents, an island specific profile of poverty would have been a useful analytical tool to target future development interventions.

As per the study cited above (1987), the maximum expenditure of households is on rice, coconut and fish and constitutes 64.9 per cent of the total expenses, which increases to more than 70 per cent in the Amini group of islands. The income elasticity of demand, therefore, can only be noticed for the higher expenditure group. The disparity with respect to consumer expenditure is negligible for different expenditure classes. But the concentration ratio is higher in Andrott and lowest in Bitra. Coconut cultivation is a major source of income constituting nearly 31 per cent of total earnings of households. This, too, differs from island to island—it is less than 8 per cent in Minicoy and 55 per cent in Amini. Ninety six per cent of households have some sort of income from land which is higher in Andrott and lowest in Bitra. More than three quarters of households have some livestock, mostly poultry. Most livestock products are used for home consumption rather than for sale. Income from livestock constituted 3 per cent of the total household earnings. Income from fishing also shows a skewed pattern across the islands. In Andrott and Kavaratti, fish catch does not even meet local demand. Fish constitute only 7.2 per cent of a family's monthly earnings. But variation is observed across islands; it is 30 per cent of Agatti's households, 70 per cent of Bitra's and only 23 per cent of Andrott's. Coconut tree climbing provides around 15 days a month of employment to one-fifth of households. Coir twisting largely employs women folk but provides only 2 per cent of the total earnings of the households. The households engaged in coir twisting also differ from island to island. It is only 8 per cent in Minicoy and more than 70 per cent in the Amini group of islands. In Minicoy island 86 per cent of households have one person employed as seaman in an Indian or foreign shipping company who remits money regularly and which makes Minicoy the richest of all islands. Government has emerged as the single major employer. A majority of the families in Kavaratti have one member holding a government job. Income from government jobs constitutes 16 per cent of the total earnings of Lakshadweep households. In Andrott, the priestly class of *Thangals* who go out for preaching have one-third of total earnings from this source. Traders, carpenters, blacksmiths, barbers, coconut tree tappers, jaggery and vinegar makers, boat owners and other different occupations are practised in the territory. Per capita monthly income is higher in Minicoy, followed by Andrott; it is lowest in Kiltan. Strangely, per capita monthly consumption expenditure is much less than the per capita monthly earnings. This may be due to subsidised food items and energy, free education and medical care and easy availability of coconut and fish from the sea for consumption. The dried parts of coconut trees are used as firewood. The population of the islands mostly invest in gold ornaments and do not have bank deposits. Income is obviously more unequally distributed than expenditure. The ratio is lowest in Bitra and the concentration is higher in Andrott. Inequality in income distribution is maximum in Andrott, minimum in Bitra.

Asset Distribution

With regard to distribution of assets, according to the same (1987) study the total of average values of various items is higher in Andrott and lowest in Chetlat. Land is the largest component of assets of Lakshadweep households and more than half of them have some landed property. Fifty seven per cent of households have *pucca* houses, 31 semi-*pucca* and 12 per cent *kutcha*. The *inter se* proportion of the three types is skewed across islands. It is the highest in Minicoy, followed by Kavaratti while the largest number of *kutcha* houses are in Amini. Livestock distribution is also skewed in favour of islands where fodder is available, such as Minicoy, Kavaratti and Andrott while it is the lowest in Kiltan. Even though fishing is a widespread

7. Abraham, 1987.

activity, less than half of the households possess fishing nets. This position may have changed with poverty alleviation programmes catering to this requirement. As regards consumer goods among households, Minicoy is the richest and Amini the poorest. Andrott, Agatti, Kavaratti and Kalpeni have households ranging from 10 to 18 per cent which possess gold ornaments. Most households have a bike or a motorboat. Motorboats have been supplied by the administration to various islanders at subsidised rates. Islanders keep liquid cash in their houses. The banking habit is low as Muslims do not like receiving interest from their deposits. The absence of any crime explains the ease with which the people keep liquid cash in hand.

Indebtedness is very low in the island since owing to religious factors people do not like to borrow money or lend it for interest. The networth of islanders may be higher than people elsewhere in respect of households with some liabilities. Minicoy households have the lowest level of liabilities. Of the money borrowed, a high percentage is used for consumption purposes and very little for production. The consumption loan in the case of Lakshadweep islands is used for construction of houses, litigation and land disputes and not food items. But loans are mostly taken from friends, relatives or merchants and it is only in one-fourth of the cases that institutional agencies are approached. The loan from non-institutional sources is interest-free. The institutional loan is obtained by mortgaging coconut trees. Unlike interest earning, there is no stigma attached to lending and getting mortgaged coconut trees in return. This system was usually prevalent among the poor who ended up losing their trees owing to their inability to pay the loans. This practice is declining now with the availability of institutional loans. Across the islands, Kadmat has the maximum number of household liabilities while the minimum is in Minicoy.

There is a skewed distribution of assets in households across the islands. Two per cent of the total households fall in the highest asset category accounting for roughly 11 per cent of the total value of the assets. These households belonged to Amini, Andrott and Kavaratti islands and they own large landed property. The bottom 28 per cent of the households share a meagre 3 per cent of the total value of assets whereas 24 per cent households had 66 per cent share of the total value assets. The concentration of total value of assets is the lowest in Minicoy and the highest in Kadmat. But noticeable inequality in distribution of assets is found in all islands except Minicoy and Bitra. The significant feature is that the concentration of assets is much higher than concentration of income and consumption for Lakshadweep households. The situation has definitely improved in the last two decades as the socioeconomic indicators have improved a lot.

Quality of Life

The planning process for the UT of Lakshadweep which began in 1956 has helped in achieving tremendous progress in the field of education, health, employment and quality of life of the citizen and their per capita earnings.

According to 2001 Census Lakshadweep ranks IIIrd among all states/UTs in literacy. Out of the total enrolment in the schools, 47.92 per cent are girls. Gender gap is negligible and efforts are on to bring all girl child to school in order to reduce further gender gap. Literacy rate has been increasing progressively, especially female literacy rates. As per 1991 Census female literacy rates in the UT was 72.89 which has increased to 87.52 per cent according to 2001 Census. Lakshadweep is the Ist UT to introduce computer education at all schools.

TABLE 1.1

Literacy Rate (2001 Census)

(Per Cent)

States/UT	*Literacy Rate*		
	Male	*Female*	*Total*
Lakshadweep	**93.15**	**81.56**	**87.52**
Karnataka	76.29	57.45	67.04
Kerala	94.20	87.86	90.92
Tamil Nadu	82.33	64.55	73.47
All-India	75.96	54.28	65.49

Source: Selected Socio Economic Statistics India 2002.

The coverage and quality of healthcare has been improved by introducing modern technology and as of now Lakshadweep has one of the lowest death rate and lower infant and maternal mortality rates as compared to other states in India.

Lakshadweep is having the lowest poverty ratio in India as per *National Human Development Report 2001*. In the last survey conducted in the UT only 885 families were reported under Below Poverty Line. No incidence of child labour has been reported in this UT. Nearly 241 active Self-Help Groups (SHGs) are functioning in this UT.

The work force participation rate, however, is low and more so in case of female work force, in Lakshadweep as compared to the other parts of the country. Another notable feature is that there is not much gap between the participation rate of work force in rural areas and urban areas.

The employment has increased very rapidly during 1993-94 to 1999-2000 in Lakshadweep. The employment growth among women was many times faster than their male counterparts during this period, depicting a major shift in the previous scenario.

On an experimental basis National Institute of Ocean Technology (NIOT), Chennai, has set up a one lakh litre capacity Low Temperature Thermal Desalination Plant at Kavaratti in May 2005. With this the drinking water problem has been solved to a large extent at Kavaratti, the capital territory. Water supply scheme has been introduced in all the islands with the target to provide potable water supply to all households by 2010.

All the inhabited islands including Bangaram have been electrified and power supply is available 24X7 without any interruption.

The per capita consumption expenditure is significantly high in Lakshadweep depicting comparatively higher quality of life in the island.

TABLE 1.2

Health Indicators

(Per Thousand)

States/UT	*Birth Rate*			*Death Rate*			*Infant Mortality Rate*		
	Rural	*Urban*	*Total*	*Rural*	*Urban*	*Total*	*Rural*	*Urban*	*Total*
Lakshadweep	**22.1**	**18.7**	**20.4**	**4.7**	**5.2**	**5.0**	**34**	**33**	**33**
Karnataka	23.6	19.0	22.2	8.2	6.4	7.6	69	27	58
Kerala	17.4	16.6	17.2	6.8	6.1	6.6	12	9	11
Tamil Nadu	19.6	17.8	19.0	8.4	6.0	7.6	54	35	49
All-India	27.1	20.2	25.4	9.0	6.3	8.4	72	42	66

Source: Selected Socio Economic Statistics India 2002.

TABLE 1.3

Human Poverty Index–1991

States/UT	*Rural*		*Urban*		*Combined*	
	Value	*Rank*	*Value*	*Rank*	*Value*	*Rank*
Lakshadweep	**15.67**	**2**	**12.26**	**2**	**13.89**	**1**
Karnataka	35.28	16	21.59	19	30.99	16
Kerala	24.57	6	17.23	8	22.73	7
Tamil Nadu	30.31	12	18.61	15	26.45	11
All-India	42.25		23.03		37.42	

Source: National Human Development Report 2001.

TABLE 1.4

Work Force Participation

States/UT	*Rural*			*Urban*			*Total*		
	Male	*Female*	*Person*	*Male*	*Female*	*Person*	*Male*	*Female*	*Person*
Lakshadweep	**40.70**	**6.07**	**23.77**	**44.75**	**8.61**	**27.28**	**42.51**	**7.19**	**25.33**
Karnataka	58.32	39.86	49.20	54.11	16.06	35.67	56.87	31.88	44.60
Kerala	50.22	15.88	32.56	50.78	13.55	31.65	50.36	15.28	32.32
Tamil Nadu	59.38	41.33	50.39	56.37	18.42	37.59	58.06	31.32	44.78
All-India	52.36	30.98	41.97	50.85	11.55	32.23	51.93	25.68	39.26

Source: Selected Socio-Economic Statistics India 2002.

TABLE 1.5

Growth in Employment—Combined

(Per Cent Per Annum)

States/UT	1993-94 to 1999-2000		
	Male	Female	Person
Lakshadweep	**3.8**	**11.0**	**5.2**
Karnataka	2.0	0.8	1.6
Kerala	1.6	1.4	1.6
Tamil Nadu	1.4	-0.3	0.8
All-India	1.9	0.9	1.6

Source: National Human Development Report 2001.

Also the per capita consumption expenditure has increased sharply during the period 1993-94 to 1999-2000.

In urban areas of Lakshadweep, 82 per cent of houses were *pucca* houses in 1993-94 as per *National Human Development Report 2001*. Even the rural areas have 60.30 per cent *pucca* houses. Lakshadweep stands apart from other states as far as development in this field is concerned.

Concluding Remarks

The analysis of the agrarian and social structure both between islands and within them shows that social differentiation has historical roots and survives even after agrarian reforms were carried out. In fact, historically, this differentiation was not less sharp than what was prevalent in the mainland societies. What is not known is whether the development process over the years has been able to bridge these social divisions, reinforced or aggravated them. As no study to throw light on this aspect is available, the future development strategy to be adopted for the state development report must take this into account, more so, if the paradigm of development adopted for the UT is committed to prevent social inequalities from emerging through various development programmes and the basic egalitarian structure is to be maintained. The Minicoy island situation can provide useful ideas and experiences in this direction.

The information contained in the above analysis also brings out that inter-island disparity exists which is not merely related to physical resource endowment but also in terms of human resource development. This

TABLE 1.6

Per Capita Consumption Expenditure

(Rs. Per Month)

States/UT	1993-94			1999-2000		
	Rural	Urban	Combined	Rural	Urban	Combined
Lakshadweep	**526.32**	**507.63**	**515.17**	**876.19**	**1018.25**	**967.35**
Karnataka	269.40	423.10	318.47	499.78	910.99	638.81
Kerala	390.40	493.80	419.08	765.70	932.61	816.76
Tamil Nadu	293.60	438.30	344.31	513.97	971.61	681.37
All-India	281.40	458.00	328.18	486.08	854.96	590.98

Source: National Human Development Report 2001.

TABLE 1.7

Households with *Pucca* Houses

(Percentage)

States/UT	1981			1991			1993-94	
	Rural	Urban	Combined	Rural	Urban	Combined	Rural	Urban
Lakshadweep	**49.75**	**74.90**	**61.71**	**83.91**	**92.84**	**88.84**	**60.30**	**82.00**
Karnataka	19.19	54.64	29.33	30.44	69.43	42.54	28.70	67.20
Kerala	35.07	56.08	38.80	51.56	69.06	55.97	51.50	67.70
Tamil Nadu	25.57	60.74	36.62	34.60	69.08	45.54	36.40	64.10
All-India	22.53	64.70	32.67	30.59	72.75	41.61	29.20	70.70

Source: National Human Development Report 2001.

feature is broadly similar to the kind of regional imbalances which are noticed in larger mainland states. It is, therefore, necessary that the perspective for the growth and development of Lakshadweep maps out a well thought out mechanism for balancing growth and building up an island specific development plan within the ambit of its overall framework.

The tension between non-indigenous people and the local population which is quite common in mainland states is also non-existent here. This is the result of the conscious steps taken by the government (such as Entry Permit, Land Laws, etc.) to check migration and to create positive disincentives for migrants to come over to the islands and stay here permanently. Given the extremely fragile resource base of the islands, their carrying capacity can under no circumstances absorb migrants. They would even find it difficult to absorb the growing local population unless out-migration is positively encouraged. This also underlines the need for identifying areas and activities (such as computer servicing), encouraging and supporting local population in enhancing their skill base so that they are able to provide high quality services comparable to mainland.

The agrarian structure is skewed even after land reforms have been carried out. The structure of land-holdings is unequal particularly in the operational side. The inequalities are also witnessed in asset distribution which is largely related to the agrarian structure. The expenditure distribution however is more egalitarian which is explained by highly subsidised food commodities, access to free education and health facilities provided by the government and limited avenues of expenditure within the islands on non-essential commodities. The State Development Report should, therefore, keep in view the need for more egalitarian asset and income distribution. Specific approaches may be outlined for this purpose. This, incidentally, will help neutralise inter-island disparities that exist at present as well.

Skill endowment relatable to specific social groups as well as to islands have been brought out in the above note. Admittedly, this is of a very low level though it was and still is quite important for the present development economy of island societies. The development strategy should explore whether strategies of skill development for future growth can build on this foundation besides taking up new areas. Such strategy would have great distributional advantages and influence both asset and income distribution since these skills are mostly possessed by lower level classes. This approach would also be necessary in order that these skills do not go into disuse and people are weaned away from the dependency syndrome.

It is now being increasingly appreciated that the various development initiatives particularly for augmenting incomes, building up infrastructure and processing and marketing of agricultural and industrial produce could fall through if not pursued with adequate foresight and professional rigour in planning and project appraisal and management. This could lead to considerable inefficiency of investment as well as wastage of resources. The experience gained in respect of such projects also illuminates the technocratic approach that often dominates the process of development planning with no countervailing pressure from peoples' organisations to temper it. Any approach for a long-term and sustainable development of the region should recommend a structure of decision making which not merely involves the local people in a major way far beyond the present framework of *panchayati raj* but also ensures that such failures are not repeated. There is also strong need for building up expertise of sound financial analysis in project preparation and appraisal even after granting that the island situation would demand a different calculus of cost and social benefits. The resources invested in production capacity underutilised or created in excess of the assured availability of inputs has a huge opportunity cost for the people of the islands as well as the government. Any adverse experiences would slow down future investments and shake people's confidence in the administration's capability to deliver. It should be a matter of concern for the decision makers as well.

It is also necessary to caution the administration in Lakshadweep against implementing various centrally sponsored schemes as a matter of routine and primarily because resources are flowing to the island territory through them. Replication of schemes taken up elsewhere without a rigorous evaluation of their relevance is neither appropriate nor productive. The island situation is entirely different from the mainland. Even in the mainland, the situation in various states is not similar while the central programmes draw up a standardised schematic structure. Quite often, states in the mainland also complain that they should be given freedom to decide the schemes to be taken up rather than be asked to implement the standardised schemes. For the island territory, implementing certain central scheme would not only be wastage of resources but would create externalities which are adverse for the people or environment. It will needlessly engage implementing bureaucracy in programmes which are not needed and divert attention and resources from those where positive impact can be created. The agriculture and animal husbandry sector is a good example of the kind of dis-functionalities created by some such schemes. The State Development Report should, therefore, specifically incorporate a discussion on this subject with strong emphasis on the mechanism to evaluate the type of central schemes to be implemented. As there are limited areas where development programmes can be taken without creating adverse impact on some aspect of island situation, central schemes should be accepted only when they fit into an already worked out conceptual frame for the UT. No scheme should be implemented just because additional money is flowing through it.

This also brings to the centre stage the question of selection of technology for development projects. Technological choices are not neutral, either to the environment or to people. Past experience shows that neither of the two aspects appears to have been adequately scrutinised and evaluated. Various technological interventions suggested in this report for power generation, desalination of water, fishing storage, transportation, solid waste disposal, etc. should go through a rigorous appraisal in respect of these two aspects besides the financial and management analysis. There is need for recommending a comprehensive mechanism for appraisal of technology from all these angles before a project based on it is taken up for preparation. Needless to say that people's organisations should be meaningfully involved in the process of this appraisal and necessary technological/scientific information should be placed before them in a demystified language.

The development experience also exposes the fragility of market intervention through the state that has been pursued for commercial disposal of the produce/products. The states' record in marketing has been dismal all over the country. With a higher level of production/extraction envisaged in various proposals of future development, state marketing could become even more inviable than it is at present. People in Lakshadweep have not been exposed to private markets and have so far been protected against their uncertainty and volatility. This is not good for them or for the stability of various development initiatives focusing on extraction, production, and value addition. People should be encouraged to face markets so that they develop entrepreneurship and risk taking capacity particularly in the current global economic environment. The state may forge necessary linkages and develop base level infrastructure for people to get integrated to markets.

Chapter 2

Economic Issues

Profile of the Islands

The Union Territory of Lakshadweep is an archipelago of 36 small and tiny islands located 220-440 kilometres off the Malabar Coast, between 8° and 12° 30' North latitude and 71° and 74° East longitude. There are 12 major islands and lagoons (Agatti, Andrott, Amini, Bangaram, Bitra, Chetlat, Kadmat, Kalpeni, Kavaratti, Kiltan, Suheli and Minicoy), three submerged reefs (Baliapani, Cheriapani, Perumalpur) and five banks (Bassas de Pedro, Sessostris, Coradivh, Aminipetti, Elikapeni). The Lakshadweep group of islands covers an area of 32 sq km with Kavaratti as the headquarters. All Lakshadweep islands are of coral origin and some of them like Minicoy, Kalpeni, Kadmat, Kiltan and Chetlat are typical atolls. Geologically, Lakshadweep islands are considered to be a continuation of the Aravalli system of rocks of Rajasthan and Gujarat. Of all the 28 States and 7 Union Territories, Lakshadweep is the smallest in terms of both area and population.[1]

Even though the islands in Lakshadweep measure in all only 32 sq km in area, the lagoons, which form integral part of the islands, measure 4,200 sq km. The territorial waters of Lakshadweep are about 20,000 sq km and the Exclusive Economic Zone, about 4,00,000 sq km.[2] This makes the islands extremely crucial from the economic point of view as well. The nearest ports to Lakshadweep are Calicut (346 km), Kochi (404 km) and Mangalore (352 km). The airport in Lakshadweep is located at Agatti from which Indian Airlines operates regular flights to Kochi and during some months also to Goa.

The temperature in Lakshadweep Islands remains moderate all through the year, ranging between about 24 and 32 degrees Celsius. During the period 1992 to 2001, the annual rainfall recorded at Minicoy and Agatti ranged from 1500 to 1857 mm and between 1090 and 1858 mm, respectively. Almost 75-80 per cent of the rainfall occurs during the months of May to December. Such a climatic pattern, coupled with other natural and ecological factors such as the Eddie oceanic currents are believed to be the main factors behind the origin and development of these coral islands. The soils are highly calcareous in nature.

The ecology of the Lakshadweep Islands comprises not merely the landmass, but the continuum of the ocean, the reefs in the shape of atolls, lagoons, shores and the landmass. The deep seas are host to innumerable varieties of flora and fauna, like most other oceans. The reefs and the lagoons, however, offer the uniqueness to the ecology of these islands, primarily due to the corals and the inhabiting polyps. The vegetation of the reefs and the lagoons comprises mainly the strand corals of 78 enumerated species of which about 80 per cent is occupied by the blue coral 'heliophora'. The available (listed) fauna include sponges (41 species), turtles (4 species), fish (601 species), birds (101 species) and echinoderms (10 species). The landmass is practically covered fully by coconut palms in the inhabited as well as uninhabited islands.

The demography of Lakshadweep exhibits certain features that are highly significant but often unique as well. For instance, its population density at 1,894 per sq km is far higher than the average for India (324) and its gender ratio at 947 is skewed though better than the all-

1. Area and population data of the various States and UTs is placed in Annexure A-3.

2. The limits for territorial waters, continental shelf and the exclusive economic zone have been prescribed under the Territorial Waters, Continental Shelf, Exclusive Economic Zone and Other Maritime Zones Act, 1976 as 12, 24 and 200 nautical miles, respectively, from the nearest point of the shore (1 nautical mile=1.852 km). Total area of territorial waters of India is 3,14,400 sq km.

India figure of 933 (2001 Census). The literacy rate in Lakshadweep at 87.52 per cent (2001) is among the highest in the country, being next only to Kerala (90.92) and Mizoram (88.49). In terms of literacy rate among Scheduled Tribe population, Lakshadweep (80.58 per cent) stands next only to Mizoram (82.73 per cent) and is way ahead of the all-India average of 29.60 per cent (1991 Census[3]). In terms of the popular health indicators such as crude birth and death rates, infant mortality rate, maternal mortality rate and life expectancy at birth, Lakshadweep stands ahead of the all-India average.[4]

The entire indigenous population of this island territory has been classified as Scheduled Tribe and constitutes 93.15 per cent of the island population (1991 Census).[5] In terms of religious classification, the entire indigenous population is Muslim.

Lakshadweep was accorded special status under the administrative arrangements of the British Government. Even today, it continues to be governed by special laws, primarily on account of its strategic location and environmentally sensitive character. A note on the special status of Lakshadweep may be seen at Annexure A-2.

All the islands of Lakshadweep, inhabited or otherwise, constitute one district with headquarters at Kavaratti. Since 1983, the *Tehsil* system has been replaced by Revenue Sub-Divisional System. The Uni-district territory consists of nine Revenue sub-divisions which are grouped into four major sub-divisions (Minicoy, Kavaratti, Andrott, Amini) and five minor sub-divisions (Kalpeni, Agatti, Kadmat, Kiltan, Chetlat). The sub-divisions are headed by Deputy Collector (for Minicoy), Sub-Divisional Officers (for other major subdivisions) and Addl. Sub-Divisional Officer's (for minor subdivisions). Under the *panchayati raj* system, it has a two tier set up, with one District *Panchayat* and 10 Village (*Dweep*) *Panchayats*, at the rate of one for each of the inhabited islands. In the Lok Sabha, Lakshadweep contributes one seat.

The UT Administration is headed by the administrator who is a senior officer of the Indian Administrative Service and is appointed by the President of India under Article 239 of the Constitution. He is assisted by 2 IAS officers, Collector-cum-Development Commissioner, and Managing Director (Lakshadweep Development Corporation Ltd.); 2 IPS officers, SP and Commandant (Indian Reserve Battalion); 1 IFS officer, 13 Delhi, Andaman-Nicobar and Lakshadweep (DANICs) Civil Service officers, various other officers from the local cadres.

The economic activities in Lakshadweep depend on the land, the surrounding water bodies, the lagoons, coral reefs and the ocean. The landmass is limited and the soil has unique characteristics. The scope for industrial development has severe limitations in view of the ecological and cost related factors. The prospects for economic activities have to focus mainly on agriculture and allied activities, fisheries and tourism and supplementary activities in the sectors of animal husbandry and small scale and cottage industries.

Agriculture

Agriculture, along with fisheries, is the most widely prevalent economic activity in the territory. Almost all the households own small or marginal pieces of agricultural land, as is evidenced by the fact that the number of agricultural holdings is 10,209 (2000-01) as against the estimated population of about 60,650. However, over 87 per cent of the operational holdings are of less than 0.5 hectare size. The trend of the landholding pattern shows rapid fragmentation and an increasing pressure on the land.[6]

Of the total geographical area of 3,200 hectares, the net sown area in Lakshadweep is 2,579 hectares, which works out to a little over 80 per cent of the total geographical area of the island. The net sown area has shown a small decline over the past 10 years as in 1992-93, it was 2,755 hectares. However, the area sown more than once has remained constant at 1,404 hectares. Details for recent representative years are given in Table 2.1.

The cultivable soils in the various islands of Lakshadweep are generally of coral material and have a gentle slope. The potable water table is shallow and continuous extraction from the wells inevitably leads to ingress of brackish water.

Characterisation of the Soils[7]

These islands were created due to weathering of corals into sand and their deposits. The soils are

3. The 2001 Census figures on this score are yet to be announced.
4. This is discussed in more details in Chapter 4.
5. Results of Census 2001 in this regard are awaited (as of 31st December, 2004).
6. Statistics for the operational holdings for 1990-91 and 2000-01 (Provisional) are placed in Annexure A-4.A and A-4.B.
7. Island-wise characterisation of soils is placed at Annexure A-5.

TABLE 2.1

Land Utilisation Statistics of Lakshadweep

(Items A to D in Hectares)

Land Use	*1994-95*	*1996-97*	*1998-99*	*2000-01*	*2001-02*	*2003-04*
A. Total geographical area	3,200	3,200	3,200	3,200	3,200	3,200
B. Area not available for cultivation	445	445	446	621	621	621
C. Net sown area	2,755	2,755	2,754	2,579	2,579	2,579
D. Area sown more than once	1,504	1,403	1,404	1,404	1,404	1,401
E. Ratio of C to A	86.1%	86.1%	86.1%	80.6%	80.6%	80.59%

Source: Basic Statistics 2003-2004, Lakshadweep Administration.

geologically very young and rich in calcium carbonates of aquatic origin. The content of calcium carbonate ranges from 92 to 98 per cent. The landscape is generally plain, gently sloping and elevated 2-5 m above mean sea level. Soils derived from coral limestone, are light textured with very little clay, calcium carbonate equivalent ranging from 72-99 per cent and are predominantly sandy. As compared to the rest of the Indian soils, they have very high organic carbon ranging from 0.77 to 4.78 per cent. They are very rich in nitrogen, phosphorus and certain micronutrients. Deficiencies of potash, iron, zinc and copper are quite widespread due to their calcareousness and sandy nature. The soils are highly calcareous, alkaline (pH up to 8.5), structure less and poor in available nitrogen and potassium. The soils are moderately deep to very deep (80-140 cm depth). The texture of the surface soil is sand in the west and turns to sandy loam in the east and throughout a transitional central zone with loamy sand texture. Subsoil is loamy sand or sand. Generally the clay content is below 10 per cent and sand, above 90 per cent. With reference to physico-chemical characteristics, pH ranges from 7.9 to 8.7 with very low electrical conductivity of 0.23 ds/m. Cation exchange capacity (CEC) is also very low (3.8 to 8.4 cmol (+) kg^{-1}). Organic carbon ranges from 0.20 to 2.01. Population of bacteria, fungi and actinomycetes is high in all soils (4.5–8.5 lakh cfu/g soil—actinomycetes). Soils are quite deep except for a few cases of shallow and gravely areas as detailed in Table 2.2. They have well defined A horizon (plough layer), absence of B horizon and thick C horizon (parent material). All these features indicate that the soils are very young and in the developing process. They are single grained virgin material without any structural development. Soil depth is limited by the presence of a hard pan or shallow ground water (Table 2.2).

TABLE 2.2

Depth-wise Distribution of Soils of Lakshadweep

Depth Class	*Area (ha)*	*Per Cent of Total*
Very deep soils	809	(32.5)
Deep soils	424	(17.0)
Moderately deep soils	967	(38.8)
Moderately shallow soils	151	(06.0)
Shallow soils	143	(05.7)
Total	**2494**	

Source: Draft chapter on Agriculture & Horticulture, prepared by the Indian Council of Agricultural Research.

Soils are predominantly light textured and well drained. Unlike mainland soils, the islands' sand is rich in calcium carbonate ($CaCO_3$) and poor in silica and sesquioxides. Clay content is generally less than 10 per cent and only in a few cases it may approach 20 per cent. Therefore soils are predominantly coarse textured, i.e., sand, loamy sand and sandy loam. Light texture provides high infiltration rate and recharging of ground water. In spite of high rainfall, most of the rainwater goes into *in situ* infiltration in these sandy soils.

The islands are nearly flat with a gentle slope. The distribution of slope classes is given in Table 2.3.

TABLE 2.3

Distribution of Land in Different Slope Classes

Slope Class	*Area (ha)*	*(Per cent of Total)*
Nearly level (A-slope)	1330	(53.3)
Very gently sloping (B-slope)	1154	(46.3)
Gently sloping (C-slope)	10	(0.4)
Total	**2494**	

Source: Draft chapter on Agriculture & Horticulture, prepared by the Indian Council of Agricultural Research.

Since land is gently sloping and sandy with high infiltration, overall erosion is not a major issue except along the coastline owing to beating by the waves, apart from human interventions. About 90 per cent of the island area is covered by a thick canopy of high-density palms. Rainfall is intercepted by the leaves and reaches ground level as non-erosive stem flow or reconstituted drops. There is no direct beating or dispersion of soil surface by the kinetic energy of rain drops. High infiltration rate does not allow critical concentration of water to produce runoff and soil erosion. It will also be helpful to develop vegetative lining of the coast that would facilitate wave breaking and thus protect the shore. Out of the total flat land area of 2494 ha, 2211 ha (i.e., 89 per cent) is classified as slightly eroded, while the remaining is moderately eroded.

Fortunately, most of the soils being sandy are well drained and can support good growth of plants and vegetation. This characteristic is important from the point of view of water logging, land use and biomass productivity. Out of the total flat land area of 2494 ha, 2107 ha (i.e., 85 per cent) is classified as excessively drained, while the remaining is imperfectly drained. The permanent limitations of erosion, drainage and shallowness/gravelness are not very severe.

Climatic Conditions

Rains are the most important fresh water resource for crop/biomass production, livestock rearing, aquaculture, domestic consumption and environmental services. Precipitation in the range of 1255 to 1934 mm depending upon the island is fairly distributed from May to November. The other advantage is that there is some rainfall in the remaining months of the year to provide proper moisture for maintaining growth throughout the year of a typical humid tropical climate. Annual rainfall generally decreases whereas the southwest monsoon increases from south to north. Rainfall in the southern islands is more uniformly distributed as compared to the northern islands. June to September rainfall is 70 per cent of the annual in the north and only 56 per cent in the south islands. The southern island receives 20 per cent and northern 15 per cent of the annual rainfall during October and November. June is the rainiest month contributing 25 per cent in the north and less than 20 per cent of annual rain in the south. Rainfall decreases progressively after June in the north whereas the south experiences a secondary maximum in October (bi-modal) owing to the influence of the northeast monsoon. Yearly variation in rainfall also increases from south to north. On an average the number of rainy days (72.5 mm rainfall) in a year was 80 at Amini (north) and 94 in Minicoy (south). The air is humid throughout the year, the relative humidity being always over 70 to 75 per cent. The humid tropical monsoon climate with mean monthly temperature ranging from 25-30°C is ideal for harvesting of sunshine, utilisation of moisture and biomass production throughout the year. Climatic data of selected islands is given in Annexure A-6.

Cropping Pattern

Coconut is the main crop in all the islands and has been grown for centuries. Owing to the rapid subdivision and fragmentation of holdings, the farmers practice very close planting and strikingly plant more seedlings on the boundaries or corners to mark their fields, thus creating overcrowding of palms in all the islands. An average of 400-500 coconut palms of all ages are available in one hectare of land as against 170-200 normally recommended for optimum yield. This has resulted in a very low yield even in the absence of any major diseases.

Other fruit crops such as banana, papaya, breadfruit, drumstick, sweet potato, water melon, acid lime and, to a lesser extent, guava, pomegranate, sapota and vegetable crops such as brinjal, chilli, tomato, amaranthus, cucumber, snake gourd and pumpkin as well as tubers such as tapioca and sweet potato are also becoming popular, often as intercrop with coconut. Vanilla, a high value crop, was introduced in 2001 but its adaptability under the island conditions is yet to pick up. The use of chemical fertilisers is practically banned in the islands, on ecological considerations.

Coconut is the most popular crop in Lakshadweep. The total harvest of coconut varies from year to year, and stood at 531 lakh nuts in the year 2001-02 (Table 2.4).

Even though it is a small region and has only about 2700 ha of lands under coconut, which is 0.14 per cent of the all-India figure of 18.92 lakh ha, its production of coconut at 531 lakh nuts amounted to 0.41 per cent of the all-India production figure of 12821.7 lakh nuts (2001-02).

Despite the overall very high level of productivity of coconut, there is a very significant inter-island variation in these respects and Amini, for example, reports as high as 35,405 nuts per ha whereas Minicoy has only 498. The total number of yielding coconut palms is 6,51,626, which makes the average yield per palm to be of the order of 81 nuts with inter-island variation

TABLE 2.4

Area, Production and Productivity of Coconut Cultivation in States, UTs and All-India Average[8]

State/UT	2000-01			2001-02		
	Area ('000 ha)	Production (Million Nuts)	Productivity (Nuts/ha)	Area ('000 ha)	Production (Million Nuts)	Productivity (Nuts/ha)
Andhra Pradesh	102.6	1092.7	10650	104.0	1129.1	10857
Assam	21.0	136.0	6476	21.1	163.6	7754
Goa	25.0	125.1	5004	25.0	125.1	5004
Karnataka	333.8	1754.2	5255	373.7	1523.4	4077
Kerala	925.8	5536	5980	939.5	5744	6114
Maharashtra	16.8	244.4	14548	16.8	193.8	11536
Orissa	17.7	109.9	6209	17.3	142.4	8231
Tamil Nadu	323.5	3192	9867	335.8	3293.6	9808
Tripura	3.1	7.0	2258	3.3	7.0	2121
West Bengal	24.5	330.5	13490	25.6	331.6	12953
A&N Islands	25.2	89.0	3532	25.2	89.7	3560
Lakshadweep	**2.7**	**36.9**	**13667**	**2.7**	**53.1**	**19667**
Pondicherry	2.2	24.7	11227	2.3	25.3	11000
All-India	1823.9	12678.4	6951	1892.3	12821.7	6776

Source: ICAR.

ranging from 132 in Agatti to just about 5 in Minicoy (2001-02). The significant level of inter-island variation in productivity indicates the need and scope for improvement. It can be taken up in low-lying areas where water availability is adequate.

Although productivity of coconut cultivation in terms of nuts per hectare, stands the highest in the country, it can be improved in terms of size of the nuts. The number of palms per hectare, which stands on an average at 241 and goes much higher in some of the islands, needs to be brought down to 180-200 as the existing high density reduces the availability of sunlight for the coconut palms as well as land for intercropping. Efforts for intercropping in a scientific way need to be initiated on a pilot basis and popularised further after closely monitoring the effect of the pilot efforts. This will call for enhanced level of research and extension activities in this respect by institutions such as the ICAR station of Central Plantation Crops and Research Institute, Minicoy.

Product Diversification and Value Addition

Lakshadweep being coconut territory, coconut productivity plays an important role in improving economic status of the Island. Now productivity level has almost reached to the saturation level. Increase in population is mounting pressure on resources available in the Territory. In order to meet the requirement of growing population for a comfortable life, income generated from copra alone will not be sufficient to meet the increasing demand. The only way out is to go for product diversification and value addition.

The coconut tree is a very useful plant. Each part of the tree is useful. On an average thousand nuts yield one quintal copra, 60 kg of fibre and 1000 coconuts shells and it is possible to add value to the crop through its various products namely:

i) Vinegar—a permanent natural preservative, ingredient for pickles, salads, soups, curry, etc.

ii) Jaggery—a colloidal sugary substance made out of coconut *neera* (toddy) used for making a variety of snacks, a best substitute for jams, for making cool drinks, etc.

iii) Desiccated coconut powder—Powder made out of fresh coconut by mechanical processing. Processes involved are removing of shells without breaking kernel, outer skin is peeled, cleaned and crushed in the desiccator machine After desiccation, the powder is dried in the driers maintaining 40-60°C for 30-45 minutes, packed and marketed; used mainly for

8. Source: *Directorate of Economics and Statistics*, Ministry of Agriculture, GoI.

confectionery items, many other variety dishes, curries, etc.

iv) Snowball tender coconut—Eight to nine months old tender coconut is dehusked and shells removed using a machine without touching the kernel content, kernel ball is fixed in an ice cream bowl and served with a straw fixed in the eye of the kernel ball. Water can be consumed using straw and kernel eaten later.

v) Ball copra—It is conversion of raw coconut into copra without breaking it into two pieces, nuts allowed to dry till shell is separated from the kernel and dried, ball copra is comparatively clean, fetches good value in the market, long shelf life, north Indian's prefer especially for religious functions.

vi) Coconut milk—Coconut cream is the processed milk extracted from fresh matured coconuts. It is an instant product, which can be either used directly or diluted with water to make various preparations such as curries, sweets, desserts, puddings, etc. It can also be used in the manufacture of bakery products and for flavouring foodstuffs. Processed and packed coconut cream has a shelf life of six months.

vii) Coconut fibre products—curled coir fibre, coir rope, yarn, coir mats and matting, pressed board, fibre brush, geo-jute for soil erosion, etc.

viii) Extraction of coconut oil and Virgin coconut oil.

ix) Converting waste coconut pith into usable manure, briquettes.

x) Coconut shell for Handicrafts, activated carbon, shell powder, etc.

xi) Coconut tree stem—construction material, quality furniture, boat making, etc.

xii) Rib of coconut leaf—Broom and Handicrafts

Other than DCP, Coconut milk/cream and Coconut fibre, other products mentioned above are not being produced in an organised manner in Lakshadweep. Farmers need to be motivated for such ventures for a sustainable economic prosperity.

Agro Management

In order to be economically competitive and environmentally sustainable, alternative varieties, practices and better management of agricultural fields are called for. Cultivation of other fruits, vegetables, trees, etc. is necessary to reduce the risk factor. Hybrid dwarf coconuts have become available and need to be promoted more vigorously among the farmers. Coconut plantations should be thinned by removal of unthrifty senile/uneconomical old palms. Other measures identified in this direction are as follows:

- Extensive intercrop management needs to be popularised by cultivating crops other than coconut, adaptable to the agro-climatic conditions of the territory in the interspaces of the coconut plantation such as papaya, fruits, vegetables, pulses, vanilla and tuber crops.
- Encourage production and usage of organic bio-fertilisers and pith-plus compost and discourage the use of chemical fertilisers and pesticides, eliminating these altogether in a phased manner in favour of organic farming.
- Control of pests such as rhinoceros beetle, rodents, coconut mite which affect the coconut and other pests such as scales, whitefly, serpentine leaf minors, aphids, ladybird beetle, fruit borer and fruit flies which affect the intercrops.
- Control of diseases like bud rot, stem bleeding, leaf spot, sheath rot, button-shedding, bunchy top, mosaic, little leaf and nematodes.
- Banana cultivation, which was popularised by the department some time ago in all the inhabited islands, should be discontinued immediately in view of the heavy evapo-transpiration rate of banana trees (more than 15 litres per day per tree is required for irrigation owing to the sandy nature of the soil).
- Rainwater harvesting and conservation for the development of rainfed areas and promotion of on farm water management, water saving technologies and devices (e.g., Sprinkler/Drip Irrigation) for increasing water use efficiency need promotion.
- There should be greater partnership between Lakshadweep development agencies, ICAR in Minicoy and Krishi Vigyan Kendra (KVK) in Kiltan to lay special thrust on research for efficient water utilisation and conservation.
- Promotion of water saving methods and devices such as drip/sprinkler irrigation, encouraging water conservation and recycling of household

TABLE 2.5

Production of Milk and Poultry Eggs in Lakshadweep

	1996-97	*1997-98*	*1998-99*	*1999-2000*	*2000-01*	*2001-02*	*2002-03*	*2003-04*	*2004-05*
				Milk Production ('000 Litres)					
Govt. Units	0.28	0.28	0.15	0.33	0.48	0.34	0.31	0.25	0.27
Private Units	8.12	12.42	10.81	10.05	12.48	12.78	13.17	11.08	12.30
Total	**8.40**	**12.70**	**10.96**	**10.38**	**12.96**	**13.12**	**13.48**	**11.33**	**12.57**
				Egg Production (Numbers)					
Govt. Units	0.74	1.06	1.76	1.37	1.83	2.92	1.96	4.66	3.13
Private Units	42.77	57.80	58.27	66.83	77.17	79.34	83.38	105.46	116.63
Total	**43.51**	**58.86**	**60.03**	**68.20**	**79.00**	**82.26**	**85.34**	**110.12**	**119.76**

Source: Lakshadweep Administration.

water should be prioritised. There is also a need for value addition to the fibre products, for which institutional support from various agencies is required.

- The soils being highly porous and rainfall being high, there is the possibility of intense leaching losses of nutrients as well as pollution of water with nitrates. To overcome this, the Department of Agriculture should perhaps promote only slow release nitrogenous fertilisers such as neem cake blended urea, urea formaldehyde, lac coated urea and applying the fertilisers in four splits for better fertiliser management. This should be pursued within the overall goal of a phased elimination of the use of chemical fertilisers.
- Foliar application of nutrients for vegetables, banana and other low canopy horticultural crops may be adopted to prevent leaching losses. Green manure crops supplied with potassium (K) and magnesium (Mg) and micronutrients will help in meeting the requirements of coconuts partially on their incorporation.
- Use of pesticides and fungicide should be minimised and more emphasis should be given to biological and agronomical control of pests and diseases, to prevent pollution hazards.
- The rat menace attacking the coconut plantations needs to be controlled scientifically.
- Fishing waste at present is put back into the sea, which is environmentally undesirable and could also be used as manure.
- Use of bio-fertilisers, vermicomposts and green manure should be encouraged.

Animal Husbandry

Current Status

Animal husbandry in Lakshadweep islands mainly consists of poultry and goat rearing, with cattle coming thereafter. Besides being subsidiary economic activity these also provide useful by-products for preparation of organic manure. However, owing to the scarcity of grazing lands and traditional factors, household farming of cattle is being practised instead of organised farming. In tune with the religious beliefs of the local people, pigs and dogs are non-existent on the islands. As per the 17th Livestock Census (2002) the number of cattle was 4,206, goats,46,333 and poultry birds, 1,30,651, ducks,10,740, turkey,1,476, other livestock (Japanese Quail and Guinea Fowl, etc.), 5006.[9] Total production of milk and poultry eggs in Lakshadweep in government farms and in the private units during the recent years is given in Table 2.5.

The per capita availability and requirement of meat, eggs and milk are indicated in Table 2.6.

TABLE 2.6

Availability and Requirement of Eggs, Meat and Milk (2004-05)

Item	*Availability (2004-05)*	*Per Capita Availability*	*Requirement*
Egg	119.76 Lakh	156 Nos./annum	125 Lakhs
Milk	1257 MT	54 gram/day	5800 MT
Meat	250 MT	3.9 kg/annum	1425 MT

Source: Department of Animal Husbandry, Lakshadweep Administration.

9. Livestock population for the years 1972-2002 and Island-wise projections for 2002 are at Annexure A-7.A & A-7.B.

Nearly 90 per cent of total households are rearing two to three goats for meat purposes and also to meet their daily requirement of milk to some extent. In spite of a large number of households rearing goats, the availability of goat milk and meat is meagre. Cattle, both for meat and milk are mainly imported from coastal cities such as Mangalore and Calicut. As there are no quarantine infrastructure facilities available at Mangalore and Calicut ports, the purchased animals on arrival are kept in quarantine before these are introduced in the islands, with a view to prevent entry of diseases.

There are three veterinary hospitals and six veterinary dispensaries (Clinics), run by the government to provide veterinary healthcare. There are eight government hatcheries that have a capacity to produce up to 3 lakh chicks and the actual production during 2004-05 was 1.7 lakh.

Fodder development units are functioning in the islands of Andrott and Minicoy. These units meet only the minimum requirement of animals since large-scale fodder cultivation is not possible owing to scarcity of land and sweet water.

Recommended Approach

In Lakshadweep commercial livestock farming is neither feasible nor advisable. Keeping small units of cows and goats under stall-feeding should be an ideal model to meet the requirement of livestock products and for supplemental income. A cattle farmer on an average can earn around Rs. 50 per day from a one/two cow unit which is sufficient for a family of two to three members.

Poultry offers a viable commercial proposition and farmers could be encouraged to establish large units (more than 1000 birds). Government's intervention would be very helpful, by way of extending financial assistance for ensuring availability of feed at affordable price, marketing support, development of infrastructure such as cold storage and insurance coverage, etc. as also to facilitate development of organised poultry farming.

For better production and adaptability, new strains of poultry suitable to the island conditions may be developed in consultation with various poultry institutes/ universities. Diversified poultry activities such as rearing of ducks, quails, turkey and guinea fowl should be promoted to supplement egg and meat production. Adoption of backyard poultry has shown remarkable results. It should be continued with various strains developed by the concerned research institutions. Rearing of parent stocks of layers, broilers and other avian species should be strengthened in various islands to support hatching operations.

The scope for goat rearing especially among the womenfolk is large in the islands. However, the need is to adopt scientific breeding methods to improve body weights and prolificacy. Genetic upgradation of the present goat population should be attempted through crossbreeding with high yielding milch and large body size meat breeds. Artificial insemination in goats should also be introduced. Moreover, scientific rearing and feeding of goats should be emphasised to check indiscriminate grazing of the scant vegetative growth in the islands. Bucks should be maintained in Lakshadweep islands for providing natural service.

As for cattle rearing, at present around 1000 crossbreeds of Jersey, Holstein Friesian and Brown Swiss are available. It would be desirable to restrict the crossbred population to one breed cross for ease of maintaining the breed populations. Considering the hot and humid climatic conditions of Lakshadweep, it is advisable to maintain Jersey Crossbreds. Subsequent breeding and improvements using semen of proven crossbred bulls should be put in place. Presently there are five Artificial Insemination Centres (AI) in different islands. The AI network needs to be extended to other islands where the cattle population is sizeable. Efforts should be made to provide doorstep AI services to the farmers. Sufficient number of AI workers should be trained to provide breeding services at the farmer's door. The facilities of liquid nitrogen both for storage and distribution of semen should be strengthened.

While cattle fodder is generally available locally, the feed requirements are brought in from the mainland. Present consumption of livestock feed is about 2000 MT per annum. This is expected to increase to 3000 MT in the coming years. Large quantities of coconut cake and fish meal are available in Lakshadweep. It should be convenient and economical to start small feed mixing units in the islands with large poultry and goat populations. Such an approach while allowing use of local available feed inputs would also reduce the feed cost.

Efforts should be made to ensure better livestock health in the islands. Simultaneous efforts are necessary to prevent the entry of any disease from outside through introduction of livestock and livestock products. Animals required for both milk and meat for the islands are brought from coastal cities like Calicut and Mangalore. There is no infrastructure facility available in these ports to adopt quarantine certification service. In the present context, it is necessary to establish a quarantine unit to ensure prevention of diseases from the mainland.

Other measures suggested are as follows:

- Disease diagnostic laboratories/disease information units should be established at the major islands.
- A feed analysis laboratory should be established at the capital island Kavaratti for ensuring good quality fresh feeds.
- Mass vaccination against dreadful diseases should be taken up to declare the territory a "disease free zone."
- A veterinary medical store at Kavaratti should be established to ensure buffer stock of emergency medicines/vaccines/diagnostics.
- Mobile Veterinary Units in all major islands should be established to make available veterinary aids at farmers' doorsteps.
- Owing to the geographical isolation of the islands from each other, it is difficult to transport men and materials for timely vaccination and medication whenever any outbreak of disease occurs. In order to address disease contingencies, a convenient mechanised boat having navigational aids should be made available to the department of Animal Husbandry.
- There is only one slaughterhouse at the capital island Kavaratti. Small slaughterhouses should be established in other major islands so as to produce clean and hygienic meat and also provide training to technicians and butchers working in them.
- An institutional mechanism to train women and farmers involved in various animal husbandry activities and apprising them with the latest technical know-how should be put in place.

Soil and Water Conservation

Unlike the mainland, seasonal or perennial streams, lakes, ponds or wetlands do not exist in the Lakshadweep islands. The overall climate is of a humid, tropical, monsoon type and possibilities of snowfall, which would melt gradually and provide off rainy season flows, are completely non-existent. The topography is almost flat, soils are sandy, highly permeable and even local surface runoff marks are not seen. The size of the islands is so small that water runoff, if any, cannot attain critical concentration to make even a small stream. It is all *in situ* infiltration of rainwater into the ground.

The mean annual rainfall ranges from 1715 mm in Amini to 1934 mm in Minicoy but 80 per cent is received from May to November when roof harvesting would be sufficient to meet domestic requirements. Five almost rainless months from December to April are critical for water conservation. Since rainfall is high, soils are sandy and highly permeable with level topography, recharging potentials are extremely good. Infiltrated rainwater being of good quality always floats on relatively denser saline aquifers with a sharp boundary in all coastal and island ecosystems. However, the floating fresh water zone is of limited thickness.

Almost every household has one to two shallow dug wells for skimming floating fresh water for washing, bathing, livestock or even drinking during critical periods of the year. However, this water is limited in quantity and its salinity level increases as a function of time during withdrawal in the rainless period of five months. Sometimes they abandon the well if the water quality becomes too poor. Contamination of this shallow ground water is a serious threat in all the islands. Most of the latrines are based on soak pit since sewerage treatment system is not provided. Even defecation and urination made on the ground in the open has high probability of contaminating very shallow ground water especially during the rainy season because of the high infiltration rate of the sandy soil. Hence, extraction of shallow ground water for drinking is full of health hazards. Desalinisation of saline water is quite expensive and energy demanding. Thus, the need for harvesting and extracting rainwater on a scientific basis has become very acute.

Rainwater Harvesting Techniques

The traditional open wells, which are a type of subsurface fresh water skimming system, can be improved substantially. Open dug wells being used to skim fresh water floating over a relatively denser saline layer have limited capacity. Their yield can be enhanced by laying filter pipes (collector pipe) horizontally into the fresh water layer and connecting it to the dug sump wells. In this way fresh water from 40-50 m horizontal distances can be collected into the open dug wells constructed with RCC rings.

Another option is roof water harvesting. The potential of harvesting rain falling on the roof is available for providing reliable drinking water. Fortunately sloping roofs of GI sheets are common all over the islands. Each storage structure can be filled and refilled many times during the rainy season and hence a system has to be designed for the dry season of five to six months. An approximate exercise was done by assuming a runoff coefficient of 0.8 from a GI sheet roof. It was assumed to provide five litres/day of drinking water per person for the dry period of four to six months of different islands. For an average family size of five, the requirement was assumed to vary from three to five kilolitres. Per family investment ranged from Rs. 8,000 to Rs. 13,000 depending upon the island. This also works out to be Rs. 1,600 to Rs. 2,600 per person with a weighted average of Rs. 2,080 per person. Overall investment of Rs. 1.50 crore will be required to cover 70,000 people living in these islands.

The existing schemes for rainwater harvesting need to be integrated with this suggested approach. It is also desirable to make the rainwater harvesting structures mandatory for all future civil constructions. In respect of construction undertaken by private individuals, suitable financial subsidies may also be extended.

Soil Erosion and Conservation

The thick canopy of coconut palms that covers almost every inch of the islands, breaks the kinetic velocity of the rainwater. There is a thick growth of grasses and shrubs especially where there are no coconut trees and this provides adequate ground cover to neutralise the beating effect of rain drops. Further, the highly porous nature of the soil induces the falling rainwater to percolate down the soils *in situ*. These phenomena minimise the chances of soil erosion and maximise the opportunities of recharging aquifers which are the back bones of the present domestic water use. Therefore, conservation measures of the mainland such as trenching, contour, field or compartment bunding are not required.

However, coastal erosion by the sea waves is quite prevalent. Unfortunately coastal or wetland vegetation like that of mangroves elsewhere, which offers a very effective wave breaking system, is generally absent in these islands. Some coastal vegetation has been observed in Bangaram and Minicoy (Keorha) but most other islands are devoid of such vegetative protection. Depending upon the orientation of the islands, direction of monsoon storms and the waves, erosion in one part and soil accretion or deposition on other parts of the same island appear quite common. The lagoon structure associated with an island is also important in guiding soil erosion or deposition (accretion) of weathered material.

Wave breaking concrete solid blocks (tetrapods) have been used in the past. These blocks are very expensive and optimisation of their utility is uppermost. They are also not aesthetically very pleasing and restrict the enjoyment of the beaches. Instead of these, solid block concrete rings or squares may be used and appropriate vegetation such as bamboo, casurina or rapidly spreading or crawling type vegetation observed in Bangaram may be planted within these concrete rings or squares. Such vegetation will provide better anchorage of concrete rings or squares and also provide a canopy to absorb waves. This will also provide additional energy (carbon) source for aquatic fauna and will enhance biodiversity, besides giving a pleasing appearance.

Fisheries and Ocean Development

Marine fishery is one of the core economic activities in Lakshadweep. The number of fishermen engaged in this sector is 8,060 (2003-04), which is about 25 per cent of the total working population. The main fishing season in the islands extends from October to May, the peak period being December to March. Tuna forms 87 per cent of the fishery and apart from this, a wide variety of fishes such as pelagic sharks, seer fishes, perches, barracudas, garfish, rainbow runner and carangids are available in the area (See Annexure A-8). Major fishing methods employed are pole and line fishing, trolling, hand lining and gill netting. Total fish catch, which mainly consists of tuna (70-75 per cent), ranges from 10 to 14 thousand tonnes annually, with 12,800 tonnes valued at Rs. 25.60 crore in 2001 and around 10,300 tonnes valued at Rs. 20.06 crores in 2003.[10] Fishing activities operate through 1500 boats, with 500 of them being mechanised. Commercially exploitable fishery resources are estimated to be of the order of 1.50 lakh tonnes per annum. Cold storage facilities for fisheries with capacity ranging between 5 and 10 tonnes each are available in the islands of Agatti, Andrott, Kavaratti, Minicoy and Chetlat. Export of fish products (specially dried fish called *Mas* and salt dried shark) ranges from 1,100 to 1,500 tonnes annually, with an exception of 1,845 tonnes in 1998.[11]

10. *Lakshadweep: Basic Statistics 2003-04*, Lakshadweep Administration (p.34).

11. *Lakshadweep: Basic Statistics 2003-04*, Lakshadweep Administration (p.37).

The extensive exclusive economic zone of 4 lakh sq km that surrounds Lakshadweep provides ample opportunities to exploit the fishery resources from the vast oceanic depths. There are over 600 species of marine fish, of which 300 are ornamental. The other aquatic species available includes 111 species of coral, 82 species of seaweed, 52 species of crabs, 2 of lobsters, 48 gastropods, 12 bivalves, 41 sponges, 10 echinoderms, and 4 species of turtles. The present level of fish catch is almost negligible compared to the available potential. A strategy to periodically monitor the movement of the various varieties of fishes, prawns, shrimps, etc. utilising satellite imagery and other modern techniques needs to be developed. Simultaneously, sophisticated vessels to enable a scientific approach to the catch, storing the catch in cold conditions on the high seas, and subsequent handling and storage at the shore, processing and packaging etc., need to be worked out in detail. Above all, further avenues for marketing of the fish produce are required to be explored. For this purpose, institutions such as the Marine Products Export Development Authority need to be involved in a big way.

The vast oceanic surroundings offer the scope for high value commercial activities such as production of pearls through oyster culture (molluscan culture), ornamental fisheries, etc. also needs to be pursued.

Tuna Fisheries

A reasonable estimate of the exploitation potential of tuna around Lakshadweep is 50,000 tonnes, while the present production is only about 10,000 tonnes. Agatti, Minicoy, Bitra and Suheli are the four major tuna landing centres in Lakshadweep. The skipjack tuna, *Katsuwonus pelamis* accounts for 82 per cent of the tuna caught followed by yellowfin tuna, *Thunnus albacares*. Tuna fishing in almost all the islands except Andrott and to a certain extent Kalpeni, is conducted using pole and line live-bait technique and trolling. The use of mechanised boats for pole and line fishing has resulted in considerable increase in the catch per boat. However, in pole and line fishing only fishes available in surface shoals/schools can be targeted by the gear and irrespective of the availability of the number of fish, only the ones attracted/lured towards the bait can be caught. The craft presently in vogue is also a hindrance in augmentation of the production beyond a certain level because of the size and power of the vessel and the frugal facilities on board for living, fishing and storage. Fishermen largely target a single species, i.e., skipjack tuna, caught by the pole and line method. Further, lack of shore-based infrastructure such as ice plants, tunnel freezers, cold storages and means of transportation required for multi-day fishing, restricts fishers from undertaking multi-day fishing trips.

Presently, most of the pole and line fishing islands are already saturated with the units. However, the present crafts and gears can effectively be deployed and utilised for enhancing the production in the mother ship type fishing and dory fishing, using them as tools and fishing platforms and transferring the catches into the storage, freezer vessels with essential supplies. This also fits into the situation where it is difficult to provide large infrastructure facilities for operation of bigger vessels. Thus, it is better to introduce mother vessels/collector vessels. Such vessels can take a number of smaller fishing boats to far away fishing grounds. Recent innovations introduced in some of the boats include use of mechanical splashers and GPS system that need to be extended to other vessels.

The drift gill netting with mesh regulations (100-150 mm) has proved successful in Andrott since its introduction in 1994 and is an alternative method worth trying on a large-scale, as the time and energy spent for the method is almost half that of the pole and line fishing and independent of live bait availability. However, the ideal time of operation for the gear is during night hours. Management options include introduction of new generation pole and line fishing vessels with multi-day fishing ability and experimental fishing by purse seines.

As already mentioned, fishing in the islands is largely confined to skipjack tuna. There exists immense potential for deep-sea fishing for yellowfin tuna that has a huge export market in Japan and the Far East. The Lakshadweep Development Corporation has established that tuna long line fishing is viable, with a potential of export of 50 metric tonnes of yellowfin tuna every month. The possibilities of operating long line for yellowfin tuna in the region can be examined by conducting experimental fishing and provision of credit facilities along with development of markets in the mainland. Adequate attention also needs to be paid to monitoring the tuna environment and satellite data for increasing the catch.

The following measures are proposed to augment the tuna production instantly at least to double the present level:

- Provisions for fitting sprayers in all the pole and line units to increase efficiency and to reduce the manpower.

- Training and utilising unskilled surplus (caused due to the automation) fishermen in the productive field either by introducing new units or by putting into operation the 'step-knee' units of pole and line fisheries.
- Adopting the diversified and combination methods such as pole and line-cum-gill netting, gill netting-cum-long lining-cum-trolling, etc.
- Increasing the endurance of the existing Pablo boats in line with dory fishing or mother ship type fishing.
- Distributing and deploying more units, preferably the combination vessels around Suheli Par, Bitra, Perumal Par, Valyapaniyam, Cheriyapaniyam, Elikalpeni Bank, Investigator Bank, Mankunn and Pitti areas.
- Introducing bottom set gill netting, light fishing, trap fishing, etc. inside and outside the lagoons of Suheli, Bitra, Bangaram-Tinnakara-Parali, Perumal Par, Cheriyapaniyam, Valyapaniyam and Kalpeni-Chriyam.
- Installation of stationary Fish Aggregation Devices (FADs) to attract tuna and other fishes.
- Proper utilisation of tuna ensilages for both economic and health well-being.
- Popularisation of tuna and tuna products in the internal markets for increasing the demand.
- Training of local fishermen to equip them to handle the technologically advanced devices.
- Opening avenues to facilitate the export of the Lakshadweep fishes including tuna.

Live-bait Resources

Baitfish comprises small fishes collected from the lagoon or reef areas and put into the sea to attract tuna schools within the range of the boat. Live-baits are of paramount importance for the success of pole and line operations for skipjack. Major fishing areas for live-baits are Minicoy, Agatti, Suheli, Perumal Par, Bitra, Valiapani and Cheriapani. The important groups exploited at Minicoy are clupeids, caesionids and apogonids while the clupeid, *Spratelloides delicatulus* is the only species caught as bait in other islands. Increase in the number of pole and line units consequent on mechanisation of boats has resulted in the progressive increase in the demand for live-baits and their shortage is found to be a major constraint for pole and line operations in the islands especially after mechanisation.

Non-availability of live-baits in required quantities can be attributed to tampering of the lagoon ecosystem, seasonality in the recruitment pattern of migrant species and exploitation pressure. Attempts to culture important live-baits such as *Chromis caeruleus* and *Spratelloides delicatulus* are being made by the Central Marine Fisheries Research Institute (CMFRI). In the northern islands, rational exploitation of *S. delicatulus*, which is the only species used for tuna pole and line fishing, could be advised and management measures for the maintenance of stocks implemented. Fishermen need to be encouraged to exploit alternate species belonging to Pomacentridae, Apogonidae and Caesionidae families, that are associated with coral colonies in deeper regions of the lagoon. Necessary infrastructure and facilities for collection and transport of live-baits from the lagoons need to be provided by the Department of Fisheries. Possibilities of culturing *Chromis caeruleus, Chromis ternatensis* and *Lepidozygus tapeinosoma*, which are hardy and form a good percentage in the live-bait catches during certain seasons, could be explored. Shelter for the island fishermen and warehouse for their fish, etc. are required to be provided on the mainland in areas such as Mangalore, Kochi and Calicut.

Tuna Products

In Lakshadweep, the bulk of the surplus catch of tuna after local consumption is processed into a traditional product called *masmin*, a boiled, smoked and sun dried product with a shelf life of about a year. The average annual production of *masmin* in Lakshadweep is presently around 1,200 tonnes valued at Rs. 10 crore. *Masmin* is packed in gunny bags and transported to the mainland by mechanised country crafts or ships and sold to dealers in Calicut, Mangalore and Tuticorin. The current price of *masmin* ranges from Rs. 80-100 per kg depending on catch and season. A small portion of the tuna caught is canned in the government canning factory set up in Minicoy in 1969, which has an installed capacity of 1500 cans per 8 hours. An ice plant of 5 tonnes and a cold storage of 20 tonnes capacity are attached to this facility. The present average production during a season is around 1,12,000 cans. The products from this factory are received well both in home and foreign markets. However, it is at present just breaking even with the cost of the tins being very high, taxes levied on the cans and competition from imported cans.

The local demand for tuna being limited, adequate attention has to be given for the storage, processing and marketing of the catches. The production capacity of the tuna canning plant has to be increased to cope with the increased tuna landings. Transportation and marketing of tuna in the mainland after freezing can also be considered. Further, *masmin* deteriorates on keeping for several months by beetle infestation. Steps have to be taken to improve the quality depending on the market preferences on the mainland and elsewhere. A large quantity of firewood is consumed for the preparation of *masmin* and shortage of firewood is already felt in some of the islands. Use of alternate sources of energy needs to be explored to remedy the situation. The packaging of *masmin* should be improved to make it more hygienic and attractive, while increasing the shelf life.

Utilisation of Fish Wastes

An estimated annual average of 1,847 tonnes of valuable proteins and calcium are wasted as the ensilages in the form of head, bones, liver, ovaries, guts, etc. from the tuna catches. About 400 tonnes of fish meal valued at a minimum of Rs. 20 lakh can be produced annually from these wastes. This will facilitate extra income, increased employment opportunities and improve the overall health and hygienic condition of the islanders by reducing the health hazards owing to the decomposed wastes.

Other Fish Resources

Apart from tuna, there are other fish resources such as snappers, groupers, flying fishes, barracudas, carangids, wahoo (*Acanthocybium solandri*), rainbow runner (*Elagatis bipinnulatus*), Dolphin fish (*Coryphaena hippurus*), perches, sharks and rays, that are either totally neglected or exploited to the barest minimum for personal uses alone from the nearest grounds (reefs and lagoons). Constituting about a fourth of the total production, they are mainly exploited by traditional gear such as the hook and line, harpooning, surface trolling, dragnets and cast nets. As the traditional methods of capture of fishes other than tuna have not undergone any change, landings of these fishes have not shown any significant increase. The magnitude of the landings of other fishes depends on the fluctuation in the availability of tuna shoals around the islands. Diversified fishing efforts such as long lining for sharks, drift gillnetting coupled with improvements in crafts to fish in distant waters would help a long way in tapping these resources.

Ornamental Fish Resources

A good number of species in the lagoon and reefs of Lakshadweep are valuable ornamental fishes. Export of ornamental fishes on a limited scale can be attempted with suitable arrangements for storage, transportation and marketing. It has been estimated that about 8.6 million fishes belonging to 165 species of 20 families could be fished every year. However, any indiscriminate exploitation can disturb the balance in the associations of different organisms leading to loss of biodiversity and environmental degradation. The following aspects need consideration before exploitation and export of ornamental fishes from the lagoons and reef flats of different islands is taken up on a commercial scale:

- Impact of exploitation of ornamental fishes will have to be carefully and continually monitored with suitable regulations to prevent any undesirable decline in the fish populations.
- Fishing for ornamental fishes should essentially be carried out by non-destructive methods such as trap fishing and hand-net fishing, as it ensures collection of only the required species in desired numbers and hence needs to be considered seriously while formulating strategies for commercial exploitation.
- Some species of wrasses (*Halichoeres centriquadrus, H. marginatus, H. kawarin, Stethojulis axillaris*), damsel fishes (*Dascyllus aruanus, Chromis caeruleus, Abudefduf saxatilis, A. sexfasciatus, A. glaucus*), surgeon fishes (*Acanthurus triostegus, A. leucosternon*), parrot fishes (*Callyodon taeniurus, C. scaber*), butterfly fishes (*Chaetodon auriga, C. citrinellus*) and puffer fishes (*Canthigaster marginatus*) offer immense potential for exploitation and export, and call for developing markets for these fishes.
- Careful vigil is necessary to see that the corals are not damaged while collecting fishes living among them or in their vicinity.
- Exploitation and export have to be routed through a single agency to ensure close monitoring, maintenance of information on species-wise numbers caught and exported.
- One of the lagoons has to be left unexploited to serve as a sanctuary and help in preserving the biodiversity.
- Care should be taken against extensive exploitation of such species which may endanger their existence.

Seaweed Resources

Resource assessment surveys in the Laccadive Archipelago carried out by the Central Marine Fisheries Research Institute, Kochi and the Central Salt and Marine Chemicals Research Institute, Bhavnagar indicate nearly 10,000-19,000 tonnes (wet biomass) of standing crop of seaweed comprising 114 species belonging to 62 genera. Twenty five per cent of this standing crop comprises seaweeds such as *Gelidiella acerosa* and *Gracilaria edulis* that can be exploited for the production of commercially important polysacccharides like *agar-agar* and *Turbinaria* and *Sargassum* spp. for alginic acid. The rest include edible and carageenan yielding species. These resources can be tapped for industrial purposes by regulated harvest as well as mariculture in lagoons.

Gelidiella acerosa is found to be growing luxuriantly in Kadmat and Gracilaria edulis in Agatti and Kavaratti Islands, which offer an immediately exploitable resource for setting up an *agar-agar* production unit. As many seaweed-based industries are coming up in India and the raw material supply from natural seaweed beds is inadequate to meet the growing demand of the industries, it has now become essential as also feasible to attempt mariculture of these resources. The availability of seedling stock, suitable site for farming (calm lagoons), highly nutritive and clear, high saline water devoid of silt and sediments are big assets for promoting mariculture of seaweeds in Lakshadweep.

It is desirable to put in place suitable institutional arrangements for exploiting seaweed resources. While the nodal responsibility for this purpose may be assigned to the Lakshadweep Administration, the technical support and involvement of national institutions such as the National Institute of Ocean Technology, Central Salt and Marine Research Institute, and the like, should be provided as a built in arrangement.

Mariculture Potential

Molluscan Culture

Marine pearl culture, using the pearl oyster, *Pinctada fucata* has been identified by the CMFRI, Kochi, as a technology ideally suited for transfer to Lakshadweep Islands. Based on this, the Institute conducted a demonstration trial at Bangaram Island in 1987 with the active participation of the Fisheries Department of the UT. This successful trial led to the initiation of a National Agricultural Technology Project (NATP) funded scheme on transfer of marine pearl culture technology in Minicoy Island in 2001. The scheme is currently in operation and pearl production trials are underway. Vast lagoons such as Bitra, Bangaram, Suheli, Kalpeni and Minicoy can be utilised for pearl culture. Implanted and conditioned oysters can be procured from CMFRI and reared up to the required period and the pearls extracted.

Seaweed Culture

Graci/aria edulis has been introduced and acclimatised in Minicoy lagoon for mariculture purposes in the year 1989-90. Optimum physical requirements and other husbandry practices for the mariculture of this species have been identified and a 7-10 fold increase in yield of *Gracilaria edulis* can be achieved. However, grazing by herbivorous fishes is a major constraint. Other species identified for mariculture include the carrageenan yielding red seaweed, *Kappaphycus striatus* and *Eucheuma cattani.* Since these are cultivated in porous polythene bags suspended from long lines, grazing can be controlled to a large extent. Preliminary studies indicate excellent prospects of augmenting production of valuable carageenan yielding seaweed through mariculture in the Laccadive seas besides providing job opportunities in the sector.

Floating Cage Culture

Fattening of fishes and lobsters in cages placed in vast lagoons like Suheli, Bitra, Bangaram, Kalpeni and Minicoy can be carried out after pilot trials.

Aqua-Tourism

Tourism on the lines of the Australian coral reef management system may be adopted for these areas, wherein tourism does not affect the coralline ecology. Necessary steps to provide facilities such as boats and gear for sport fishing as part of tourism development may be taken at suitable locations.

Marine Parks

The terrestrial and marine habitats of Lakshadweep are fast changing and conservation measures are urgently called for in some of these islands to preserve and protect these critical habitats for scientific, cultural and economic purposes. Selection of coral preserves and establishment of parks in and around some of the islands may serve this purpose.

Turtle Farm

Lakshadweep is one of the few places in the Indian

Ocean where the green turtle, *Chelonia mydas* nests. It has been observed that about 30 green turtles nest in Suheli Valiyakara. A small turtle farm can be established in Suheli Valiyakara with an annual stocking of 200 neonates of *Chelonia mydas*. As Agatti is strategically located with airport facility, a Sea Turtle and Dolphin Park may be established for tourist attraction at Agatti near the port tower area after obtaining technical opinion for constructing a civil structure in the said area.

Ocean Development Authority

The exploitation of the vast potential of economic wealth from the ocean contained in the exclusive economic zone of Lakshadweep can be facilitated by setting up an Ocean Development Authority, suitably empowered on the lines of the existing Island Development Authority.

An Action Plan for the fisheries sector on the above lines is placed at Annexure A-9.

Cooperation and Civil Supplies

Due to the peculiar conditions of Lakshadweep, the Department of Cooperation is entrusted with dual statutory responsibilities of the Cooperative Societies on one hand and administration, implementation and monitoring of Public Distribution System on the other hand. The basic information on Cooperative Societies in Lakshweep is given in Table 2.7

Vision for Future

Marketing

The mainstay of the people of Lakshadweep is fishing and coconut cultivation. There are no primary or secondary markets in the islands for copra and the copra producers in the island take their produce to mainland marketing centres like Mangalore and Calicut. Fishermen of Lakshadweep islands specialise in catching tuna fish which has a ready market in Sri. Lanka and Southeast Asia. Dried tuna is exported to the above countries via Tuticorin in Tamil Nadu. Copra and tuna are highly seasonal produce in the conditions of Lakshadweep, the main season being from October to April. There is no organised marketing set up and strategy, so the average fisherman of the islands is not in a position to hold back his produce till such time as market condition becomes favourable for the seller. A strategy has to be evolved to procure dried *Mas* from the islands and market them through Cooperative Societies/ Lakshadweep Development Corporation as in the case of copra.

During the main marketing season the cooperative societies should have sufficient funds at their disposal for procurement of Copra as well as *Mas*, lest the small producers would be forced to sell their produce to private merchants even at a loss. The Government of India has sanctioned a one time grant of Rs. 5 crore for marketing of copra by Lakshadweep Cooperative Marketing Federation during Tenth Five-year Plan. This

TABLE 2.7

Basic Statistics on Cooperative Societies (as on 31.03.2005)

Sl.No.	*Name of Society*	*No.*	*Membership*	*Share Capital (In Lakhs)*		*Govt. Loan Outstanding*	*Turnover*
				Govt.	*Others.*		
1.	L.C.M.F.	1	80	15.30	3.32	378.13	1316.00
2.	I.C.S. & M.S.	10	48102	11.70	5.10	54.25	1420.80
3.	G.E.C.S. & C.	6	3571	0.55	0.72	7.88	69.45
4.	S.C.S.	9	8589	8.17	17.89	94.56	132.31
5.	L.C.C.S.	5	1113	0.44	0.29	8.98	3.23
6.	IND.C.S.	15	1964	1.50	1.26	—	—
7.	F.C.S.	6	513	5.25	0.18	—	—
8.	L.W.T.C.S.	1	30	3.00	0.93	0.11	—
9.	Student Consumer Stores.	2	258	0.20	0.00	—	—
	Total	**55**	**64220**	**46.11**	**29.69**	**543.91**	**2941.79**

Source: Department of Cooperation and Civil Supplies, UT of Lakshadweep.

amount is not sufficient to meet the full requirements. The approximate market value of copra and *mas* is estimated to be about Rs. 40 crores. Lakshadweep Cooperative Marketing Federation and Cooperative Societies have to raise funds to meet the full demand for marketing capital.

Since the main marketing centres for mas and copra are situated in Mainland centres like, Mangalore, Tuticorin, Calicut, etc. it is necessary to build required infrastructure like storage and warehousing facilities, which would enable the producers of the island to be in a better bargaining position.

Revival Package for Cooperative Credit Institutions

The Government of India, committed to increasing the flow of credit to rural agricultural purposes, has prepared a revival package for Cooperative Credit Institutions which is aimed at reviving the short term rural Cooperative Credit Structures (CCS) and make it a well managed and vibrant medium to serve the credit needs of rural India. The assistance for this for Lakshadweep is awaited from Government of India.

Public Distribution System

The basic information about Public Distribution System in Lakshadweep is furnished in Table 2.8 to Table 2.10.

The Public Distribution System in Lakshadweep is channelised through a network of Cooperative Societies. Lakshadweep Cooperative Marketing Federation, an apex body of Cooperative Societies situated in the islands is designated as the wholesale agent of Administration under Public Distribution System. It's main role is procurement & transportation of essential commodities. The 10 primary Cooperative Supply & Marketing Societies, 1 each in the 10 inhabitant islands act as the retail agents under Public Distribution System. Their main role is to stock the essential commodities in the islands and distribute them to the consumers through their retail outlets.

Considering the peculiar geographical situation and logistic problems the Government of India is allocating rice and wheat on an yearly basis, sugar and Kerosene oil on half-yearly basis. On the basis of the allocation orders issued by the Government of India, Public Distribution System items are lifted from the Central Agencies like Food Corporation of India (FCI) and India Oil Corporation (IOC) and transported to the islands in the administration's cargo barges and private motorised sailing vessels. The essential commodities procured are stored in the islands in government godowns as well as the godowns of Cooperative/Supply and Marketing Societies, which have combined storage capacity of about 6673 MT. These essential commodities are distributed to the consumers in the islands through Fair Price Shops working under the Cooperative Societies, each one of which has a coverage of less than 2000 people living within a radius of 1.5 kilometres.

Vision for Future

Door Delivery Of Essential Commodities and Other Consumer Goods

In the case of UT of Lakshadweep, core essential commodities and all other consumer goods are sold to consumers through the retail outlets of Cooperative Societies, which also serve as Fair Price Shops. The

TABLE 2.8

Basic Statistics on Public Distribution System-Beneficiaries

Sl.No.	*Name of Island*	*APL*	*BPL*	*AAY*	*AP*	*Total*
1	Kavaratti	2759	41	17	9	2826
2	Kalpeni	1155	104	30	5	1294
3	Amini	1727	76	59	7	1869
4	Andrott	2507	46	74	5	2632
5	Minicoy	1617	12	31	4	1664
6	Agathi	1404	31	5	6	1446
7	Kadmat	1436	126	45	5	1612
8	Kiltan	935	74	38	3	1050
9	Chetlat	640	41	27	3	711
10	Bitra	170	7	10	1	188
		14350	558	336	48	15292

Source: Department of Civil Supplies & Cooperation, UTL Administration.

TABLE 2.9

Basic Statistics on Public Distribution System–Foodgrain Requirement

Sl.No.	Name of Islands	Fair Price Shop	Monthly Requirements		
			Rice (MT)	Sugar (MT)	K.Oil Barrels
1	Kavaratti	6	85	12.5	50
2	Kalpeni	3	50	7.5	40
3	Amini	4	75	9.5	40
4	Andrott	5	100	14.5	50
5	Minicoy	4	60	13	100
6	Agathi	3	60	8.2	35
7	Kadmat	4	50	7	40
8	Kiltan	3	32	5	20
9	Chetlat	2	20	3.8	20
10	Bitra	1	3	0.4	5
	Total	**35**	**535**	**81.4**	**400**

Source: Department of Cooperation and Civil Supplies, UT of Lakshadweep.

TABLE 2.10

Basic Statistics on Public Distribution System—Storage Facilities

Sl.No.	Name of Island	Storage Facilities Available		Total
		Storage Capacity under Govt.	Storage Capacity under Coop. Sector	
1	Kavaratti	500	252	752
2	Kalpeni	252	300	552
3	Amini	252	700	952
4	Andrott	252	700	952
5	Minicoy	252	700	952
6	Agathi	252	400	652
7	Kadmat	275	400	675
8	Kiltan	168	400	568
9	Chetlat	168	400	568
10	Bitra	50	0	50
	Total	**2421**	**4252**	**6673**

Source: Department of Cooperation and Civil Supplies, UT of Lakshadweep.

next step is to achieve the objective of door delivery of essential commodities and other consumer durables.

Extension of LPG Distribution in All the Islands

Due to various constraints, particularly the transport bottleneck, the facility of LPG distribution could not be extended to Lakshadweep Islands till 1989. From 1989 till date the facility could be extended only in two of the islands namely Kavaratti and Minicoy.

There is great demand for extension of LPG facility to all other islands not only because the use of LPG is more convenient, but also because of non-availability of conventional fuels like coconut husk, which are increasingly being used for processing of Tuna fish to make *Mas*. In view of the public demand, required land for construction of LPG godowns have already been identified in all the islands. Unfortunately, the marketing facility could not be extended to other islands because of transport bottleneck. In the absence of a dedicated LPG ship, LPG cylinders are transported as deck cargo in cargo barges. However, the administration is exploring the possibility of acquiring an LPG ship with a view to extend the marketing facilities of LPG to remaining islands as well, which is likely to take a considerable time.

There are additional multiple handlings involved in the transportation of LPG Cylinders from mainland to island. Hence the actual cost per cylinder would be almost 35 to 40 per cent higher than the cost of the cylinders sold at mainland. In view of this and also in view of the fact that the Lakshadweep islands are backward and isolated, the Government of India had already instructed the Indian Oil Corporation (IOC) to bear full transportation charges.

Tourism

The Tourism sector has good potential for not only creating employment opportunities but also earning foreign exchange. In Lakshadweep, nature is at its colourful and pristine best. As an archipelago, the islands have a land area of 32 sq km surrounded by 4200 sq km of lagoon. It is one of the most spectacular tropical island systems of the world. Though the islands are near the equator, the climatic temperature is usually much lower than that of the neighbouring mainland. The average temperature ranges from 23° to 33° Celsius, which is suitable for the existence and growth of corals. The serene and still ambience of the island system totally rejuvenates visitors. Lakshadweep is home to many rare species of marine life and is perhaps the biggest natural underwater zoo in the world. The waters are calm and ideal for water sports such as diving, snorkelling, windsurfing, parasailing, etc. The fact that the visitors to the islands see before them the unfolding drama of evolution of the only islands in the country formed as a result of coral activity, makes it the only place of its kind. The southwest monsoon winds blow the coral dust in the same direction every year, which is why most of the islands have a north-south orientation. The islands are described as a coral paradise. These present a breath taking spectacle of sparkling coral reefs encircling a placid and tranquil lagoon and palm covered tiny islands. Lakshadweep has, therefore, the potential of growing into a top destination for beach tourism and water sports.

Even though the beauty and peace of these islands make these a haven for tourists, yet, the restrictions imposed on the entry of visitors and the remoteness of the islands from the mainland coupled with inadequate means of commutation, have led to only a modest level of tourism related activities for the economy of the territory. The total arrival of tourists in Lakshadweep has hovered around the figure of 4,000 annually inclusive of domestic as well as foreign. Among the inhabited islands, the more famous ones for the visitors are Bangaram, Kadmat, Minicoy and Agatti. The uninhabited islands offer an abode for a variety of flora and fauna. One such island, Pitti, is famous as a birds' island.

Tourism offers a potential for growth of the island economy. It generates employment for the local people and earns foreign exchange. While Kavaratti is the administrative headquarters of the islands as well as the most developed one; the only airport in Lakshadweep is located in Agatti and therefore Agatti is popularly known as the Gateway to Lakshadweep. Kalpeni is known for its scenic beauty with small islets called Tilakkam and Pitti. A huge lagoon encloses all of them. This lagoon is especially rich in coral life. A peculiar feature of the Kalpeni atoll is the huge storm bank of coral debris along the eastern and southeastern shoreline. Kadmat has become the focal point of tourist activities in Lakshadweep owing to the water sports institute and scuba diving centre. It is also known as 'Honeymoon Paradise' mainly because of the long sandy beaches with a beautiful shallow lagoon on the west. Minicoy is the southern most island with a lighthouse and has one of the largest lagoons. The uninhabited Bangaram Island has lately been developed as a tourist centre and is open to foreign tourists apart from Agatti, Kadmat, Thinnakara and Cheriyam. Some of the interesting water sports available in the above mentioned islands are wind surfing, scuba diving, parasailing and water skiing. However, the normal life of the islands is not disturbed by the tourism industry. Very few tourists visit the other islands mainly because of transportation problems.

The promotion of tourism in Lakshadweep has been entrusted to the Society for Promotion of Recreation & Nature Tourism (SPORTS). It is a registered society managed by senior officers of the administration and prominent citizens of Lakshadweep. The society operates tourist packages from Kochi to some of the islands such as Minicoy, Kalpeni, Kavaratti and Kadmat. It mainly operates two types of packages. The first one is a day package called "Coral Reef". Tourists explore the islands during the day and travel onboard at night; it covers three islands, namely, Minicoy, Kalpeni and Kavaratti in its five day voyage. The second package is a staying package called "Marine Wealth Awareness Programme", in which the tourists stay at Kavaratti and Kadmat for three days. It also operates a seven-day diving package at Kadmat for beginners and advance divers.

The tourist facilities developed so far in the islands include family huts (45), private huts (7), honeymoon

TABLE 2.11

Tourists Accommodation Facilities in Lakshadweep (as in 2002-03)

Island	*Family Huts*	*Beds*	*Restaurants*	*Honey-moon Huts*	*Beds*	*Executive Huts (AC)*	*Beds*	*Pre-fab Huts*	*Beds*	*Private Huts*	*Beds*	*Total Bed Capacity*
Kavaratti	5	10	1	-	-	-	-	-	-	-	-	10
Bangaram	30	60	1	-	-	-	-	-	-	-	-	60
Kadmat	10	20	1	8	16	8	22	1	2	-	-	60
Kalpeni	-	-	1	-	-	-	-	-	-	4	8	8
Minicoy	-	-	2	-	-	10	20	-	-	3	6	26
Agatti	-	-	-	-	-	10	20	-	-	-	-	20
Total	**45**	**90**	**6**	**8**	**16**	**28**	**62**	**1**	**2**	**7**	**14**	**184**

Source: Basic Statistics of Union Territory of Lakshadweep – 2003-2004.

huts (8), executive huts (28), prefabricated hut (1) and restaurants (6). Out of 13 islands identified for tourism development, only 6 have these facilities whereas 7 islands namely Agatti, Amini, Andrott, Bitra, Chetlat, Kiltan, Suheli and Cheriyam do not have tourist facilities (Table 2.11).

The actual arrival of tourists to this region has hovered around the figure of 4,000 for the past several years. The details are given in Table 2.12.

TABLE 2.12

Tourist Arrivals in Lakshadweep

Year	*No. of Tourists*		
	Indian	*Foreign*	*Total*
1992-93	2287	1150	3437
1993-94	2965	408	3373
1994-95	3166	1059	4225
1995-96	3470	1210	4680
1996-97	3502	1359	4861
1997-98	2900	1223	4123
1998-99	1999	736	2735
1999-00	1379	741	2120
2000-01	2992	871	3863
2001-02	3259	539	3798
2002-03	4151	580	4731
2003-04	4045	656	4701

Source: Basic Statistics 2003-04, Lakshadweep Administration.

The figures above indicate a decline in tourist arrivals, more noticeably in the case of foreigners. Inadequate communication facilities and restrictions on visitors are the main reasons behind the low level of tourism activities in these islands. A recent study report has projected the tourist arrivals to grow significantly in the coming years, reaching the level of 38,000 by 2020-21, Annexure A-10. However, careless growth of tourism is likely to harm the fragile ecosystem of the region.

The approach to the growth and development of tourism in this territory should keep in focus the need to maintain and nurture, besides the ecology, the local culture and traditions. This is particularly important as the very small size of the local population and the rather rudimentary level of the local economy make these vulnerable to getting overwhelmed by the externalities that come along with modernity. Analysis of the strengths, weaknesses, opportunities and threats of the tourism potential in Lakshadweep Islands gives a useful insight into the possible approaches.

The strength of Lakshadweep for growth as a tourism centre lies in the location of the islands, the scenic beauty, nature and climate of islands, the blue water lagoons, the coral reefs, the unspoilt virgin beaches, the calm waters ideal for water sports such as diving, snorkelling, windsurfing and parasailing and the many rare species of marine life and perhaps the biggest natural underwater zoo in the world that the islands and the adjoining biodiversity offers. These factors are further helped by the low crime rate of the islands and the helpful and friendly attitude of the local people.

The weaknesses of Lakshadweep lies primarily in the low carrying capacity of the islands, the absence of quality accommodation and food facilities, transport bottlenecks in terms of mainland-island and inter-island connectivity, lack of land based tourism attractions such as amusement parks, shopping arcades, entertainment plazas, fun cities, health resorts, trekking/skiing, adventure sports avenues, etc. and inadequate publicity.

In the midst of such strengths and weaknesses, Lakshadweep does seem to have adequate opportunities for growth as a still larger tourist centre. It has, for instance, ample scope for development of aqua sports and for the development of diving packages for divers. The beaches, lagoons, and the sea, all offer considerable scope for a variety of tourism activities. Among the options to be considered for promotion of tourism are the Mauritius Model and the Maldives Model. Both these models focus on high-end tourists and provide them with luxurious comfort. In fact, the Maldives Model has gone farther in this concept. In either model, government's direct investment is very small and yet the government retains its regulatory role and earns considerable revenues as well. As different from the Maldives Model is the model of nature tourism as well as marine tourism.

It is also necessary to keep in view the possible threats to the ecological, social and cultural environment of these islands from the traditional approaches to tourism growth and development. Environmental pollution of the beaches, soils and the frugal water bodies of the islands is very much a possibility. Sewage and garbage disposal, which are already a major problem, are most likely to worsen with the inflow of tourists unless due care is taken. Large-scale construction activities would bring in the problems of pollution, besides causing serious disturbance to the surface by building construction. The islanders also feel concerned about cultural pollution that could come along with the growth of tourism. For instance, consumption of alcohol is taboo in these islands and, therefore, the tourism policy ought not to frustrate such values of the people.

The example of the Maldives needs to be studied to work out a model for appropriate growth and development of tourism in Lakshadweep. It may be recalled that the Maldives model has led to a fast growth of high-end tourism. There are, however, concerns expressed over the adverse fall out, particularly ecological, in pursuing that model. A careful review of such concerns needs to be made while adopting the strategy for tourism promotion for Lakshadweep. The issue of selective high-end tourism versus mass tourism has also generated considerable debate. As the islands have very limited capacity to entertain large populations even of visitors, the tourism policy should discourage the same. In such contexts, the cruise-based tourism approach appears to be a viable proposition, wherein the tourists come from the mainland in cruises, spend the nights on the cruise and visit the various islands during the daytime.

In any model of tourism development, it will also be necessary to keep certain concepts intact. These will include preservation of the environment and the ecology, physical, economic and social security of the islanders, and provision of quality services to the visitors. While private sector participation is highly desirable, such participation, if followed straight on the pattern of the mainland developments, may have a serious fall out for the islands. The fragile social strength of the islanders coupled with their small numbers will not be able to survive any large inflow of private capital that comes to thrive on the biodiversity of the islands. It is also necessary to ensure that the economic fruits of growth and development of tourism reach the islanders. To achieve these ends, the government would need to retain and exercise its regulatory role with greater vigilance and also protect the economic, social and cultural interests of the islanders.

Industries

Industrial activity in Lakshadweep centres around coir and fish. The ecological and environment considerations prevent the setting up of large-scale industrial units in these islands as is done for the mainland states. The strategy for the industrialisation of Lakshadweep will have to focus on fisheries and agro-based units of medium and small-scales. However, the ecological parameters may be taken into account before initiating any industry. For instance, though the territory abounds in corals, picking them is prohibited on ecological considerations, thus leaving no scope for any economic activity. There are 41 registered industrial units in the government sector and 504 in the private sector (2001-02). All the units in the private sector are small and medium scale dealing with coir, fish and various support activities. In the government sector, there are seven coir fibre factories, a printing press, a hosiery factory, a tuna-canning factory and two boat building yards. The level of industrial development in Lakshadweep remains modest.

Fortunately, each part of the coconut palms and fruit lends itself for value addition. The nut can be converted into a variety of products such as desiccated coconut powder, vinegar, jaggery, snowball tender coconut (water and kernel can both be consumed), ball copra, coconut milk having less fat content and coconut cream. The value added products from coconut fibre include curled coir fibre, coir rope, yarn, coir mats and matting, pressed board, fibre brush, geo-jute for land slope stabilisation, etc. though some of these possibilities are not fully exploited yet. Coconut oil is most commonly used for kitchen purposes, cosmetics, toiletries, and medicinal preparations, as also for industrial usage. The waste coconut pith can be converted into usable manure. Coconut shell, which is largely being wasted in most of the islands, can be converted into charcoal. Coconut stem, rib of the coconut leaf, coconut shell, etc. can be utilised for making handicraft items.

There is also scope for value addition to the fibre products for which the institutional support of the Coir Board, Kerala may be required. The Board can set up a Field Unit in Lakshadweep for the development and provision of marketing support for coir products from Lakshadweep.

Coconut shell (estimated to be around 2000 tonne) may be utilised for handicrafts, activated charcoal manufacturing and shell powder. Coconut tree stems in addition to their use as construction material, can be utilised for manufacturing of quality furniture and boats on commercial basis.

Though a large amount of fish is captured and vast unexploited potential exists in the islands, present processing facilities are not adequate. Fish-based industries such as canning, oil extraction and pickle production may be geared up. Value addition by processing, minimising spoilage and avoiding glut in the market will certainly increase returns to the fishing families.

Besides fishing, the islanders are traditionally famous for their boat making skills. Such skills need to be revived and upgraded to provide economic value.

Brand name development for Lakshadweep fish, coconut and the related products as 100 per cent organic products is highly desirable. A marketing network to reach these products in larger cities such as Delhi, Kolkata, etc. also needs to be pursued.

Care is required to ensure that the setback to the entrepreneurial efforts experienced in the past, as was brought out in Chapter I of this report, does not recur. This will require a coordinated effort on the part of the various agencies involved, coupled with a proactive administrative mechanism and close involvement of the local institutions as well. The Island Development Authority should also undertake periodic monitoring and review of the outcome of the development efforts and programmes.

Savings and Investments

Detailed data on savings and investment in various sectors particularly in the household sector and the private sector are not available. However, the information in respect of bank deposits and budgetary capital expenditure by the Lakshadweep Administration will give some idea in this respect (Table 2.13).

TABLE 2.13

Recent Trends in Bank Deposits and Budgetary Capital Expenditure by Lakshadweep Administration (LDA) in Lakshadweep[12]

Year	*Bank Deposits (As on 31st March)*		*Cap. Exp. by LDA (During the Year)*	
	Rs. in Lakhs	*Annual Growth (%)*	*Rs. in Lakhs*	*Annual Growth (%)*
1997-98	3836		1708	
1998-99	5355	39.60	2348	37.49
1999-00	6271	17.11	2383	1.48
2000-01	5553	-11.45	6042	153.54
2001-02	6791	22.29	7986	32.18
2002-03 (R.E.)	N.A.	N.A.	6285	-21.30

Source: Basic Statistics of Union Territory of Lakshadweep: 2001-2002 and Budget data.

As for supra-regional investments, the Central Statistical Organisation (CSO) data give the status in respect of communications (public sector), banking and insurance, and Central Government Administration. Year-wise information in these respects for recent years is given in Table 2.14.

The information given in the above tables indicates that the level of investments from the banking and insurance sectors in Lakshadweep is low. It is possible that the more affluent individuals and institutions keep their investments in the main land based institutions. However, there is no denying that the bulk of investments are in the Government/public sector. As for the Government budgetary expenditure, more than 70 per cent is in terms of revenue expenditure, leaving a low amount for capital investment.[13] The strategy for

12. *Source:* For bank data, *Basic Statistics of Lakshadweep 2001-02*, Lakshadweep Administration and for budgetary data, Demands for Grants of MHA.

13. Trends in bank deposits and budgetary capital expenditure by the Lakshadweep Administration have been placed in Annexure A-12.

TABLE 2.14

Estimates of GSDP/NSDP of Lakshadweep from Supra-regional Sectors at Current Prices[14]

(Rs. Lakh)

Sl. No.	*Sectors*	*1997-98*		*1998-99*		*1999-2000*		*2000-01(R)*		*2002-03(Q)*	
		GSDP	*NSDP*	*GSDP*	*NSDP*	*GSDP*	*NSDP*	*GSDP*	*NSDP*	*GSDP*	*NSDP*
1.	Railways	-	-	-	-	-	-	-	-	-	-
2.	Communication*	155	114	202	156	218	165	243	182	252	184
3.	Banking & Insurance	134	131	154	148	154	147	197	190	250	236
4.	Central Govt. Administration	5902	5310	6858	6244	8427	7718	8599	7890	8997	8279

Note: R: Revised; Q: Quick estimates; *: Public Sector

Source: Basic Statistics of Union Territory of Lakshadweep – 2003-04.

economic growth of the region lies in tapping the savings of the private sector and also in attracting private sector investment. Tourism, shipping, air services, industry, fishery etc. offer ample scope for the purpose.

14. *Source: Basic Statistics of Lakshadweep 2001-02*, Lakshadweep Administration. The same information, at constant prices, is placed at Annexure A-11.

Chapter 3

Infrastructure

Energy

The tiny islands of Lakshadweep surrounded by ecologically delicate coral shelves and lagoons and nestled in the midst of the deep sea, pose a unique challenge for planners, builders and managers of infrastructure including sources of energy and means of transport and communication.

Power Generation and Consumption

Electricity generation in all the islands is mainly through diesel generators. The Electricity Department lifts about 66 lakh litres of HSD oil annually from the Indian Oil Corporation depot at Calicut. The oil is loaded into 200 litre barrels, which are transported by barges to the offshore of the reef. The barrels are again unloaded on barges for transportation to the jetties on the islands. On land, the barrels are transported by small trucks from the jetty to the island stockyard for storage. The whole process of transportation of diesel is tedious, cumbersome and costly. The Ministry of Petroleum and Natural Gas, through the Indian Oil Corporation, has undertaken to set up suitable oil storage tanks in select locations in Lakshadweep.

Lakshadweep has achieved 100 per cent electrification of households in all the inhabited islands. There are 14,474 domestic, 237 industrial and 2,809 commercial consumers in these islands. The time series data on installed capacity, generation and actual consumption of power in the recent years are given in Table 3.1.

It is apparent that utilisation of the generated power has improved from the level of 71-75 per cent in the early 1990s to 87-88 per cent in the recent years.

TABLE 3.1

Power Generation and Consumption in Lakshadweep

Year	*Installed Capacity kW*	*Generation '000 kWh*	*Consumption '000 kWh*	*Industrial Consumption '000 kWh*	*Share of Industrial Consumption (5/4) (%)*	*Ratio of Consumption to Generation (4/3) (%)*
1	*2*	*3*	*4*	*5*	*6*	*7*
1993-94	5014	12812	9149	516	5.64	71.41
1994-95	5270	14498	10355	698	6.74	71.42
1995-96	6921	15410	11098	719	6.48	72.02
1996-97	6919	16796	12545	483	3.85	74.69
1997-98	8120	18396	14051	372	2.65	76.38
1998-99	9965	18849	16501	1071	6.49	87.54
1999-00	9972	19398	17122	557	3.25	88.27
2000-01	9922	19820	17387	496	2.85	87.72
2001-02	9837	19856	17386	430	2.47	87.56
2002-03	9887	20379	18228	437	2.35	89.44
2003-04	9878	21352	18965	413	2.18	88.82

Source: Lakshadweep: Basic Statistics 2003-04, Lakshadweep Administration.

The distribution of electricity in Lakshadweep is through 11 KV and 415 Volt systems. The transmission and distribution (T&D) losses have been reduced to about 10 per cent, made possible owing to replacement of overhead lines by underground cable and modernisation of power systems. The administration has targeted to bring down the T&D losses to 8 per cent by the end of Tenth Five-year Plan.

An interesting feature of the power supply management system in Lakshadweep is that there are no meter readers and the consumers themselves take their respective meter readings and credit the required amount with the administration.

Cost of Electricity Generation and Tariff Structure

The cost of generation per kWh was Rs. 4.55 in 1993-94, which increased to Rs. 8.86 in 2002-03, indicating a net increase in cost by Rs. 4.31 per kWh during this period. The annual growth rate of the cost of power during this period was 6.88 per cent. The revenue realised was Rs. 102 lakh in 1993-94, which increased to Rs. 774 lakh in 2002-03, indicating an annual growth rate of 22.46 per cent, which is very high as compared to the growth of the cost of generation. Revenue realised as percentage of total expenditure was very low 15.86 per cent in 1993-94, which increased to 34.76 per cent in 2002-03. The cost of generation far exceeds the revenue that is realised and there is a large gap between the expenditure and the revenue generated (Table 3.2).

Electricity tariffs, however, are regularly revised and were last revised in April 2000. The present tariff structure is as follows:

		(Rs./Unit)
Domestic	0–50 units: 1.50;	0–100 units: 2.50;
	0–200 units: 3.50;	200 and above: 4.00
Industrial		4.50
Commercial and Street lighting		6.50

While the average cost of electricity generation is Rs. 8 to 9 per kWh, the average tariff charged to the consumers is only Rs. 3.50, indicating high subsidy. However, in view of the location disadvantage and remoteness of the territory and also the necessity of electricity in daily life, its subsidised supply appears justified.

Problems Associated with the Current System

Electricity generation by diesel generating sets is not only an expensive proposition, it is also a cause of concern because of its adverse impact on the ecology and environment. The highly fragile ecology of Lakshadweep faces serious adverse consequences of air, water or noise pollution, which are inevitably associated

TABLE 3.2

Cost and Revenue from Power Generation in Lakshadweep

	Year										Growth Rate
	1993-94	1994-95	1995-96	1996-97	1997-98	1998-99	1999-2000	2000-01	2001-02	2002-03	
Cost of Generation (Rs. Per kWh)	4.55	5.01	5.44	6.00	6.16	6.36	7.32	7.77	8.22	8.86	6.88
Cost of HSD Per Litre (Rs.)	9.50	11.00	12.25	13.50	14.85	16.50	18.00	19.50	22.00	22.28	8.89
Expenditure Per Annum (Rs. Lakhs)	641	750	817	1059	1134	1201	1420	1972	2079	2228	13.27
Revenue Realised (Rs. Lakhs)	102	112	136	170	240	307	453	555	713	774	22.46
% of Revenue Realised	15.86	14.99	16.59	16.08	21.14	25.55	31.89	28.17	34.28	34.76	
Revenue Realised Per Unit (Rs.)	0.95	1.01	1.08	1.20	1.57	1.63	2.64	3.63	4.15	4.27	16.20
Loss Per Annum (Rs. Lakhs)	539	637	681	889	894	894	968	1416	1355	1453	10.43

Source: Lakshadweep Administration.

with power generation through diesel sets. Moreover, as the soil in these islands is highly porous, the seepage of oil from diesel generators as well as during transportation at various places such as loading and unloading locations, jetty, powerhouse, etc. and supply/ storage in damaged leaky barrels pollute the water and the soil. The presence, accumulation and increasing concentration of oil and grease will have adverse effects on coral reproduction, growth rate, photosynthesis, cell structure, colonisation capacities, feeding and behavioural responses in the long-term. For humans, consumption of water containing fuel oils or their derivatives is reported to be carcinogenic on a long-term basis.

Another problem is that due to the high density of coconut trees and high velocity of wind, trapping of overhead lines and the snapping of conductors are frequent. Further, the saline atmosphere causes corrosion of joints of metal parts, leading to disruptions in the power supply. These also contribute to heavy distribution losses in the islands.

Non-Conventional Energy Sources

The environment and ecology related problems accruing to the existing diesel based power generation system in the island can to some extent be addressed by increasing usage of new renewable alternative sources of energy such as solar, wind and biomass. Such schemes for alternative and renewable energy sources will lead to saving of precious fossil fuel and therefore have a significant beneficial impact. Another option, of wave energy, also exists but the technology is still not developed for its adoption on a commercial scale.

Solar Energy

Geographical location, ecological considerations and energy demand pattern of Lakshadweep make solar energy, through the solar photovoltaic (SPV) generation, one of the most appropriate options to meet the energy demand of the island. The average solar radiation over the islands is 4.932 kWh/sq.m/day, which indicates a vast potential for harnessing solar energy. Using the monthly radiation data and taking into account the 11 per cent efficiency of the solar panels and effective number of sunshine hours, dust, cloud cover, etc. the generation of about 8.4 million units of electricity per annum has been estimated from 0.139 sq km area (about 4.6 per cent of the total islands area) assumed to be available for SPV power plants as per the details given in Annexure A-13.A & A-13.B. Island-wise annual electricity generation potential through solar energy is given in Table 3.3.

TABLE 3.3

Annual Solar Energy Potential in Different Islands

Sl.No.	*Island*	*Annual Electricity Generation Potential (in Thousand kWh)*
1.	Minicoy	1259.80
2.	Kavaratti	1211.00
3.	Amini	743.20
4.	Andrott	1388.90
5.	Kalpeni	800.60
6.	Agatti	1113.40
7.	Kadmat	895.30
8.	Kiltan	467.80
9.	Chetlat	327.10
10.	Bitra	28.70
11.	Bangaram	166.40
	Total	**8402.20**

Source: Ministry of Non-Conventional Energy Sources.

There are at present six SPV power generation stations with total peak generation capacity of 685 kW. Five more such plants are under erection, with peak generation capacity of 400 kW in all. Actual electricity generated through SPV systems during the year 2002-2003 was 10,61,806 kWh which amounted to about 5 per cent of the total power generation. The energy produced from these power plants of 1 MW capacity is expected to save diesel fuel equivalent to approximately 5.6 lakh litres per annum.

The main limitation for the application of solar-based technology in these islands is the large land area requirement for setting up the solar photovoltaic power plants. Almost the entire territory is covered under dense coconut plantation, which is the main crop for income generation. This limits the availability of free land in these islands very severely. Whatever land is available, as also the rooftops, face lack of sunlight owing to the dense coconut tree cover. Owing to these reasons, stand-alone solar home lighting systems are also not feasible for lighting in these islands. As the large-scale solar energy based power generation systems require large uncovered areas, such plants can be set up in the lagoons.

Wind Energy

Wind resource assessment had been undertaken by the Ministry of Non-conventional Energy Sources in association with the local Electricity Department at two locations namely Agatti and Minicoy Islands. The wind resource survey analysis (Annexure A-14, indicates that between May and November, only the months of June, July and August have the highest wind speeds of about 8 to 9 m/s. The remaining months have hourly wind speeds greater than 2.8 m/s and there is no significant variation in the hourly wind speeds in a typical month. Wind energy has, therefore, the potential for energy generation in Lakshadweep.

Based on the available data for the island, a rough estimate of the electricity generation potential through wind energy for each island is given in Table 3.4.

TABLE 3.4

Estimated Potential for Electricity Generation through Wind Energy

Sl.No.	*Island*	*Annual Electricity Generation Potential (in Thousand kWh)*
1.	Minicoy	1239.5
2.	Kavaratti	1239.3
3.	Amini	929.5
4.	Andrott	1239.3
5.	Kalpeni	929.5
6.	Agatti	929.5
7.	Kadmat	1239.3
8.	Kiltan	433.7
9.	Chetlat	309.8
10.	Bitra	62.00
11.	Bangaram	124.00
	Total	**8675.4**

Source: Ministry of Non-Conventional Energy Sources.

Another favourable point for wind electric generators is that they cause relatively small adverse impact owing to marginal land requirement and removal of vegetation. The beneficial impacts of these systems depend, to a large extent, on the height and location of the tower and wind pattern.

There are a few limitations in promoting wind energy for electricity generation in these islands, which include inadequate shipping and unloading facilities in the islands for the equipment and machinery heavier than two tonnes. In view of this, wind electric generators up to 100 kW capacities seem to be feasible for installation in these islands. Another limitation is the mast height of the generator, which needs to be higher than that of the coconut trees so that the available wind speed is fully utilised. The minimum clear area around the wind generators and the strong foundation requirements could also be a limitation.

The feasibility for installation of an offshore wind farm may also be considered for greater levels of power generation, as this could possibly offset the capital cost and would also not pose any additional stress on the already scarce land resources. This, however, can be a technical challenge. The Centre for Wind Energy Technology (C-WET) Chennai, an institution of the Ministry of Non-Conventional Energy Sources can be assigned the responsibility to assess the feasibility in this regard.

Biomass Power

Biomass power for generation of grid quality power, based on available biomass resources in the islands, appears to be another important renewable energy source. Coconut is the major economic crop of the territory with an annual production reaching 53 million nuts during 2001-02. *Copra* is produced from the coconut and the dried husk is used for fibre extraction. There is, however, a very large quantity of unused biomass such as dried husk, leaves or cadjins, shells and sawmill biomass. The unused biomass in the islands is a major environmental problem, which may be tackled by utilising it for power generation through biomass gasifiers.

In Kavaratti Island, it is estimated that about 4,776 tonnes of total biomass from coconut is available for electricity generation through biomass gasification. The Electricity Department has installed a 250 kW biomass gasifier at Kavaratti that consumes 350 kg of biomass per hour. It is estimated that the biomass requirement is only 2,100 tonnes (43.5 per cent of total availability of biomass) for 250 kW capacity biomass gasifier for 6000 hours operation (250 days per year). The Electricity Department is, however, facing a lot of difficulty in successfully running the gasifier due to technical problems. Servicing of equipment is likely to be an impediment for successful implementation of biomass gasification in the islands.

Based on the experience in Kavaratti Island, estimation, given below, has been made for other islands in Lakshadweep for biomass availability and electricity generation potential (Table 3.5).

Problems Associated with Biomass Gasifiers

Though the pollution potential of biomass gasifiers is relatively low, it does produce airborne emission such as SO_2, NO_x and CO_2, though at a reduced level compared to coal or hydrocarbons. The land requirement for storage of biomass and plant is also relatively high. The biomass and water requirement are

TABLE 3.5

Island-wise Biomass Availability and Electricity Generation Potential

Sl.No.	Island	*Coconut Harvested (1998-99)**	*Biomass Available from Husk (Tonnes)*	*Biomass Available from Shells (Tonnes)*	*Biomass Available from Cadjins (Tonnes)*	*Total Biomass Available (Tonnes)*	*Approximate Annual Electricity Generation Potential ('000 kWh)***
1.	Agatti	28,00,000	896	210	1680	2786	796
2.	Andrott	43,90,000	1405	329	2634	4368	1248
3.	Amini	43,70,000	1398	328	2622	4348	1242
4.	Bitra	1,40,000	45	11	84	139	40
5.	Chetlat	13,50,000	432	101	810	1343	384
6.	Minicoy	26,70,000	854	200	1602	2657	759
7.	Kalpeni	31,70,000	1014	238	1902	3154	901
8.	Kadmat	35,40,000	1133	266	2124	3522	1006
9.	Kavaratti	38,00,000	1216	285	2280	3781	1080
10.	Kiltan	17,70,000	566	133	1062	1761	503
	Total	**280,00,000**	**8959**	**2101**	**16800**	**27859**	**7959**

Note: **: Using 40 per cent of total available biomass.

* *Source: Basic Statistics 1995-1996*, Department of Planning & Statistics, Lakshadweep, Kavaratti.

very high for most popular biomass gasifiers (Direct fixed system). As the land and water resources are both critical to the island system, any stress on these is considered undesirable. Yet another concern is that the enhanced levels of biomass requirements for biomass gasifiers may result in stress on biomass. However, on the whole, the concept of biomass based power generation seems to have considerable merit and deserves serious consideration.

Wave Energy

In India the first pilot wave power plant was established in the sea off Vizhinjam at Thiruvananthapuram. The 150 kW capacity Oscillating Wave Column (OWC) device deployed at 12 m depth is connected to the main breakwater of the Vizhinjam fishing harbour. The site was considered suitable because of higher wave power availability, easy access to deeper waters and availability of other local infrastructure facilities, in addition to the location being cyclone-free. The success of this project has led to the designing of a 1.5 MW plant in the breakwater of the fishing harbour at Thangassery Kollam, Kerala.

Wave power cannot be economical as a stand-alone facility at the present level of development. To make it viable it has to be developed as a multipurpose scheme. Harbour protection, coastal erosion control, mariculture, desalination, seafood processing, coastal waterways, tourism, etc. can be coupled with wave power schemes. However, the situation in the Lakshadweep islands is favourable for wave power generation, even as a stand-alone system considering the non-availability of other sources and high cost of diesel power generation.

The Centre for Earth Sciences Studies, Thiruvanthapuram had undertaken a study sponsored by the Department of Ocean Development and prepared a project report for tapping wave power in Lakshadweep Island in the year 1992. As per this study, wave based power generation may be appropriate during the rainy season when intense wave conditions prevail. The recorded wave data had shown that the wave power potential is higher at the Lakshadweep location than that at Vizhinjam, where the wave power plant has been set up. Further detailed studies for assessing the potential and possibilities of wave power generation need to be conducted.

Energy from Waste

Various organic biodegradable wastes and effluents such as sewage, night soil, fish wastes, slaughterhouse wastes, etc. are being generated in the islands, which are leading to acute problems of ground water/ environmental pollution, endangering the health of the inhabitants. All such wastes/effluents may be gainfully utilised in Anaerobic Digestion plants for generation of biogas, which can be used as fuel for direct thermal applications (cooking, water heating, etc.) or even for power generation, with the attendant benefit of abatement of environmental pollution. A detailed feasibility study may be carried out in this regard.

Conclusions

The Electricity Department, Lakshadweep has estimated that electricity demand is increasing at the rate of around nine per cent per annum. Accordingly, the peak demand at the end of the Eleventh Plan period will be about 12 MW. The substantial energy demand, which is presently met through conventional power using diesel can be substituted to a large extent with renewable energy sources, which will not only lead to reduced dependence on diesel but also help in protecting the ecology and environment of the islands.

In order to minimise the consumption of diesel to the extent possible for power generation and to supplement it through renewable energy technologies, the following steps are proposed:

- The existing 6 grid interactive SPV power plants of aggregate capacity of 650 kWp installed at Agatti, Kiltan, Minicoy, Andrott, Kavaratti and Kadmat island and 3 SPV power plants of an aggregate capacity of 300 kWp under installation at Amini, Chetlat and Kalpeni islands can be augmented to higher capacity.
- More SPV power plants may be installed, depending upon the availability of land.
- Preliminary investigations of wind resource assessment undertaken at Agatti and Minicoy islands indicate the feasibility for installation of wind electric generator of up to 100 kW capacities in Lakshadweep Islands, particularly during the monsoon. Feasibility for setting up an offshore wind farm should also be explored.
- Unused/surplus biomass mainly from coconut plantations can be utilised for electricity generation through gasification technology. However, the technical problems in the existing 250 kW biomass gasifier installed at Kavaratti need to be removed first.
- Hybrid stand-alone systems based on SPV, wind and biomass for various applications including power generation can be taken up in decentralised mode for isolated locations and areas in the islands.
- Detailed study for assessing the potential and possibilities of wave power generation in the islands needs to be undertaken.
- Anaerobic Digestion plants to utilise the domestic sewage, night soil and other organic degradable wastes like fish waste, slaughterhouse waste, etc. for biogas generation, may be set up.

It may also be stated that despite the emphasis proposed for alternative sources, the conventional diesel oil based power generation will have to continue to be a significant source for power for the coming years, at least till the alternatives stabilise on a commercially viable scale. It will be desirable to consider the scope for improvements in the diesel based generation systems. The present system of power generation may be revitalised through scrapping and replacing the existing redundant and inefficient diesel power generating sets.

At the same time, the experience of implementation of projects and schemes for energy generation through alternative energy sources gained so far in Lakshadweep as well as in other places needs to be reviewed. In fact, in Lakshadweep itself, the experience has been very good, as has been brought on record. The main constraint is the availability of land, that too without obstruction to solar radiation. There have been suggestions made to the effect that the solar panels be set up in the lagoons. While this appears a good alternative to the land, the ecological impact on the lagoons needs to be carefully studied before adopting it.

Other micro-level energy saving measures, such as smokeless *chullas*, windmill based water lifting devices, high efficiency kerosene stoves and pressure cookers should be popularised to bring about fuel savings.

Shipping

Fishing, coconut plantation and coir twisting are the only means of livelihood of Lakshadweep islanders. There is no agricultural activity in the Islands other than coconut cultivation and hence all food articles including rice, wheat, sugar, pulses, potato, onions, etc. are transported from the mainland. Similarly, there is no major industrial activity in the Islands other than some small or cottage industry. Thus, all commodities such as building materials, fuel, clothing, all daily essentials, etc. are also transported from the mainland. There are no major hospitals, schools and colleges in most of the islands. The people perforce have to travel to the mainland or from one island to the other for receiving medical treatment or for education. Shipping services are the primary means of transportation of men and material between the Islands and the mainland as well as in the inter-island sectors. With the growth of population and increase in the propensity to travel among the islanders for various developmental activities, the transportation requirements of the islanders are constantly on the rise.

The islands are surrounded by lagoons which are fenced by coral reefs all round. These reefs provide a natural shelter from rough seas, besides adding beauty to the islands. However, at the same time, these reefs restrict the navigability of the islands owing to shallow depth of water over the reefs. The islands are navigated by small and low draught vessels through some limited navigable entry points of these reefs where the navigable depth of water over the reef is available.

Thus, the main problem is that vessels with drafts more than two metres cannot enter the lagoons. Hence, embarkation and disembarkation of passengers and cargo at most of the islands are carried out in open sea and then brought to the islands and *vice versa* by small launches or country boats. This makes the whole exercise of embarkation and disembarkation very risky; expensive and time consuming.

Passenger shipping is provided by the administration, which maintains and operates passenger ships as well as passenger-cum-cargo ships. The mainland-island passenger-cum-cargo services are provided mainly by five ships that have a total passenger capacity of 1,485 and cargo capacity of 235 tonnes. Some of the ships are ageing and are in the process of replacement, besides addition of new ships. Two fast ferry aluminium hull (catamaran type) vessels with 100 passengers capacity have also been operating since 1991 for the inter-island traffic and these handle about 30 per cent of the inter-island passenger traffic. Total passenger traffic carried by various ships and ferries during the recent years is of the order of 1.5 lakh, which comprised about one-third inter-island passengers and two thirds, between the mainland and the islands (See Annexures A-15.A, A-15.B and A-15.C).

The data in the Table 3.6 indicate that while the mainland-islands traffic is going up, the inter-island traffic is declining. This indicates the increasing dependence of the islanders on the mainland rather than on the islands.

With the upgradation/addition of passenger ships as per currently approved schemes, the annual passenger carrying capacity of the mainland-islands shipping services will go up to 1 lakh in 2006-07 and 1.70 lakh from 2007-08 (See Annexure A-16).

Cargo movement is done mainly through private vessels though most of the passenger ships carry some cargo also. Cargo transported by various ships/vessels during 2001-02 was of the order of 1.81 lakh metric tonnes, which included 1.53 lakh MT by cargo vessels and 0.28 lakh MT by ships (Table 3.7).

TABLE 3.6

Trends in Passenger Traffic

Year	*Mainland-Islands*	*Inter-Island*	*Total*
1991-92	67,646	43,589	111,235
1992-93	64,526	48,385	112,911
1993-94	73,277	68,377	141,654
1994-95	81,114	79,794	160,908
1995-96	84,188	68,710	152,898
1996-97	86,610	64,845	151,455
1997-98	92,430	63,618	156,048
1998-99	87,811	51,610	139,421
1999-00	82,165	41,603	123,768
2000-01	86,692	43,955	130,647
2001-02	89,162	47,407	136,569
2002-03	105,107	50,972	156,079
2003-04	105,714	53,992	159,706
2004-05	107,950	54,943	162,893

Source: Lakshadweep Administration.

TABLE 3.7

Trends in Cargo Traffic

Year	*In Govt. Ships*	*In Private MSVs*	*Total*
1990-91	12,077	28,381	40,458
1991-92	11,825	27,017	38,842
1992-93	12,045	30,900	42,945
1993-94	16,267	37355	53,622
1994-95	16,166	43,859	60,025
1995-96	19,887	73,175	93,062
1996-97	21,897	75,310	97,207
1997-98	22,694	75,643	98,337
1998-99	25,882	76,498	102,380
1999-00	25,279	157,201	182,480
2000-01	29,669	120,494	150,163
2001-02	28,450	152,981	181,431
2002-03	27,475	158,072	185,547
2003-04	25,697	—	—
2004-05	29,650	—	—

Source: Lakshadweep Administration.

Projections for cargo traffic growth, based on linear extrapolation of the past trends, indicate that it would touch 3 lakh tonnes by 2008-09 and close to 4 lakh tonnes by 2014-15 (See Annexure A-17).

The problems faced by the shipping sector in Lakshadweep were examined by a committee constituted by the GoI in February 2000 under the chairmanship of the Joint Secretary (Shipping). The Committee made various useful suggestions to improve the passenger and cargo shipping services. A Perspective Plan for

Shipping Requirements in Lakshadweep has also been prepared. The updated status of the problems and the solutions is as follows:

Embarkation and Disembarkation of Passengers and Cargo

The main problem of navigation here is that vessels with drafts more than two metres cannot enter the lagoons. Hence, embarkation and disembarkation of the passengers and cargo is usually carried out in open sea and then brought to the Islands and *vice versa* by small launches or country boats. As the discharge of cargo takes place in open sea, the speed of operation is very low and there is also a loss of cargo during discharge. Inclement weather and sea conditions make it difficult for the cargo vessels to operate with full capacity for about three months in a year (June to August) as during this period cargo discharge at open sea outside the lagoons becomes extremely difficult. All this makes the whole exercise of embarkation and disembarkation very risky, expensive and time consuming. It also reduces the capacity utilisation of the ships, particularly for cargo operations. Passengers too suffer considerable misery on this score.

Environmental considerations make it difficult to increase the depth of the water in the lagoons of the islands and hence large size vessels having drafts higher than two metres cannot enter the lagoons to berth at jetties of the islands. Hence, it is necessary to provide floating embarkation/disembarkation facility in the open sea where larger vessels can anchor.

It is also necessary to deploy shallow draft all weather self-propelled steel barges, each for landing of about 100–150 passengers on deck, in each of the islands where the large mainland-island vessels would be calling. These small barges would have to be fitted with gangways/ladders and should have large deck areas. Barges have been chosen keeping in mind that this type of floating vessels has high stability.

Maintenance of Ships

The repair and maintenance costs of the existing vessels are rather high, which could be due to dependence on a single ship repair yard. Currently, the administration is heavily dependent on the Shipping Corporation of India Ltd. for ship management. An element of competition needs to be introduced for ship repair and maintenance jobs to minimise the costs and improve the efficiency. However, timely and economic completion of such repair and quality of work should not be compromised.

It is also desirable to train the islanders in ship maintenance. This should make the operations more cost-effective and also promote local employment prospects. The ITI, Kavaratti can also be suitably involved in these efforts.

The territory needs dry-dock facilities for ship repairs and maintenance. However, scarcity of land prevents setting of this infrastructure in any of the constituent islands. Such facilities can be set up in the lagoons, subject, however, to environmental sustainability.

Berthing Facilities at the Mainland Ports

Availability of berthing facilities for the ships of the administration at mainland ports is becoming a major problem. Berths have to be made available for passenger ships on priority. In the absence of open berths very often passenger ships have to be berthed in closed wharfs at Cochin, which creates problem for the passengers. At the moment the administration is operating 12 different types and sizes of ships. The perspective plan for shipping requirements in Lakshadweep recommends acquisition of 18 different types and sizes of ships. When these are inducted into service, berthing for the administration's ships on the mainland will become a serious problem. Because of various limitations the Port Trust/Port Authorities are unable to provide berths for the administration's ships on priority. The permanent solution for the problem is construction of dedicated berthing and terminal facilities for the administration's own ships at the mainland ports. Keeping this requirement in mind a scheme has been included in the Tenth Five-year Plan for construction of dedicated berths not only in major ports but also in the minor ports of Beypore and Azhikal in Kerala state where infrastructure and facilities can be provided. The matter was further taken up and pursued with Cochin Port Trust which has agreed in principle for providing required land for construction of dedicated berth at Cochin Port Trust for UTL ships. Cochin Port Trust has informed that the proposed berth can be located in between the South Coal Berth and the workshop jetty and a preliminary estimate has been prepared and estimated cost comes up to Rs. 20 crores. The facilities proposed comprise of the following:

(i) Construction of a main berth 300 m long and 12 m wide connecting the shore with 2 approach bridges each 10 m wide.

(ii) Passenger waiting hall of 500 m^2 having adequate facilities.

(iii) Cargo storage/handling facilities of 500 m^2.

(iv) Service facilities like water supply, electricity, road, etc.

Further as the water frontage available on W/Island is limited, the Port Trust is not in a position to make available the berth in the exclusive custody of Lakshadweep Administration and has proposed an arrangement in which the capital investment for the construction will be met by Lakshadweep Administration as grant-in-aid and the berth will be owned and maintained by the Port Trust. The berth will be made available to UTL as and when required on priority. As the ownership rights was not found acceptable, UTL Administration has further taken up with Cochin Port Trust for transferring the ownership of the berth/water front on the proposed site. In response Cochin Port Trust has informed that the UTL proposal for construction of the berth is under active consideration. As regard with the terms and conditions of lease of water area, construction of berth, etc. is to be discussed and finalised with Cochin Port Trust. Meantime as requested by CPT for an appreciation of the Port area requirements, the details of number and size of vessels expected to be at Kochi Port have already been furnished. The matter is under active consideration

Subsidies in Passenger Fare

Passenger fares for shipping services are highly subsidised. The fare for the 220 nautical mile journey between Kochi and Kavaratti is around Rs. 200 only (2nd Class). However, considering the inevitability of the journeys for the islanders to and from the mainland as well as between the islands, the fare subsidies are justified and need to be continued. However, it needs to be reviewed if the same level of subsidy will be required for journey by air too.

Once these major bottlenecks are overcome, it should become possible to provide regular and dependable shipping services which is the key to the socioeconomic development of the territory.

Road Communication

All the islands of Lakshadweep are serviced by all weather cement concrete roads providing at least the main connectivity within each island. Each island is serviced by a main road and branch routes. The situation in this regard seems satisfactory. Road construction and maintenance is handled by the administration as well as by the district *panchayat*.[1]

The islands being small in expanse, do not necessarily require four wheelers for commutation and, therefore, two wheelers have remained popular. The number of motorised vehicles in Lakshadweep in 2001-2002 was 418, which includes 13 government vehicles and remaining 405 private vehicles. More than three-fourths of the registered vehicles are motor cycles (327). Other types of vehicles are tillers (28, including 6 belonging to the government), autorickshaws (18), LCVs (19), mopeds (12), jeeps and vans (9), tractors (4) and 1 car. Intra-island movement of humans and goods is heavily dependent on roads. Additionally, good roads are essential for promotion of tourism too.

Now, more attention is required for maintenance of the roads than construction of fresh roads, as the main roads are largely in place. Some interior roads such as those along the wharfs, coastal ring roads and linking roads are required. Arrangement for public transport can also be considered, to facilitate the movement of people as well as goods.

The process of transportation, storage and handling of diesel and petrol has been highly cumbersome and fraught with environmental hazards for Lakshadweep. It is desirable to discourage the use of such transport vehicles that use diesel or petrol. Instead, electric powered vehicles need to be popularised.

The possibilities of introduction of natural gas based transport vehicles also needs to be explored, as these are much more eco-friendly. However, alongside, the preparatory efforts for transportation, storage and distribution of the gas, including the compressed natural gas (CNG) need to be initiated.

Telecommunication

Telecommunication facilities are relevant in every part of the country, but more so in Lakshadweep, in view of the remoteness of the islands. The sub-sectors to be considered in this context include, besides landline telephones, mobile telephones, public call facilities, telegraph facilities, and internet connectivity.

Telephone

The New Telecom Policy 1999, had stipulated that all villages should be covered by telecom facility by the end of 2002. Lakshadweep has already achieved this target. All the inhabited islands in Lakshadweep have telephone exchanges of the Digital Electronic type. Telephone facilities, mobile as well as landline, in Lakshadweep are currently being provided by the Bharat

1. Details of construction of rural roads during the Eighth, Ninth and Tenth Plans are placed at Annexure A-18.

Sanchar Nigam Ltd. (BSNL). The total equipped capacity of the 10 telephone exchanges in Lakshadweep is 11,776, while the connections taken were 8,794 with 68 applicants in the waiting list, as on 30.11.2002. By and large, landline facilities are available on demand. STD/ISD facility is available to all subscribers. Though the islands are far apart, subscribers of each island can dial other numbers in every island by dialing the directory number at 180 seconds pulse. Island-wise details of the telephone lines and teledensity are given in Table 3.8.

The telecom penetration, which is assessed in terms of teledensity, that is, the number of telephones per 100 population, was 14.5 for all the 10 islands together. As for inter-island variation, the teledensity varies between 11.5 (Amini) and 18.5 (Kalpeni). All the 10 inhabited islands have telephone exchanges and public telephones. Six islands, Kavaratti, Minicoy, Kalpeni, Andrott, Agatti and Kiltan, are linked by satellite channels to the national network via digital connectivity. Other islands are up-linked through UHF systems via Kiltan. It is proposed to establish Digital Satellite connectivity with all islands by installing satellite terminals in the remaining four islands.

Telegraph

A central telegraph office is functioning at Kavaratti, while telecom centres are functioning in all other eight islands (except Bitra). Fax facility is available in all the 10 islands.

Internet

An Internet node has been provided at Kavaratti, which facilitates Internet access at local call rates from Kavaratti. The Internet access at local call rate is also available from Agatti, Amini, Andrott, Minicoy, Kadmat, Kalpeni and Kiltan. There were 36 Internet customers in Lakshadweep Islands as on 30.11.2002. An Internet PCO is functioning at Kavaratti.

The targets for growth set for the telephone and internet connections have been largely met during the recent years, as the details in Table 3.9 will indicate.

The data show the increasing popularity of Public Call Offices (PCOs) and Internet connections. The quality of the telephone services has been satisfactory in Lakshadweep. The call completion rate figures of local, junction and STD calls during the months of September 2002 to November 2002 varied from 68.2 per cent to 71.9 per cent, 55.2 per cent to 56.5 per cent and 54.1 per cent to 55.2 per cent respectively. In Lakshadweep, owing to the satellite connectivity, it has not been technically feasible so far to replace the multiple access rural radio (MARR) system by wireless in local loop (WLL) system. Efforts are being made to bring in upgraded WLL system to make it functional on satellite media so as to improve the speed and efficiency of connectivity.

Civil Aviation

One of the main reasons why the islands have remained backward and remote is that there are no

TABLE 3.8

Island-wise Number of Telephone Exchanges, Capacity and Teledensity (As on 30-11-2002)

Island	*No. of Exchanges*	*Equipped Capacity*	*Expansion undertaken in Equipped Capacity*	*No. of Working Connections*	*No. of Non-working Connections*	*Total Connections (Working and Non-working)*	*Teledensity (in Per Cent)*	*Waiting List*
1. Agatti	1	1000	-	832	12	844	11.9	1
2. Amini	1	1000	600	835	8	843	11.5	5
3. Andrott	1	1400	-	1369	12	1381	12.9	8
4. Bitra	1	184	632	38	0	38	14.4	-
5. Chetlat	1	368	-	352	5	357	15.6	23
6. Kadmat	1	1000	-	792	9	801	15.1	0
7. Kalpeni	1	1000	-	791	9	800	18.5	5
8. Kavaratti (U)	1	3424	-	1681	77	1758	17.4	0
9. Kiltan	1	1000	-	579	10	589	16.1	0
10. Minicoy	1	1400	600	1368	15	1383	14.6	15
Lakshadweep	**10**	**11776**	**1832**	**8637**	**157**	**8794**	**14.5**	**57**

Source: BSNL (Kerala).

TABLE 3.9

Growth of Telephones and Internet in Lakshadweep during 1997-2003

Year	*Telephone*	*PCO (STD Booth)*	*PCO Local*	*Internet Customer*	*Internet PCO*
1997-98					
i) Target	6374	24	3	-	-
ii) Achievement	5690	24	3	-	-
iii) % Achievement	(89.26)	(100)	(100)	-	-
1998-99					
i) Target	7214	29	5	-	-
ii) Achievement	7214	29	5	-	-
iii) % Achievement	(100)	(100)	(100)	-	-
1999-2000					
i) Target	7834	32	6	-	-
ii) Achievement	7733	32	6	-	-
iii) % Achievement	(98.71)	(100)	(100)	-	-
2000-01					
i) Target	8221	32	7	21	1
ii) Achievement	8221	32	7	21	1
iii) % Achievement	(100)	(100)	(100)	(100)	(100)
2001-02					
i) Target	8679	34	9	27	1
ii) Achievement	8636	34	9	27	1
iii) % Achievement	(99.50)	(100)	(100)	(100)	(100)
2002-03 (As on 31St Dec., 2002)					
i) Target	8775	46	9	36	1
ii) Achievement	8707	46	9	36	1
iii) % Achievement	(99.22)	(100)	(100)	(100)	(100)
Growth Rate	**8.88**	**13.89**	**14.65**	**19**	-

Note: Figures within parentheses are percentage to total target.

Source: BSNL (Kerala Circle).

regular means of communication between the islands and the mainland. They are also considered remote because there is no method of commuting to them on a daily basis from the mainland. While the ships do provide access, they are slow and far between. The only way to remove this feeling of remoteness and provide regular access would be to have regular air service between the islands and mainland and inter-island.

At present, air services are provided to Lakshadweep by the nationalised carrier, Indian Airlines, which connects Agatti to Kochi and Goa. The aircraft deployed is usually the Dornier type (15 seater). Besides, the Lakshadweep Administration operates helicopter services for inter-island connectivity as well as for providing commutation, particularly for emergency evacuation, to the mainland. The frequency of the air services is low and the costs to the passengers, high. Availability of faster means of communication through frequent and affordable air services is necessary for the effective integration—economic or otherwise—of the islands with the rest of the country. The main possibilities in this regard have been identified as follows:

a. ***More aircraft and airstrips:*** Air service may be extended, besides Agatti, to five larger islands, namely Minicoy, Andrott, Kavaratti, Kadmat and Kiltan. The proposal is to use a small fixed wing aircraft/seaplanes capable of seating about five to six passengers. These aircraft are currently being made in India. They would be much like the "Islanders" which are owned by the Indian Navy. The aircraft proposed to be used needs a runway length of 500 to 700 metres. In fact, the aircraft can operate from an unprepared airstrip also. These islands would also require airstrips of 500 metres each that comply with all safety requirements. There are reports that the seaplanes could be made to land and take off from the lagoons, thus obviating the need of building more runways or of extending the existing runways. This aspect needs to be studied further.

b. ***Subsidy on airfare***: While the journey on the passenger ships operated by the administration is heavily subsidised, the air journey to and from Lakshadweep has remained prohibitively costly. Ship journeys undoubtedly take far more time. There are also indications to the effect that the economic cost of air travel is less than that of ship travel. More detailed studies need to be undertaken in this respect and if it turns out to be true, then the infrastructure for air journeys should be strengthened and suitable subsidies extended to the islanders for air travel.

c. ***Extension of runway at Agatti airport***: Agatti airport, the only airport in Lakshadweep, can facilitate landing of aircraft with carrying capacity of less than 70 passengers. This is totally inadequate. There is urgent need to extend the runway to facilitate landing of bigger aircraft such as like Air Bus/Boeing 737 which would be useful not only for tourism and other civilian requirements but also for the defence forces. Larger aircraft will enable the carrier airlines to reduce the fares too. This will possibly require connecting the adjoining island of Kalpitty by way of a bridge and extending the runway from the existing length of 1350 metres by another 700 metres.

d. ***Infrastructure at the airport***: The economic growth of Lakshadweep would get a fillip if facilities are created to boost the export of the local produce such as fish and fishery products. This will require an extension of the existing runway of Agatti airport, as stated above. Besides, the infrastructure of Agatti airport needs to be upgraded to facilitate such export related activities.

Chapter 4

Human Development

Assessment of the levels of human development has been refined over the years. The Human Development Index (HDI), developed by the Planning Commission, is a composite of variables capturing attainments in the three dimensions of human development, namely, economic, education and health. These have been considered on the basis of per capita monthly expenditure adjusted for inequality; a combination of literacy rate and intensity of formal education; and a combination of life expectancy at age one and infant mortality rate. The position in respect of the various Union Territories and the all-India position are given in the Table 4.1. For the sake of benchmarking, the position in respect of Kerala, the immediate neighbour to Lakshadweep and one of the well-developed states of the country, is also indicated in Table 4.1.

TABLE 4.1

Human Development Index of the Union Territories, Kerala and India 1981 and 1991

	1981		*1991*	
	Value	*Rank*	*Value*	*Rank*
A & N Islands	0.394	11	0.574	5
Chandigarh	0.550	1	0.674	1
D & N Haveli	0.276	25	0.361	25
Daman & Diu	0.438	6	0.544	8
Delhi	0.495	3	0.624	2
Lakshadweep	**0.434**	**7**	**0.532**	**10**
Pondicherry	0.386	12	0.571	6
Kerala	0.500	2	0.591	3
All-India	0.302		0.381	5

Source: National Human Development Report 2001, Planning Commission, March 2002.

It may be seen in the above figures that Lakshadweep has declined in its relative position, from seventh rank in 1981 to tenth rank in 1991. Such a composite index is not available in respect of the Union Territories for recent years. However, sectoral indices relating to population characteristics, employment, literacy, public health and poverty will give some indication in the matter.

Population Density

Lakshadweep is the tiniest member among all the states and union territories of the country, in terms of both population (60,650) and geographical area (32 sq km).[1] Yet, Lakshadweep leads most other states and Union territories in terms of population density, as Table 4.2 shows.

Thus, during the period 1981-2001, the population density of Lakshadweep has gone up significantly, from 1,250 persons per sq km to 1,895, which is far higher than the corresponding all-India average figures of 216 and 324, respectively. The population density (2001) of Lakshadweep at 1,895 is more than double that of Kerala (819).

Of the total population of Lakshadweep, which was 60,650 as per the 2001 Census, 33,683, or 55.54 per cent, was classified as rural and the remaining 26,967, or 44.46 per cent as urban, in terms of Census norms for urban-rural classification of area and population. Out of the total population of 60,650, the child population (0–6 years) was 9,091, that is, 14.99 per cent. In the 1991 Census, the corresponding figures were 51,707 and 9,464 respectively. This indicates shrink in the size of the family.

The average annual compound growth rate of population of Lakshadweep, which was 2.51 per cent for

1. The Provisional Census figures for 2001 had indicated the population as 60,595. The Final Census figures are reported as 60,650.

TABLE 4.2

Geographical Area and Population of Union Territories, Kerala and India

	Area ('000 sq km)	Population ('000)			Population Density (persons/sq km)		
		2001	1991	1981	2001	1991	1981
A & N Islands	8.25	356	281	189	43	34	23
Chandigarh	0.11	901	642	452	7,903	5,632	3,965
D & N Haveli	0.49	220	138	104	449	281	212
Daman & Diu	0.11	158	102	79	1,411	911	705
Delhi	1.48	13,783	9,421	6,220	9,294	6,353	4,194
Lakshadweep	**0.03**	**61**	**52**	**40**	**1,895**	**1,625**	**1,250**
Pondicherry	0.49	974	808	604	1,979	1,642	1,228
Kerala	38.86	31,839	29,099	25,454	819	749	655
All-India	3,166	1,027,015	846,303	683,329	324	267	216

Note: Details in respect of all the States and UTs are given in Annexure A-19.

Source: Census of India, 2001.

TABLE 4.3

Area and Population of Inhabited Islands of Lakshadweep—2001 Census

Island		Area (sq km)	Male	Female	Total Population	Share of Female (%)	Females per 1000 Males	Population per sq km
1	Minicoy	4.37	4,617	4,878	9,495	51.38	1,057	2,173
2	Kalpeni	2.28	2,278	2,043	4,321	47.23	897	1,895
3	Andrott	4.84	5,357	5,370	10,727	50.04	1,002	2,216
4	Agatti	2.71	3,633	3,376	7,009	48.17	929	2,586
5	Kavaratti	3.63	5,586	4,533	10,119	44.83	811	2,788
6	Amini	2.59	3,737	3,616	7,353	49.22	968	2,839
7	Kadmat	3.12	2,691	2,643	5,334	49.52	982	1,710
8	Kiltan	1.63	1,844	1,825	3,669	49.59	990	2,251
9	Chetlat	1.04	1,173	1,118	2,291	48.32	953	2,203
10	Bitra	0.10	159	108	267	40.15	679	2,670
11	Bangaram*	0.58	56	9	65	13.85	161	112
	Total	**26.89**	**31,131**	**29,519**	**60,650**	**48.65**	**948**	**2,255**

Note: The density of population has been calculated on the basis of land use area of the individual islands and not the total island area.

* Bangaram–a tourists' island–is added/included in Agatti for demographic/statistical analysis.

Source: Lakshadweep Basic Statistics 2003-2004, Department of Economics & Statistics, Lakshadweep, Table-1 (p.10).

the decade 1981-1991, came down to 1.59 for 1991-2001, while the corresponding all-India figures stood at 2.13 and 1.95, respectively.[2] The estimated population of Lakshadweep in the coming years, based upon the past trends, indicates that it will reach the level of 70,322 by 2011,[3] which will mean a population density of 2,198 persons per km of landmass.

The dispersal of population density among the inhabited islands of Lakshadweep exhibits considerable variation Table 4.3.

2. *Basic Statistics 2003-2004*, Lakshadweep Administration, Table 1 (p.10) and Census of India, Provisional Population Totals, Paper 1 of 2001, Statement 4 (pp.42-43).

3. *Basic Statistics 2003-2004*, Lakshadweep Administration Table 15 (pp.17).

Bitra is the smallest in area having a population of 267 persons and Bangaram Island (previously uninhabited) has a population of only 65 persons (2001). Island-wise population details over the last five censuses have been placed at Annexure A-19.

Gender Ratio

The data given in Table 4.3 also indicate the inter-island disparity in the gender ratio. However, compared to most other Indian states and union territories, the gender ratio in Lakshadweep has been much better though not the ideal, as the details for the years 1981, 1991 and 2001 given in Annexures A-20 and A-21 will indicate. The relevant data in respect of the various union territories, Kerala and the all-India position are as given in Table 4.4.

TABLE 4.4

Gender Ratio in the Union Territories, Kerala and All-India 1981, 1991 and 2001

Sl.No.	Female per 1000 Male		
	1981	1991	2001
1. Andaman & Nicobar Islands	760	818	846
2. Chandigarh	769	790	773
3. Dadra & Nagar Haveli	974	952	811
4. Daman & Diu	1,062	969	709
5. Delhi	808	827	821
6. Lakshadweep	**975**	**943**	**948**
7. Pondicherry	985	979	1,001
8. Kerala	1,032	1,036	1,058
All-India	934	927	933

Source: Census, 2001.

The figures in the above table indicate that measures are required for correction of gender disparity in the demography of Lakshadweep as in most other States and UTs. However, the sex ratio for the child population (0–6 years) for Lakshadweep was 941 in 1991 Census and improved to 959 in 2001, which indicates a positive trend towards gender correction in the demography of Lakshadweep. All the same, there is still need to make conscious efforts to improve the gender ratio further.

Literacy and Education

Literacy Rates

Lakshadweep has a tradition of a very high rate of literacy. In the 1981 Census, it ranked fourth among all states and UTs, and by 1991, it overtook Chandigarh to gain the third rank after Kerala and Mizoram. The same position has continued in 2001, as may be seen in the Table 4.5.[4]

As for the literacy rate among the Scheduled Tribe population, Lakshadweep at 80.58 per cent stands second, after Mizoram (82.73), which are both way ahead of the all-India Average of 29.60 per cent (1991 Census).[6] The number of illiterates (excluding the child population, i.e., 0-6 age group) in terms of Census of 2001 was 6,454 only. The literacy rate in each of the islands is between 83.68 per cent (Kiltan) and 98.33 per cent (Bangaram), indicating a low level of inter-island variation in this respect (See Annexure A-22).

The adult literacy rate[7] (1995-96, NSSO 52nd Round) in Lakshadweep at 85.63 per cent stands third after Kerala (89.47) and Mizoram (88.43) and far above the all-India average of 54.32 per cent. As per a recent house-to-house survey (September 2003) conducted by the Territory's Administration, the number of adult illiterates has been identified as 3,814.[8] The Administration has drawn up a strategy to make the Territory fully literate by the year 2005 utilising the ongoing plan schemes effectively. Some of the island

TABLE 4.5

Literacy Rates in Union Territories, Kerala and India[5]

	1981			1991			2001		
	Male	Female	Persons	Male	Female	Persons	Male	Female	Persons
A & N Islands	70.29	53.20	63.19	78.99	65.46	73.02	86.07	75.29	81.18
Chandigarh	78.89	69.31	74.81	82.04	72.34	77.81	85.65	76.65	81.76
D & N Haveli	44.64	20.37	32.70	53.56	26.98	40.71	73.32	42.99	60.03
Daman & Diu	74.50	46.70	59.90	82.66	59.40	71.20	88.40	70.37	81.09
Delhi	79.28	62.60	71.90	82.01	66.99	75.29	87.37	75.00	81.82
Lakshadweep	**81.24**	**55.32**	**68.42**	**90.18**	**72.89**	**81.78**	**93.15**	**81.56**	**87.52**
Pondicherry	77.09	53.03	65.14	83.68	65.63	74.74	88.89	74.13	81.49
Kerala	87.73	75.65	81.56	93.62	86.13	89.81	94.20	87.86	90.92
All-India	56.38	29.76	43.57	64.13	39.29	52.51	75.64	54.03	65.20

Source: National Human Development Report 2001, Planning Commission, March 2002.

4. Island-wise literacy rates are given in Annexure A-22.
5. Literacy rate is defined as the proportion of literates to the population in the age group 7+. A person is considered literate if he or she can read and write with understanding, in any language. However, a person who can merely read, but cannot write, is not recorded as literate in census.
6. National Human Development Report 2001, Planning Commission (March 2002), Table 4.6.
7. Population of 15 years and above.
8. Source: Lakshadweep Administration.

TABLE 4.6

Gross Enrolment Ratio for School Age Children (6-14 years) for 2000-2001

	Classes I-V (6-11 Years)			*Classes VI-VIII (11-14 Years)*			*Classes I-VIII (6-14 Years)*		
	Boys	*Girls*	*Total*	*Boys*	*Girls*	*Total*	*Boys*	*Girls*	*Total*
A & N Islands	87.83	91.07	89.34	89.61	87.01	88.36	88.46	89.59	88.99
Chandigarh	65.17	65.55	65.35	68.21	73.43	70.59	66.28	68.32	67.23
D & N Haveli	144.22	102.74	122.58	88.42	55.88	72.15	124.52	87.12	105.29
Daman & Diu	105.05	94.25	99.65	98.80	67.22	81.26	102.97	83.85	93.03
Delhi	60.12	62.55	61.30	52.78	53.75	53.24	57.46	59.50	58.44
Lakshadweep	**106.98**	**92.90**	**99.94**	**129.30**	**109.35**	**119.33**	**114.42**	**98.38**	**106.40**
Pondicherry	86.56	74.55	80.37	95.43	86.15	90.73	89.76	78.64	84.06
Kerala	87.71	86.54	87.14	99.80	94.76	97.33	92.32	89.68	91.03
All-India	104.91	85.92	95.66	66.68	49.94	58.64	90.26	72.36	81.58

Source: Economic Survey 2002-2003, GoI.

representatives claimed that most of the officially declared illiterates were in fact able to read and write Arabic or Mahl. This calls for a careful review of the Census figures as well as the principles.

Enrolment in Schools

Lakshadweep seems to have excelled in attracting children to the schools as the data on gross enrolment ratio, given in Table 4.6 indicates:

The gross enrolment ratio (2000-01) for Classes I to V was 99.94 (Girls: 92.90) and for Classes VI to VIII, 119.33 (Girls: 109.35). This was among the highest in the country and higher than the all-India Average of 95.66 and 58.64, respectively.[9]

Infrastructure for Education

Lakshadweep has 10 Pre-Primary Schools, 21 Junior Basic Schools, 5 Senior Basic Schools, 4 High Schools and 8 Senior Secondary Schools, besides a Navodaya Vidyalaya in Minicoy and a recently opened Kendriya Vidyalaya in Kavaratti. Recently, in the academic year starting 2005, 4 existing High schools have been upgraded into Senior Secondary Schools. This upgradation has been done to make all the islands self-sufficient in atleast primary education. Also, it is difficult for the chidren particularly, the girl student to travel to other islands for continuing studies. Moreover, the strength of students in all the islands is quite high for the upgradation of the schools. All these are in the government sector. There are no institutions of further higher/professional levels. A District Institute of Education and Training (DIET), for meeting the training and development needs of teachers was opened at Kavaratti during 2002-03, but is yet to become functional and needs to be operationalised soon. Moreover, the administration's initiative of upgrading High Schools into Senior Secondary Schools requires the support of Ministry of Human Resource Development. There is urgent need for creation of around 56 PGT posts and 10 posts of Lab. Assistants for the schools to run effectively.

All the High Schools have been provided with computer laboratories (16 PCs each) and computer teaching has been introduced in the curriculum of Classes VII and IX. Education up to Class XII is provided free except in the recently opened Kendriya Vidyalaya. Besides, students in Classes VII to X are provided with scholarships of Rs. 50 per month.

The enrolment rate in the primary and upper primary levels of schooling is fairly high, close to 100 per cent, whereas the dropout rate is less than 2 per cent, as only 312 children in the age group of 6-14 are out of school.[10]

The pupil-teacher ratio in respect of various levels of schooling (Classes I to XII) has certain significant features as the comparative data in respect of relatively better off States/UTs, given in Table 4.7. indicate.

The figures in the Table 4.7 indicate that the pupil-teacher ratio in Lakshadweep is very comfortable in respect of all classes except for the Middle School level.

9. *Economic Survey*, 2002-03, GoI, Table 9.2, p.110.

10. Source: Lakshadweep Administration; relates to 2002-03. As per *National Human Development Report 2001*, Planning Commission, the dropout rate in respect of Lakshadweep for 1998-99 was 2.89 for Classes I-V and 21.89 for Classes I-VIII.

TABLE 4.7

Pupil-Teacher Ratio as on 30th September 2001

State/UT	*Primary /Junior Basic Schools*	*Middle/Senior Basic Schools*	*High Schools*	*Higher Secondary/ Junior Colleges*
Kerala	28	28	29	19
Mizoram	21	9	15	19
A & N Islands	20	18	18	19
Lakshadweep	**27**	**48**	**9**	**21**
All-India	43	34	33	36

Source: Select Educational Statistics 2001-02, Department of Secondary & Higher Education, Ministry of HRD, 2003.

However, all the existing teachers are trained and in that respect, Lakshadweep is placed better than even Kerala or Mizoram.[11]

The need is now to constantly improve the quality of education. This has to be achieved primarily by upgrading the teaching standards, for which immediate activation of the DIET, as mentioned above, is essential. It will also be appropriate to introduce exchange programmes for teachers as well as students, with mainland institutions.

Higher Education

There are no institutions of higher/professional education such as for degree and higher courses in arts, science, humanities, engineering, medical sciences, etc. in Lakshadweep. However, seats have been reserved in the institutions of mainland states, more notably in Kerala, for students hailing from Lakshadweep. These include 46 seats in State Engineering Colleges, 19 in the Regional Engineering Colleges/National Institutes of Technology, 10 for the MBBS Course, 5 for Diploma in Hotel Management, 3 each for BAMS and Nursing, 2 each for BDS, BHMS, BSc (Agrl.), D. Pharm., Paramedical, and LLB and 35 for Diploma in Engineering, 302 for BA/BSc/B.Com., etc. Students hailing from Lakshadweep studying in the mainland institutions against reserved seats are provided with scholarships, besides reimbursement of tuition fee, hostel fee and return journey fare once a year. These reservations have so far been found to be useful.

Lakshadweep does not have any educational institution for higher/professional studies except for an Industrial Training Institute that has an intake of 20 students for 4 disciplines such as tailoring, automobile repairs, stenography and embroidery. Despite the small number for the intake, the dropout rate as well as the rate of students who fail in the courses, have been high (See Annexure A-23 and A-24). The selection of these disciplines needs to be reviewed, to make the courses market friendly.

The Tenth Plan document of Lakshadweep has emphasised the need for establishment of a Degree College in Lakshadweep.[12] However, the educational curriculum of such an institution will need to be more focused on the employment opportunities. Therefore, a Degree College with courses in vocational disciplines including B.Ed., paramedical subjects, marine fisheries, computer applications, etc. may be set up in the territory. Recently the UTL Administration has set up three degree level University Centres at Kadmat, Andrott and Kavaratti in collaboration with Calicut University.

There is a Study Centre of the Indira Gandhi National Open University in Kavaratti. Such centres need to be started in some of the other islands too, to provide a cost-effective alternative to institutions of higher learning.

Kochi and Calicut are the most popular centres for the students of Lakshadweep to pursue higher studies on the mainland. A hostel in each of these two places may be maintained by the Lakshadweep Administration for the convenience of such students.

The Education Department of the Lakshadweep Administration should, in association with the Industrial Training Institute, Kavaratti, arrange for career counselling for the youth, including the students of Classes XI and XII as well as of the ITI, to make them aware of the employment opportunities in the mainland as well. The Department of Labour & Employment, UT of Lakshadweep in collaboration with Department of Education and ITI is keen to open Career Guidance Centres in all the islands which will provide counselling to students at matric and senior secondary level about various career options, vacancies available, provide coaching and preparatory training for medical, engineering, seaman, police, home guard, armed forces, etc.

This inititiative can be bolstered with the aid of Information Technology. As a first step, the administration plans to take up computerisation of Employment Exchange at Kavaratti in 2006 which will eventually pave way for enabling the web enabled employment registration system and usher in e-governance.

11. Ibid.

12. *Draft Tenth Five Year Plan 2002-2007*, Lakshadweep, Vol. II, pp.229-242.

Public Health and Medical Care

Among the various possible indicators for the health status of the people, some of the more significant ones are crude birth rate, crude death rate, infant mortality rates, and life expectancy at birth, etc. The life expectancy at birth in respect of Lakshadweep is 65 years as against 63 years for the all-India average.[13] The status in respect of the other key parameters is examined below.

Birth Rate and Death Rate

The trend data for crude birth rate and crude death rate for the various Union Territories, Kerala and India, during the last decade are given in Table 4.8.

TABLE 4.8

Birth Rate and Death Rate in Union Territories, Kerala and India

(Per Thousand Population per year)

	Crude Birth Rate (CBR)			*Crude Death Rate (CDR)*		
	1991	*1995*	*2002*	*1991*	*1995*	*2002*
A & N Islands	20.0	18.7	16.8	5.8	5.8	5.5
Chandigarh	13.9	18.5	14.6	4.6	5.1	3.4
D & N Haveli	31.1	29.7	30.4	11.4	8.2	6.8
Daman & Diu	27.9	21.8	22.4	9.0	8.0	6.6
Delhi	24.7	23.3	17.2	6.3	6.0	5.1
Lakshadweep	**27.1**	**25.5**	**19.3**	**4.7**	**7.6**	**5.2**
Pondicherry	19.2	20.1	17.9	6.6	7.6	6.7
Kerala	18.3	18.0	16.8	6.0	6.0	6.4
All-India	29.5	28.3	25.0	9.8	9.0	8.1

Source: Health Information of India: 2003, Central Bureau of Health Intelligence, Ministry of H&FW, GoI (*http://cbhidghs.nic.in*).

It is apparent that the condition of Lakshadweep in terms of both crude birth rate and crude death rate is comparable with most other union territories and the all-India average pattern. However, compared to Kerala, its birth rate is very high.

Data for IMR, CBR, CDR, etc. from the 2001 Census are not yet available. However, for Lakshadweep and the all-India statistics, the following picture is available (Table 4.9).

Infant Mortality Rate

The infant mortality rate (IMR) has been defined as the number of children (infants) who are unable to survive even till their first birthday, out of 1000 live births. This information in respect of the various Union Territories, Kerala and the all-India position for the years 1961, 1981 and 2002 is given in Table 4.10.

Table 4.10 indicates a very significant, rather dramatic, decline in the IMR for Lakshadweep from the level of 118 in 1961, which was above the all-India average level of 115, to that of 25 in 2002, which is far less than the all-India average of 64.

Prevalent Communicable Diseases

An interesting feature of the health status of the people of the Lakshadweep islands is the extent of prevalence of certain communicable diseases, more notably acute diarrhoea and acute respiratory infection. Year-wise details are given in Table 4.11.

The incidence of acute respiratory infection has obviously been on the increase and every second person appears to be affected by it, though, the statistics of out/in-patients could include cases of repetition during the year. Even acute diarrhoea has shown very high level of prevalence with one in six persons affected by it.

The prevalence of three of the communicable diseases that are seen at a significant level in Lakshadweep, namely, Acute Diarrhoeal Disease (ADD), Acute Respiratory Infection (ARI) and pneumonia in the various Union Territories, Kerala and India, is detailed in Table 4.12.

The ratios presented in the above table confirm the high level of prevalence of at least three of the communicable diseases, namely, Acute Diarrhoeal Disease, Acute Respiratory Infection and Pneumonia, making it a serious cause of concern.

TABLE 4.9

Some Important Health Indicators for Lakshadweep *vis-à-vis* All-India-2001[14]

Indicator	*Lakshadweep*	*All-India*
Birth Rate	20.4	25.4
Death Rate	5.0	8.4
Infant Mortality Rate	33	66
Maternal Mortality Rate	0.18	4.0
Life Expectancy	65	63

Source: Registrar General of India and Lakshadweep Administration.

13. *Lakshadweep & Its People 2002-2003*, Lakshadweep Administration.

14. Source: *Sample Registration System Bulletin*, Vol. 36, No. 2, Registrar General, India, October 2002 (*www.censusindia.net*) for B.R., D.R., & IMR; and *Lakshadweep & Its People, 2002-2003*, Lakshadweep Administration, for the remaining two indicators.

TABLE 4.10

Infant Mortality Rate during the Years 1961, 1981 and 2002 in Union Territories, Kerala and India

States/UTs	*1961*	*1981*	*2002*
A & N Islands	77	69	21
Chandigarh	53	48	25
D & N Haveli	98	81	56
Daman & Diu	57	50	39
Delhi	67	54	32
Lakshadweep	**118**	**91**	**25**
Pondicherry	73	34	23
Kerala	52	42	10
All-India	115	77	64

Source: Economic Survey 2003-2004, GoI.

Infrastructure for Healthcare

Lakshadweep has no private hospitals. It is served by 2 Government Hospitals, 3 Community Health Centres (CHCs), 4 Primary Health Centres (PHCs), besides 14 Sub-Centres, 2 First-Aid Centres, 2 Ayurvedic Dispensaries, 1 Homeopathic Dispensary and a Dental Unit. These health institutions have in all 200 beds for inpatients. These institutions catered to 2,15,958 outpatients and 4,930 inpatients during 2001, whereas the number of outpatients and inpatients for the immediately preceding years was of a similar but somewhat of decreasing order.[15]

TABLE 4.11

Prevalent Communicable Diseases in Lakshadweep

(*No. of Persons*)

	1994	*1996*	*1998*	*1999*	*2000*	*2001*
Acute Diarrhoea						
Outpatients	9392	5465	5406	6589	6861	9907
Inpatients	299	615	464	582	322	286
Total	9691	6080	5870	7171	7183	10193
Acute Respiratory Infection						
Outpatients	10120	13663	10914	17684	19554	38349
Inpatients	81	311	430	519	493	654
Total	10201	13974	11344	18203	20047	39003

Source: Basic Statistics 2001-02, Lakshadweep Administration, Table 4 (pp.54-63).

TABLE 4.12

Prevalence of Certain Communicable Diseases in the Union Territories, Kerala and India

	Popn. ('000)	*No. of Cases Reported*			*Ratio to Population (Per cent)**		
	2001	*ADD-2001*	*ARI-2000*	*Pneu-2000*	*ADD-2001*	*ARI-2000*	*Pneu-2000*
A & N Islands	356	44722	65483	69	12.55	18.38	0.02
Chandigarh	901	7283	5450	2635	0.81	0.60	0.29
D & N Haveli	220	N.R.	N.R.	N.R.	-	-	-
Daman & Diu	158	631	4622	10	0.40	2.92	0.01
Delhi	13783	112568	214156	25046	0.82	1.55	0.18
Lakshadweep	**61**	**10193**	**20045**	**250**	**16.82**	**33.08**	**0.41**
Pondicherry	974	147700	42347	7431	15.17	4.35	0.76
Kerala	31839	561312	6241664	23399	1.76	19.60	0.07
All-India**	1027015	9289558	19657605	519921	0.90	1.91	0.05

Note: *: Population of 2001 Census has been retained for computing these ratios in all cases. N.R.=Not Reported.

**: All-India figures do not include some States/UTs for which data was not reported.

Source: Health Information of India: 2000 and 2001, Central Bureau of Health Intelligence, Ministry of Health and Family Welfare.

15. *Basic Statistics 2001-2002*, Lakshadweep Administration.

The number of doctors in government institutions in Lakshadweep as on 1.1.2001 was 28 besides 1 dentist, giving the doctor-population ratio as 2179, which was much higher than the corresponding figure for Pondicherry (1607) but lower than Andaman & Nicobar (3043) and Daman & Diu (5097). However, with only 1 dentist in position, the dentist-population ratio remained at the unrealistically high level of 61,000.[16]

To take care of the secondary level health services, there are 12 sanctioned posts of specialists (surgeons, physicians, obstetricians & gynaecologists, and paediatricians) in the UT of Lakshadweep. Most of them have been lying vacant for several years, however since January 2004, specialist doctors in the field of gyanaecology, paediatrics, surgery, anaesthesia, Orthopaedics, etc. belonging to Central Health Services cadre are being posted by the Ministry of Health, GoI on short-term basis. Similarly, in respect of paramedical staff, certain critical posts were vacant. For instance, all the 14 posts of Male Health Workers were vacant, as on 31.3.2001.[17] To meet the shortage of specialists, the administration has also introduced the arrangement of telemedicine, in collaboration with the Amrutha Institute of Medical Sciences (AIMS), Kochi. This has helped the situation to some extent. Availability of well-qualified medical personnel on a sustained basis, however, continues to remain a challenge. While the Island Development Authority has been seriously concerned with this problem, it can be addressed to some extent by extending the arrangements for telemedicine to all the islands.

While the administration is presently helping the critically ill persons by airlifting them to the mainland hospitals through the helicopter services. A pilot project consisting of ship-based hospital and a helicopter-based hospital may also be introduced. Such hospitals can reach the specialist medical care to larger numbers of people preventing patients from reaching the critical stage of illness. This should be more cost-effective for the administration too.

The future action plan is that the Indira Gandhi Hospital at Kavaratti would be reconstructed and upgraded into a Super Specialty Hospital with sufficient specialists. The plan of the building has been approved and construction will commence during 2006-07. Two Community Health Centres (CHC) are being upgraded to Indian Public Health Standard to make it as FRUs. Dental Units are planned for all CHCs. Indian System of Medicine will be further expended by Ayush Medical Officers in all PHCs and CHCs. The existing Ayurvedic Dispensaries at Kavaratti and Andrott will be upgraded into 10-bedded hospitals. Proposal for posts like Public Health Specialist, Radiologist, Microbilogist, Ortho Surgeon, Cardiologist and Gynaecologist have been made. Three more Ayurvedic Dispensaries are proposed for Minicoy, Amini and Agatti and two Unani Dispensaries are planned for Kalpeni and Kavaratti with sufficient infrastructural facilities and staff. There is also need for introducing Public Health Insurance Scheme for all.

The administration is also working on introducinig Health Card as a part of Lakshadweep Multi Purpose Citizen Identity Card in line with national initiative of Multi purpose National Identity Card (MINC). It will be smart card which will store various information such as name, place of birth, residence, age, medical history, economic status etc. and serve not only as an Identity Card/Voter Card/Driving License but also Health Card, Ration Card, etc. This is being done by inter-departmental group consisting of Collectorate, NIC, IT Department with the close assistance of all other departments.

Drinking Water and Sanitation

Access to Safe Sources of Drinking Water

The only source of drinking water available in this territory is rainwater, which percolates down through the porous sandy soil and floats over the subsoil saline water. However, the entire water available in the floating sweet water lens cannot be extracted on account of technical problems in continuous and uncontrolled pumping. It is estimated that sufficient quantity of drinking water is available in the subsoil taking into account transportation, limitations of extraction of the ground water and so on.

One possible reason for the high rate of prevalence of waterborne diseases is the inadequate availability of safe drinking water. As in April 2003, none of the 10 habitations (islands) of Lakshadweep were fully covered under the protected (tap) water supply programme, all were only partially covered, as per the Census data (2001).[18] Details are given in Table 4.13.

Thus, almost 95 per cent of the households in Lakshadweep get drinking water from open wells and

16. *Health Information of India: 2000 & 2001*, Central Bureau of Health Intelligence, Ministry of H&FW, GoI, Table 7.09.
17. Ibid., Table 7.13.
18. 'Ibid., Table 3.06. Island-wise details may be seen in Annexure A-25.

TABLE 4.13

Distribution of Households by Access to Different Sources of Drinking Water*

	Total	*Tap Water Supply*		*Hand Pump/Tube Well*		*Well*		*Other Sources#*	
	No.	*No.*	*% Share*	*No.*	*% Share*	*No.*	*% Share*	*No.*	*% Share*
A & N Islands	73062	55709	76.25	348	0.48	11672	15.98	5333	7.30
Chandigarh	201878	185426	91.85	16096	7.97	13	0.01	343	0.17
D & N Haveli	43973	12412	28.23	21440	48.76	8544	19.43	1577	3.59
Daman & Diu	34342	25039	72.91	8040	23.41	1181	3.44	82	0.24
Delhi	2554149	1924140	75.33	559518	21.91	1019	0.04	69472	2.72
Lakshadweep	**9240**	**283**	**3.06**	**144**	**1.56**	**8589**	**92.95**	**224**	**2.42**
Pondicherry	208655	186241	89.26	13797	6.61	5601	2.68	3016	1.45
Kerala	6595206	1345646	20.40	196655	2.98	4738954	71.85	313951	4.76
All-India	191963935	70448827	36.70	79132913	41.22	34873102	18.17	7509093	3.91

Note: *: Access to a particular source (Tap, Hand pump, etc.) includes within premises and beyond.
#: Other sources include tank, pond, lake, river, canal, spring, etc.

Source: Census, 2001.

sources other than tap water supply, hand pump or tube well.[19] The PWD has provided 1,445 taps in 8 out of the 10 islands (i.e., excluding Bitra and Minicoy). The source of water supply from these taps is open wells of which the majority have turned brackish. Supply from the functional taps is confined to about half an hour a day as no more water is available in the source wells. People therefore depend on water supply from their own backyard open wells.

The only natural source of water is ground water (subsoil water), which is replenished by rains mainly during the southwest monsoon. Even this subsoil water is not available in one of the islands namely Bitra. In this island the water supply is being managed through the Rainwater Harvesting System. Even in the other islands full requirement of water cannot be met from the ground water/subsoil water. Therefore, it has to be supplemented by adopting other systems such as Reverse Osmosis (RO), desalination plants and rainwater harvesting system. In order to meet water requirements of inhabited islands, the water supply scheme may resort to a combination of all these three water sources. A Desalination plant of one lakh litre capacity has been set up in Kavaratti by the Lakshadweep Administration with the assistance of National Institute of Ocean Technology (NIOT), Chennai in 2005. The administration proposes to replicate this in all the other islands to meet the drinking water need of the people. This will also help in bringing down the cases of waterborne diseases in islands which are very high in the islands presently.

Results of various surveys and investigations carried out by agencies such as the National Environmental Engineering Research Institute (NEERI) and Centre for Earth Science Studies (CESS) have shown the inadequacy and poor quality of the ground water. Nearly 100 per cent of the water samples showed some sort of contamination. In order to protect all the water supply sources from contamination and proper monitoring of the supply of potable water to the inhabitants of all the islands, Government of India proposed to set up a water testing laboratory in each of the islands of Lakshadweep for which necessary financial support was extended to the UT administration by the Government of India during the Eighth Plan.

Water must be managed as an economic asset rather than a free commodity in exactly the same way as any other resource. It should be treated as a resource in its totality and regeneration of sources shall be the responsibility of every user agency, whether drinking, irrigation or other uses. The comprehensive development of water resources should be opted as a strategy and the village should be considered the focal point for water development. Top to bottom arrangement is necessary to stop wastage. Supply of water to consumers should normally be based on the principle of effective demand, which should broadly correspond to the standard of services that the users are willing to maintain, operate and finance.

19. Census Commissioner of India, Census 2001, Tables on Houses, Household Amenities and Assets, Table H8.

Recently, the Lakshadweep Ground Water (Development and Control) Regulation 2001, has been promulgated on August 6, 2001. As per the regulation a Ground Water Authority has to be constituted. This Authority will have the powers to control and regulate the extraction and use of water in any form in any island in Lakshadweep. The Authority needs to be brought in soon.

Safe drinking water should be provided as per the stipulated norms on a sustainable basis to all habitations within a short time frame of, say, two years. Emphasis must be laid on stakeholders participation at all levels, from planning, design, location, implementation and management. The present practice is that water supply projects are designed and executed by the implementing departments and passed on to the end-users. Experience shows the unwillingness of the island *panchayats* to take on the responsibility for operating and maintaining them. The UT administration does not have effective machinery at the village level to maintain the assets. A radical change in the management is required. Rather than being supply-driven, the system should be demand-driven, and should take into account user preferences, private connections and related issues. People should be aware of technologies and be given the option to select the technology as well as meet the expenditure on the project. People's participation at all stages of the project implementation always helps to get over the problems of substandard materials, poor workmanship and inadequate maintenance. These problems should be addressed while preparing the plans.

Rainwater Harvesting

The highly drained and permeable soils provide good drainage and enable the rainwater to join the shallow water table and the sea, especially when an impervious coral layer is present. In such geology, fresh ground water is distributed in the form of lenses floating over deeper saline aquifers with a very limited potential. This water is generally retrieved through shallow open dug wells. Improved *Dourves* system can be used for better extraction of floating fresh water resources. This system consists of excavating a very shallow pit or well in which floating fresh water can be collected by laying a horizontal filter rather than a vertical one used in standard tube well technology. Laying a horizontal filter, say at a depth of one or two metres will help collect or skim floating lenses above the mean sea level which will get replenished with every rainfall event. Agriculture should be strategised as a rainfed crop production system rather than intensively irrigated cultivation. Rainwater harvesting, its storage and recycling has potential, especially during the high rainfall period of the monsoons. As things exist today, the freshwater lenses are very shallow and get contaminated with E-coli since latrines are designed with soak pits. This problem can be overcome to a considerable extent by resorting to better design and location of the soak pits. The availability of sweet water for households can be augmented by popularising the roof water harvesting system. There is also a case for making such a water harvesting system mandatory for all buildings. It would be worthwhile to extend budgetary subsidies for their construction.

Sanitation

Another health related social issue is that because of the absence of a systematic sewerage system, most households have constructed soak pits for disposal of latrine waste. Owing to acute pressure on the land, the soak pits have been constructed very close to the open wells. The soil being sandy and porous and the soak pits having been constructed rather unscientifically, faecal matter from the soak pits finds its way into the water in the open wells, as has been found out by the water quality testing reports in the Departments of Health and Public Works. This makes the available water supply unsafe and has been generally accepted to be the main reason behind the high rate of waterborne diseases including acute diarrhoea prevalent in the islands.

The conventional method of sewerage and sewage treatment is not feasible because of the coral sandy strata, inadequacy of space, high water table and flat terrain. There is a need to urgently explore the possibility of setting up a pilot project on disposal of waste water in the inhabited islands of Lakshadweep to study its efficacy and reliability under the prevailing local conditions and its replicability in other islands of Lakshadweep.

All existing social organisations, women's self-help groups, cooperative societies, civil societies, educational institutions, private institutions, etc. should be drawn in for effective implementation of a large-scale sanitation programme.

The Total Sanitation Campaign (TSC) approach of the restructured Centrally Sponsored Sanitation Programme (w.e.f. 1.4.1999), which is based on the successful model of Midnapur (West Bengal), may be considered for adoption in the islands in Lakshadweep with appropriate changes to suit local conditions and perception. The total sanitation programme should include safe disposal of night soil, rainwater, domestic liquid and solid wastes and not merely be restricted to construction of toilets. School Sanitation (toilet facility) should be given highest priority to inculcate safe hygienic habits among school children. The available low cost technologies for conversion of waste from the soak pits into manure need to be popularised.

In order to mobilise the required funds for rural sanitation, if necessary, financial institutions should extend loans at lower interest rates to the UT Administration for providing sanitation facilities. Various fiscal concessions such as cutting excise duty/ sales tax and changing lower electricity rates should be made available to the manufacturers of low cost sanitary materials. Private participation should be encouraged in setting up building centres and sanitary marts in rural areas to provide cost-effective sanitation technology to the households. Creation and maintenance of a data base and information base regarding various technological options, hydrogeological information, availability of building materials, design and implementation, etc. at each island level must be disseminated through *panchayats* and sanitary marts.

Management of Solid Waste

In order to keep the environment clean and healthy and also to avoid ground water contamination the UT Administration is very much concerned about the proper disposal of solid waste. There are mainly two types of such waste namely, biodegradable and non biodegradable. It is proposed that non-biodegradable items should be collected from different localities, stored in a central place, packed and sent to the mainland for final disposal. Local NGOs are to be involved in this activity. As far as biodegradable items are concerned, vermicomposting at household level has been proposed for which suitable vermicompost pots will need to be placed in each household at suitable locations for decomposition and conversion into manure. The manure produced will be utilised by the inhabitants for their kitchen gardens, etc.

Perspective Approach to Water Supply and Sanitation

In order to provide safe and adequate water supply to the people by 2021, a comprehensive water supply scheme including a Reverse Osmosis Plant (capacity 10 cum/unit/day) to be used only for cooking and drinking with 10 litre per capita per day (lpcd), Conventional Water Supply System with 40 lpcd (ground water source development, storage, disinfection and distribution), and Rainwater Harvesting (with a requirement of 10 lpcd for 120 days storage per household) have been proposed. The projected population for the various islands is given in Table 4.14.

Thus, the population of the 2001 census at 60,650, is expected to grow by about 28.20 per cent over the next 20 years, with an average decadal growth rate of 13.28 per cent, though some of the islands are expected to have a still higher rate of growth.

For a conventional water supply system, controlled pumping should be resorted to, so as to maintain the sweet water lens. The installation of reverse osmosis plants have been proposed in the estimates but this does not include source development and other infrastructure. However, depending upon the physical conditions, water supply from this plant can be provided through the distribution system laid for conventional water supply systems.

Since there is no proper waste water disposal system in the Lakshadweep islands, provision of small septic tanks has been made for each household to serve the population till 2021. After proper treatment of septic tank effluent the treated waste water can be used for agriculture and kitchen gardens. The system for the treatment of septic tank effluent needs to be designed carefully considering the hydrological conditions.

Storm water can be directly disposed of into the sea. With a provision of a separate storm water drainage system after carefully studying the geography of the area and the extent it is to be served.

It is presumed that the per capita solid waste production will be around 0.5 kg by 2021 and the organic matter contents should be about 50 per cent of the waste generated. Therefore, vermicomposting has been proposed as one of the most economical methods for producing compost from solid waste. This compost can be used for agriculture and kitchen gardens. The remaining 50 per cent solid waste can suitably be recycled and reused, keeping in view the health of the people and the environment.

A family size of 6.5 members (avg.) per family has been assumed to calculate the total number of households by 2021. With the assumptions of population growth indicated in Table 4.14, the cost estimates for providing the water supply, sanitation and solid waste disposal system over the next 20 years, are as shown in Table 4.15.

TABLE 4.14

Island–wise Projected Population for the Year 2021

Sl. No.	*Name of Island*	*Population*				
		2001 (Census)	*Decadal Growth (%)*	*2011 (Projected)*	*2021 (Projected)*	*Decadal Growth Assumed (%)*
1.	Agatti	7009	19	8085	9294	15
2.	Amini	7353	12.7	8220	9206	12
3.	Andrott	10727	15	12328	14177	15
4.	Bangaram	65	6	69	73	6
5.	Bitra	267	14.5	302	346	14.5
6.	Chetlat	2291	10.4	2527	2790	10.4
7.	Kadmat	5334	25	6117	7034	15
8.	Kalpeni	4321	5.5	4556	4806	5.5
9.	Kavaratti	10119	14.2	11549	13189	14.2
10.	Kiltan	3669	16.3	4213	4845	15
11.	Minicoy	9495	12.4	10672	11995	12.4
	Total	**60650**	**14.6**	**68638**	**77755**	**13.28**

Source: Lakshadweep Administration.

TABLE 4.15

Cost Estimates for Providing Water Supply, Sanitation and Solid Waste Disposal Systems

Rs. Crore

Sl. No.	*Name of Island*	*Population (2021-Projected)*	*No. of Households (Estimated)*	*Water Supply Systems**			*Sanitation**		*Solid Waste Disposal** (Vermicomposting)*
				R.O. Plant	*Conventional System*	*Rainwater Harvesting*	*Septic Tanks*	*Drainage System*	
1.	Agatti	9794	1430	30 (2)	186.00	176.60		50.00	
2.	Amini	9206	1416	30 (2)	184.00	170.00		25.00	
3.	Andrott	14177	2181	45 (3)	283.50	262.00		50.00	
4.	Bangaram	73	11	—	1.46	1.32		—	
5.	Bitra	346	53	15 (1)	6.92	6.36		5.00	
6.	Chetlat	2790	429	15 (1)	55.80	51.50	718.0	10.00	30.00
7.	Kadmat	7034	1082	30 (2)	140.70	130.00		25.00	
8.	Kalpeni	4806	739	30 (2)	96.12	89.00		20.00	
9.	Kavaratti	13189	2029	45 (3)	263.78	243.50		50.00	
10.	Kiltan	4845	745	30 (2)	97.00	89.40		20.00	
11.	Minicoy	11995	1845	45 (3)	240.00	221.40		50.00	
	Total	**78255**	**11960**	**315**	**1555.28**	**1441.08**	**718.0**	**305.00**	**30.00**

Note: 1. Cost estimates are indicative only.
2. These estimates do not include operation and maintenance cost.
3. Figures in brackets are the number of units of R.O. Plant proposed to be installed.
4. Water supply and sanitation schemes including solid waste disposal as proposed in this Table are in addition to the existing water supply and sanitation schemes.

Source: *: Tentative cost estimates obtained from the Water Supply Department, Ministry of Rural Development, GoI.
**: Tentative cost estimates obtained from HUDCO, Ministry of Urban Development and Poverty Alleviation, GoI.

Based on the assumptions and analysis stated above, the requirement of funds for providing water supply and sanitation including solid waste disposal for the years up to 2021, is estimated as given in Table 4.16.

TABLE 4.16

Summary of Requirements of Funds for Providing Water Supply and Sanitation including Solid Waste Disposal

Sl. No.	*Type of Scheme*	*Estimated Cost (Rs. Lakhs)*	*Basis for Arriving at Cost Estimates*	*Remarks*
1.	**Water Supply Scheme** R.O. Plant	315.00	Rs. 15 lakhs per unit exclusive of cost for source development, infrastructure and O&M.	Only for drinking and cooking purposes.
	Conventional Water Supply Scheme	1555.28	Piped Water Supply Scheme, Rs. 2000/capita. Includes source development, storage, disinfection and distribution with house service connections.	Per capita rate of supply 40 lit. Estimate does not include O&M cost.
	Rain Water Harvesting	1436.08	Rs. 12000 per household.	With 10 lpcd for a storage of 120 days for drinking and cooking for a family of 5-6 members.
2.	**Sanitation** Septic Tanks	718.00	Rs. 6000 per household.	Under Total Sanitation Campaign, effluents require further treatment.
	Drainage	305.00	Tentative Estimate depending upon geography and the extent of area.	Storm water can be disposed of into the sea.
3.	**Solid Waste Disposal**	30.00	Rs. 1 lakh/1000 tonnes of organic wastes (including Infrastructure cost).	Only organic waste is suitable for vermicomposting.
	Total	**4359.36**		

Note: The total estimated cost for providing water supply and sanitation including solid waste disposal till 2021 is Rs. 4359.36 lakhs which is substantially high. The project can be taken up in phases depending upon priority of schemes and availability of funds.

Source: Estimated based on Table 4.15.

Employment Generation

Work Participation Rate

Under the Census operations, the level of employment prevalent in Lakshadweep, as in the case of all other States/UTs, is measured by the ratios of 'Workers' and 'Non-workers' to the total population. Workers are further divided into 'Main Workers' and 'Marginal Workers'. For the Census 2001, a person who had worked during the preceding year for six months or more was classified as 'Worker' and one who had worked for less than six months, as 'Marginal Worker'. A person who did not work at all, was classified as 'Non-worker'. The ratio of total workers (Main and Marginal) to the total population is termed as the 'work participation rate', or, WPR. The WPR for Lakshadweep for the Census of 1991 and 2001 has been reported as 26.43 and 25.33 per cent, respectively. This indicates a decline in the employment opportunity for the people. The all-India average WPR for 2001 stood at 39.26. In fact, the highest figure was for Mizoram (52.70), followed by Dadra & Nagar Haveli (51.77), whereas at 25.33 per cent for Lakshadweep, it was the lowest in the country.[20]

The term 'Worker' in the Census 2001 has been further classified as 'Cultivators', 'Agricultural labourers', 'Workers in household industries' and 'Other workers'. In terms of Census 2001 (Provisional data), of the total workers in Lakshadweep, 5.93 per cent have been classified as 'Workers in household industries', and all the remaining as 'Other workers'. Lakshadweep is unique among all the States/UTs in not having a single person reporting as either 'Cultivator' or as 'Agricultural Labourer'. The reason for this situation is that the workers in the island who are engaged in coconut cultivation are classified under plantation workers and they, along with the workers engaged in fisheries, are clubbed together under the heading of 'Other workers'. Further break up of the category 'Other workers' will be known only when more detailed reports of the Census of 2001 become available.[21]

The gender gap in work participation in Lakshadweep for 2001 was 36, which was among the highest in the country, the still higher ones being Daman & Diu (48), Delhi (43), Chandigarh (42), and Andaman & Nicobar Islands (41), whereas two States/UTs equalled it (West Bengal and Pondicherry), while the all-India average stood at 2.[22]

20. Census 2001, Series 32: Lakshadweep, Provisional Population Totals, Paper 3 of 2001.

21. Ibid.
22. *Economic Survey*, GoI, 2002-03 (Table 10.11, p.222).

Labour Force Participation Rate

Yet another indicator of the employment situation is presented in terms of labour force participation rate (LFPR) in the *National Human Development Report 2001* of the Planning Commission. The LFPR has been defined as the proportion of persons in the age group 15 years and above who are either working (i.e., employed) or seeking or available for work (i.e., unemployed) but employable. The situation of LFPR in 1999-2000, as compiled by the Planning Commission through the data of 38th, 50th and 55th Rounds of NSSO Surveys, gives the following picture in respect of the various Union Territories, Kerala and All-India (Table 4.17).

TABLE 4.17

Labour Force Participation Rate (%) in the Union Territories, Kerala and India: 1999-2000

States/UTs	*Male*	*Female*	*Persons*
A & N Islands	86.4	29.7	59.7
Chandigarh	81.2	21.0	53.7
D & N Haveli	92.7	53.2	73.0
Daman & Diu	85.5	34.7	60.1
Delhi	77.7	13.6	47.6
Lakshadweep	**81.9**	**33.1**	**57.8**
Pondicherry	79.8	29.2	54.3
Kerala	80.3	35.3	57.4
All-India	83.5	38.5	61.8

Source: National Human Development Report 2001, Planning Commission, Table 2.10.

Comparison of the Census 2001 data on WPR and Planning Commission data on LFPR indicates considerable need for providing employment opportunities to the employable but unemployed population of Lakshadweep.

Status of Employment-Unemployment Scenario

The status of employment-unemployment scenario in Lakshadweep *vis-à-vis* other Union Territories, State of Kerala and the all-India situation, is given in Table 4.18 in terms of persons in the labour force and the incidence of unemployment, both as percentage of the labour force inclusive of male and female population.

The level of unemployment in Lakshadweep, despite its very small population, is very high. In fact, at 13.2 per cent, it is next only to Goa (13.6) followed by Kerala, which is way below at 8.6. Low levels of employment opportunities in the sectors of industry and agriculture, coupled with high levels of literacy seem to have brought about the high rate of unemployment in Lakshadweep.

TABLE 4.18

Status of Employment in the Union Territories, Kerala and India

States/UTs	*Persons in Labour Force (Percentage)*		*Incidence of Unemployment (As % of Labour Force)$*	
	1993-94	*1999-00*	*1993-94*	*1999-00*
A & N Islands	76.0	59.7	3.0	4.3
Chandigarh	61.7	53.7	7.1	4.2
D & N Haveli	83.8	73.0	0.7	1.2
Daman & Diu	55.0	60.1	3.0	1.9
Delhi	50.8	47.6	1.4	3.6
Lakshadweep	**54.7**	**57.8**	**16.9**	**13.2**
Pondicherry	55.5	54.3	5.1	4.1
Kerala	57.9	57.4	7.7	8.6
All-India	64.5	61.8	2.0	2.3

Note: $: The incidence of unemployment has been defined as the percentage of persons unemployed in the age group 15 years and above.
Source: National Human Development Report 2001, Planning Commission.

As per the information provided by the Labour & Employment Department of Lakshadweep, the number of registered job seekers with the Employment Exchange stood at 10,946 (as on 1.12.2003) whereas placements effected during the year till that date were only 154. Of the 10,946 job seekers, 308 were Graduates and Postgraduates, 113 were holders of Engineering Degree/Diploma, 743 were in the Plus 2 category, 4,916 were Matriculates and 4,866, below Matriculates. For a total population of the order of 61,000, these numbers appear to be very high.

There are, however, claims that many of the persons registered as unemployed are actually employed in the private sector but still report themselves as unemployed in pursuit of government jobs. A careful review of the live register is, therefore, called for.

Subject to the verification of the live register of job seekers proposed above, it can be assumed that Lakshadweep faces widespread unemployment, caused largely by the low levels of economic activities in industry and agriculture, coupled with high levels of literacy. It is not possible to foresee significant fresh investments in the industry and agriculture sectors on the pattern prevalent in the rest of the country and a different approach is called for.

The potential sectors for generating employment opportunities would be tourism, fisheries, fish and coconut/coir based industries, and agro-processing.

More detailed surveys of the employment potential of these and other sectors are required. The Industrial Training Institute (ITI) located at Kavaratti needs to reorient its coverage to include such skills that provide ready market to the trainees. A Career Guidance Centre is also required for the benefit of students and other youth of the islands.

Presently, Dr. B.R. Ambedkar Industrial Training Institute is the only ITI in the Union Territory of Lakshadweep. There are four trades in this ITI including:

i) Stenography (English).

ii) Carpenter.

iii) Cutting and Sewing.

iv) Mechanic (Diesel).

All the above trades are affiliated to NCVT, New Delhi. Approved strength of each trade is 16.

The Government of India, Ministry of Labour & Employment has identified this ITI as one of the 500 ITIs for upgradation into "Centres of Excellence" under the Centrally Sponsored Scheme. A team of Officers from Central Staff Training & Research Institute (CSTRI), Kolkata conducted a study on upgradation of this ITI and identified "Hospitality Management" course as the sector for upgradation into Centres of Excellence. The UT Administration proposes to implement their recommendation in consultation with the Institute Management Committee of the ITI.

The high level of literacy and education prevalent among the islanders could enable them to participate in the IT revolution and the call centre boom, that is sweeping many cities and towns in the country, providing gainful employment to the youth and even others as well. While such activities would have to remain in the folds of the private sector, government needs to provide the enabling environment. More particularly, government can induce the private players to set up such ventures in the islands and provide the critical infrastructure such as power and the necessary regulatory clearances.

Poverty and Inequality

Poverty Ratio

The Planning Commission has set a benchmark for the level of personal expenditure (or income) that will enable the individual to satisfy a certain minimum consumption level. The proportion of population not able to maintain the specified level of expenditure is then identified as poor. The data on poverty status for Lakshadweep, other Union Territories and States brought out by the Planning Commission for the years 1983, 1993-94 and 1999-2000 is summarised in Table 4.19.

Information presented in Table 4.19 indicates that over the 20 year period, namely, 1981 to 2000, the poverty ratio for the country declined by about 41 per cent whereas in case of Lakshadweep, it declined by 63 per cent. The most recent poverty ratio of Lakshadweep

TABLE 4.19

Population Below the Poverty Line* in the Union Territories, Kerala and India

Region	*1983*		*1993-1994*		*1999-2000*		*Poverty Line for 1999-2000*	
	No. of Persons (Lakhs)	*% of Persons*	*No. of Persons (Lakhs)*	*% of Persons*	*No. of Persons (Lakhs)*	*% of Persons*	*Rural (Rs./ Month)*	*Urban (Rs./ Month)*
A & N Islands	1.11	52.13	1.06	34.47	0.82	20.99	307.64	475.60
Chandigarh	1.19	23.79	0.80	11.35	0.51	5.75	388.15	388.15
D & N Haveli	0.18	15.67	0.77	50.84	0.33	17.14	318.63	539.71
Daman & Diu	-	-	0.18	15.80	0.06	4.44	318.63	539.71
Delhi	18.39	26.22	15.51	14.69	11.49	8.23	362.68	505.45
Lakshadweep	**0.19**	**42.36**	**0.14**	**25.04**	**0.11**	**15.60**	**374.79**	**477.06**
Pondicherry	3.28	50.06	3.31	37.40	2.41	21.67	307.64	475.60
Kerala	106.77	40.22	76.41	25.43	41.04	12.72	374.79	477.06
All-India	3,228.97	44.48	3,203.68	35.97	2,602.50	26.10	327.56	454.11

Note: *: Poverty Line is in Rupees per capita per month. In respect of the principles adopted to determine the poverty ratio in respect of Andaman & Nicobar Islands, Chandigarh, Dadra & Nagar Haveli, Daman & Diu, Pondicherry, explanatory notes in Annexure A-26 may be seen.

Source: National Human Development Report 2001, Planning Commission, March 2002.

at 15.60 per cent compares very favourably with the all-India figure of 26.10.

Per Capita Consumption Expenditure

The per capita consumption expenditure in Lakshadweep has, from 1993-94 to 1999-2000, been significantly higher than the all-India pattern as well as the neighbouring state of Kerala, as may be seen in Table 4.20.

TABLE 4.20

Per Capita Consumption Expenditure in the UTs, Kerala and India

(Rs./Month)

	1993-94			*1999-00*		
	Rural	*Urban*	*Combined*	*Rural*	*Urban*	*Combined*
A & N Islands	496	907	608	780	1,114	873
Chandigarh	463	1,028	975	989	1,435	1,383
D & N Haveli	234	442	253	561	1,207	637
Daman & Diu	452	475	463	901	979	976
Delhi	605	795	777	917	1,383	1,316
Lakshadweep	**526**	**508**	**515**	**876**	**1,018**	**967**
Pondicherry	348	420	397	598	784	732
Kerala	390	494	419	766	933	817
All-India	281	458	328	486	855	591

Source: Human Development Report, 2001, Planning Commission.

A significant feature of this index is that in 1993-1994, of all the States/UTs in India, Lakshadweep was the only one that had a higher level of per capita consumption expenditure for rural areas as compared to the urban areas. However, this distinction was lost by 1999-2000 when the per capita consumption expenditure for urban areas stood at a higher level than that for the rural areas in Lakshadweep as in all other States/UTs. It may, however, be recalled that in reality, Lakshadweep has no urban areas and the classification of certain habitations, the three islands of Amini, Kavaratti and Minicoy, as urban is purely in Census terms. Therefore, in terms of urban-rural relativities, the information for Lakshadweep given in the above table would indicate a shift in the levels of economic activities and, consequently, of prosperity towards those three islands, which are the base of most of the government offices, besides of trade and commerce.

The *inter se* ratio of food and non-food components of consumption expenditure indicate the relative prosperity of a population. It is generally accepted that poorer households would need to spend a relatively larger portion of the consumption expenditure on food items. Viewed in this context, the situation in Lakshadweep *vis-à-vis* other UTs and the national average gives the following picture (Table 4.21)

It, therefore, emerges that the ratio of consumption expenditure on food items to the total consumption expenditure is the highest for Lakshadweep among all the Union Territories in respect of the rural and urban areas, indicating a lower level of affluence among the people of Lakshadweep. There is, however, an improvement in the situation for 1999-2000 as compared to 1993-94.

TABLE 4.21

Composition of Per Capita Consumption Expenditure (Percentage)

State/UT	*Rural*				*Urban*			
	1993-94		*1999-2000*		*1993-94*		*1999-2000*	
	Food	*Non-Food*	*Food*	*Non-Food*	*Food*	*Non-Food*	*Food*	*Non-Food*
A & N Islands	63.28	36.72	61.56	38.44	43.78	56.22	51.26	48.74
Chandigarh	56.08	43.92	47.82	52.18	35.79	64.21	38.82	61.18
D & N Haveli	65.46	34.54	60.09	39.91	62.68	37.32	47.72	52.28
Daman & Diu	62.11	37.89	53.76	46.24	62.79	37.21	53.70	46.30
Delhi	63.46	36.54	44.41	55.59	48.58	51.42	41.04	58.96
Lakshadweep	**64.49**	**35.51**	**62.09**	**37.91**	**67.14**	**32.86**	**60.03**	**39.97**
Pondicherry	61.37	38.63	56.61	43.39	57.71	42.29	51.00	49.00
Kerala	60.45	39.55	53.70	46.30	53.93	46.07	49.04	50.96
All-India	63.18	36.82	59.41	40.59	54.65	45.35	48.06	51.94

Source: Human Development Report 2001, Planning Commission, March 2002.

The index of per capita consumption expenditure needs to be seen along with the measure of dispersal of the consumption expenditure among the population. This measure is given by the Gini Coefficient, which would be zero in the ideal condition of fully equitable dispersal and one, with highest inequality. The figures for Gini Coefficient are given in Table 4.22.

The Gini Coefficient for both urban and rural population for Lakshadweep is among the lowest in the country, indicating the prevalence of a fair degree of equity among the population.

TABLE 4.22

Gini Coefficient for Per Capita Consumption Expenditure

State/UT	*1993-94*		*1999-2000*	
	Rural	*Urban*	*Rural*	*Urban*
A & N Islands	0.231	0.365	0.215	0.224
Chandigarh	0.224	0.399	0.252	0.313
D & N Haveli	0.256	0.322	0.288	0.275
Daman & Diu	0.235	0.207	0.204	0.235
Delhi	0.235	0.376	0.155	0.342
Lakshadweep	**0.227**	**0.299**	**0.186**	**0.235**
Pondicherry	0.292	0.299	0.260	0.296
Kerala	0.290	0.340	0.270	0.320
All-India	0.282	0.340	0.258	0.341

Source: National Human Development Report 2001, Planning Commission, March 2002.

Chapter 5

Biodiversity and Environment Protection

Current Status and Challenges

Lying well within the tropics and extending to the equatorial belt, these islands have a tropical humid, warm and generally pleasant climate, becoming more equatorial in the southern islands of the territory. From the point of view of temperature, the climate is equable and without any distinct or well marked seasons. The Southwest monsoon period is the chief rainy season which lasts from late May to early October. The humid tropical monsoon climate with mean monthly temperature ranging from 25-30^{0}C is very ideal for harvesting of sunshine, utilisation of moisture and biomass growth throughout the year. Desirable seawater temperature also promotes growth of fishes, aquatic flora and fauna throughout the year to provide a high level of hydrobiological productivity. The hot humid climate, however, brings in a lot of diseases and pest problems. The landmass, coastline, lagoons and the reefs of Lakshadweep, along with the surrounding ocean, form a continuum of biodiversity that defy being treated in isolation. There is a close and complex interaction of coral reefs, lagoons and the sea.

The Lakshadweep islands consist of coral formations built upon the Laccadive-Chagos submarine ridge rising steeply from a depth of about 1500 m to 4000 m off the west coast of India. These islands are coralline in origin and lie on the north-south Lakshadweep ridge. They are considered to be a continuation of the Aravalli system of rocks of Rajasthan and Gujarat. A majority of the islands are blessed with large lagoons on the western side. The eastern sides are replete with rocky relicts consisting of fossiliferous, clayey conglomerates of sandstone and are subjected to heavy action of waves and wind. This area is usually devoid of any plants. On the whole, the islands are flat and scarcely rise more than three metres. They are vulnerable to storms and sea erosion.

The soil of Lakshadweep is poor, the top layer consisting chiefly of finely disintegrated coral, forming a white sandy layer with an admixture of vegetable humus. Since there is very little cultivation, except for coconut, the soil is rarely turned over, with the result that the humus layer does not go very deep. In certain islands such as Agatti, Kavaratti and Andrott, it does not exist at all since the islanders are in the habit of burning the humus. Such soils are open to wind erosion. The depth of the sand layer varies from island to island. In general, the soil is shallow in the beach and deeper towards the centre. The usual depth is about 1.0-1.75 m. At this depth there is a compact but porous crust of limestone conglomerate of about 30 cm thickness. In the islands of Minicoy, Kalpeni, and Agatti, this crust is not so well formed, being soft and powdery but in the other islands it is very hard, quarried out and used for building. On boring through the conglomerate, there is a bed of fine sand through which potable water infiltrates.

The warm tropical climate and high relative humidity are conducive for good plant growth. The vegetation of the islands is described as 'strand coral'. Absence of hills and river systems coupled with shallow soil severely limits the variety of plants that can grow in these islands, yet, nearly 400 species of plants have been reported from these islands. No endemic plants have been reported. The vegetation comprises plants of Sri Lankan, African, American, Australian, Burmese, West Indies, Chinese and Polynesian origin.

Ecologically these islands cannot be treated in isolation. There is the interaction of coral reefs, lagoons and the sea. These ecosystems harbour varieties of fauna and flora. The mucus produced by the coral plays a significant role in the coral ecosystem. These form an important food item for reef invertebrates, fish and shrimps. There are over 600 species of marine fish, of which 300 are ornamental. Seventy eight species of corals, 82 of seaweeds, 52 of crabs, 2 species lobsters, 48 of gastropods, 12 bivalves, 41 species of sponges, 10 species of echinoderms, 4 species of turtles, 601 species of fishes and 101 species of birds have been reported from these islands. The uninhabited Pitti Island is a breeding ground for many migratory birds.

The green cover of the island is mainly due to coconut groves which occupy 80-85 per cent of the green cover. The coconut cultivation and fishing activities have led to the establishment of cottage industries for rope and *copra* making and tuna fish (*mas*) making. The population of the island, which was only 13,882 in 1901, has increased to 31,810 in 1971 and 60,650 in 2001.

Corals are very fragile organisms. They indicate the health of the land, lagoon and the sea. Global factors such as climate change, pollution caused by oil spills, pesticides, sewage, dredging the reef to create wider entry points will adversely affect the coral population.

In general, the strand coral vegetation consists of various groups of plants such as algae, fungi, lichens, mosses, pteridophytes and angiosperms. Shallow reliefs are dominated by algal elements and seaweed. *Cymodocea isoetifolia, Syringodium isoetifolium* and *Thalassia hemprichii* are the three species of sea-grasses reported from there. The foreshore is free from vegetation being sandy and the backshore is composed of creepers and herbaceous plants, intermixed with shrubs and treelets in coconut groves. Broadly speaking, these plants may be grouped into herbs, shrubs, climbers/twiners, treelets and trees. Many of these are exotic. Vegetation in many of these areas is very much denuded owing to anthropogenic factors and also by grazing of goats. The islands are also home to many medicinal plants.[1]

There are several types of primary producers in the coral ecosystem. The zooxanthellae live symbiotically with the coral polyps, take up their nutritional requirements from the coral excreta and translocate nitrogen back to the corals in a quick recycling process of about four hours. Borrowing filamentous algae and calcareous algae are also associated with the corals. The latter are secondary frame builders in the reef. Benthic macroalgae like the sea-grass are the most prolific primary producers.

The islanders draw resources from the land, the lagoon, reefs and the deep sea. The reefs and lagoons provide the islanders with their basic energy needs. These include construction materials, food and cash income. Fishing and coconut cultivation are the mainstay of the economy and are important sources of protein. Scuba diving tourism is an emerging industry. Fisheries comprise commercial fishing in the deep sea and subsistence fishing in the lagoon using a variety of traditional methods. The island households use all the ecosystems within their vicinity but they put nothing back in terms of management of these free natural resources. The problems of managing these resources have been well discussed by Vineeta Hoon (2002). The human population which was 13,882 in 1901 rose to 31, 810 in 1971 and to 60,650 in 2001. The increase in population has created an ecosystem of its own in these islands. This man-made ecosystem had to depend on the natural ecosystem involving land, lagoon and sea for meeting its livelihood.

The biodiversity of the Lakshadweep Islands faces a variety of pressures and challenges from various quarters. These include the pollution of the oceans owing to the discharge of wastes and fumes from the navigating shipping vessels, while the reefs and lagoons face a similar onslaught from the ferryboats. Overexploitation of the fishery resources in the adjoining reaches and poaching by the foreign vessels add to these problems.

It is necessary to strengthen the arrangements for protection of the biodiversity of the region. This calls for augmenting the monitoring mechanism and periodic updating of the database relating to the ecology of the region. Involvement of the people in these efforts by way of awareness building measures and by giving suitable powers, and responsibilities, to the local bodies, may also be considered.

Threats to the Land and Water Bodies

The wild marine biodiversity of Lakshadweep faces many threats which can be mitigated easily. But there has to be a complete rethinking and an honest, critical dialogue between planners, the people, scientists and other groups interested in the survival of the islands. The threats to the biodiversity of the islands will be presented based on the ecological habitat ecosystem zonation.

The land, which is a thin strip of coral sand, faces multifaceted problems. These include collection of jelly (accretion deposits of coral sand/boulders) for

1. A list of the common flora of these islands may be seen in Annexure A-27 and of the medicinal plants in Annexure A-28.

construction, loss of natural vegetation including stragglers like *Mulli* (*Spinifex*) and *Ipomoea* which prevent erosion, monoculture of coconut which takes away all the nutrients, use of pesticides and chemicals which causes toxicity of the soil and the fragile ground water, construction activities which bring more land under concrete, and erosion of the beach.

The availability of sweet water bodies in these islands too is being subject to a variety of stresses. Some of these have been identified as the non-regeneration of water lens, highly extractive usage of ground water with pumps and tanks, pollution with diesel from the electricity generating units, concretisation of land which reduces the area available for percolation of rainwater, wastage of water and mixing of the sewage with freshwater lens.

Afforestation Measures

The vegetation of Lakshadweep is conspicuous by the absence of forests of any kind and the overall pattern of vegetation is almost uniform with a few exceptions in the cases of Andrott and Minicoy. The plant diversity is not large. The most common cultivated crops are coconut (*Cocos nucifera*), drum stick (*Moringa* sp.), bread fruit (*Artocarpus* sp.), banana (*Musa* sp.), colocasia (*Colocasia* sp.), chilli (*Capsicum* sp.) and cucumber (*Cucumis* sp.). Of late, plants like pepper (*Piper* sp.) and tapioca (*Manihot* sp.) have been introduced. Plants such as sea-grass namely *Thalassia* sp. and *Cymondocea* sp. grow abundantly in the surrounding lagoons. The common flora of coral sands, according to Sivadasan and Joseph (1981) are *Pemphis acidula*, *Cordia subcordata*, *Scaevola laccada*, *Thespesia populnea*, *Suriana maritime*, *Dodonaea viscose*, *Guettarda speciosa*, etc. Coconut is the only crop of economic importance in Lakshadweep and the density of trees is very high (Plate-2). Most of the vegetable crops are cultivated in coconut gardens as intercrop. *Cassytha filformis*, a noteworthy slender parasitic twiner, seems to be a potential threat to the coastal plants. *Mikania micrantha* is yet another weed spreading gregariously on fences and agricultural crops at Andrott. The flora of Lakshadweep are not very rich and almost all the plants of these islands are available in the mainland of India as well. A majority of the plants that are found growing in these islands are naturalised exotics and intruders. Nearly 400 species of plants have been collated so far.

The cumulative effect of several factors such as topography, salinity of water, wind, wave action and precipitation influence the ecology of the islands. The overall climate of Lakshadweep is humid tropical monsoon type. The monsoon is governed by cyclonic depressions which develop in the south Arabian sea and in the Bay of Bengal. In association with these, strong winds and heavy rain also occur. The mean annual rainfall ranges from 1715 (Amini) to 1934 mm (Andrott) of which 80 per cent is distributed from May to November. June is the rainiest month contributing 25 per cent of annual rainfall. As in the case of rainfall, the number of rainy days during the southwest monsoon season is also greater in the north than in the south. The length of the dry period ranges between five and six months (November to April). The temperature is generally uniform over the territory. April and May are the hottest months in the year. Mean annual temperature ranges from 27.3 to 27.9°C and the relative humidity ranges from 70-75 per cent. Throughout the year, the air is humid. Any plantation programme in the islands should be carefully programmed since the geology and soils are peculiar in many aspects. Geologically Lakshadweep islands are considered to be a continuation of the Aravalli system of rocks of Rajasthan and the Gujarat hills and not much is known about their submarine geology. Their tops are built up of coral reefs and accumulation of corals is being continued even now. The coral atolls are very rich in phosphate deposit of low grade (13.4 per cent P_2O_5). The phosphate reserve is estimated as 0.12 million tonnes and it is also reported that a large deposit of calcium carbonate exists in the surrounding lagoons.

Existing information reveals that there are no forestry resources available for the well-being of the local community. Further, on the basis of per capita requirements, the expected demand for fuel wood could be around 1,75,000 tonnes of fuel wood and for fodder the expected demand could be approximately 70,000 tonnes. The supply of fuel wood is expected to be only 20–30 per cent or even less, particularly from the agricultural residues including the supply of fuel materials from coconut plantations. Similarly, only 15-20 per cent of fodder requirement can be met from the existing biological sources. However, introduction of forestry components having potential of fuel wood, small timber, medicinal values, biofuel, etc. can be envisaged for sustainable development in this island ecosystem. The main islands are covered with green vegetation mainly comprising coconut and this green cover is 80-86 per cent.

Traditional forestry activities are not feasible in Lakshadweep as most of the landmass is already covered with coconut plantations. However, there is adequate scope for agro and farm forestry which would help in generating the islands and provide environment protection. The suggested species are jatropha *curcas* (for biofuel), *casurina equisetifolia* (for fuel, poles and pulpwood), and medicinal plants such as *emblica (amla)*, *sesbenia*, *gloriosa*, etc.

While it is imperative to introduce a variety of measures for the economic and social growth and development of the people and the region of Lakshadweep, it is also very important to ascertain the possibility of adverse impact, if any, of such measures on the delicate ecology of these islands. This may be attained by subjecting the developmental programmes and projects to detailed appraisal before launch as also during the course of implementation. Side by side, a conscious policy to recycle the various waste products and to ban the use of non-recyclable items, is definitely called for.

Agroforestry for Sustainability

The entire economic as well as the social set up of Lakshadweep depends upon, directly or indirectly, the availability of natural resources (including forest) of the mainland. Agroforestry, in this context holds great promise in augmenting wood production without any adverse effect on agriculture, land or environment. Agroforestry is a sustainable land management system which increases the overall yield of land combined with the production of crop (including tree crop). The salient features of agroforestry would be to raise fuel wood, timber and fodder, increase production of food crops, promote production of fruits, vegetables, pulses, milk and meat; conserve soil and moisture, check soil erosion and enhance soil nutrient status; and improve microclimate by enhancing the area under tree cover. It plays an important role in meeting the growing requirement of fuel, fodder and timber while maintaining an ecologically, balanced environment (Plate-3). Agroforestry is one of the best-suited systems as well as a sustainable one, for Lakshadweep islands to meet the people's demand for fuel, fodder and small timber.

In addition, based on the recent report of the Task Force on Conservation and Sustainable Use of Medicinal Plants, the Planning Commission, Government of India, has listed about 25 plant species, which are most commonly used in India which are to be evaluated for their suitability to the islands. Other nodal agencies such as CDRI, Lucknow, CIMAP, NMPB, FLHRHT, NOVOD, etc. also actively promote the use and cultivation of medicinal plants.

Tree Farming

Policy plays a vital role in providing incentives for farmers to invest in tree farming and other farm forestry systems. According to Place and Dewees (1999), policy issues on any natural resource management practice by decision makers play a major role in adoption of the concept, technology and implementation of the target. Farm forestry also involves improved technologies including multipurpose trees (MPTs) that are appropriate for the environment and consumers (farmers). This requires enhancing the partnership between researchers and farmers. Farmers also need to play a lead role in the development and testing of MPT technology, assessing on-trials, conducting researcher designed and farmer-designed trials and providing feedback to researchers on their experience. Creation and organisation of proper marketing facilities/ mechanisms for small growers and evolving minimum mandatory standards for quality control for wood based products of farm forestry origin have also to be seriously considered. Financial institutions like NABARD have a major role in promoting industries catering to value addition of agroforestry products and to strengthen institutional capabilities towards achieving this objective. This can be done only through innovative policies in the farm forestry sector, which reflect ground realities and changing priorities as well as harmonising divergent demands. Research organisations like ICFRE should provide the necessary inputs to frame such policies. According to the National Forest Policy 1988 document (GoI, 1988), forest conservation programmes cannot succeed without the willing support and cooperation of the people.

Action Plan for Greening the Islands

As mentioned earlier, the islands have a crown cover of high density, mainly with coconut crown (trees). Therefore, further greening of the islands should be need based; taking various factors into consideration such as availability of land, people's demand, species suitability including medicinal plants, marketability of the products, etc. Species of economic, social and environmental value are of importance in this context. As suggested in the earlier paragraphs, agroforestry practices are some of the best approaches for sustained production as well as to enhance the green cover of the islands. Agroforestry models which could be adopted include the following:

***Casurina equisetifolia* based Agroforestry Models**

Casurina equisetifolia is an ideal tree for agroforestry owing to its multipurpose nature to meet the requirements of fuel, poles, shelterbelts, etc. as well as its nitrogen fixing ability. It is an excellent fuel wood with high calorific value. Casurina can be introduced in the agroforestry system with already existing crops. Casurina because of its particular silvicultural characteristics and fast growth is arguably an ideal species for coastal plantations and has adapted well to the low to medium rainfall areas.

Medicinal Plants based Agroforestry Models

Introduction of important medicinal plants, which are readily marketable in agroforestry models, can meet the demand of medicinal products to a greater extent. Inter-planting medicinal herbs under the trees can be a better option to improve economic returns and ecological environment. Further, agroforestry systems play an important role in domestication and commercialisation of medicinal trees. In various places, medicinal trees incorporated in home gardens improve the diversity in the fringe areas. Development of appropriate techniques for raising medicinal trees in agroforestry and other farming systems will help in conservation of many species. Introduction of medicinal plants and trees in agroforestry systems is a novel idea and *ex-situ* conservation of important medicinal plants and trees. Medicinal trees that have high NTFP value not only provide drugs to the rural population but also generate additional employment opportunity. Establishing agroforestry models (multistorey system) with medicinal plants will enhance the production of raw material, additional income to farmers, optimum land use and one of the indirect methods of species conservation.

Multistorey Agroforestry Systems

Multistorey plantations, which will serve as shelterbelts also will be an ideal approach, in addition to what has been already mentioned (agroforestry/ home gardens, etc). Development of multi-tiered agroforestry systems will not only be highly economical but also eco-friendly as well as sustainable. It encompasses a set of land use practices which aim to realise the benefits from growing woody and herbaceous species together. Shade loving crops such as pepper and betel leaf, can be introduced in this multistoreyed system. Succession of vegetation *vis-à-vis* soil amelioration under this multistoreyed agroforestry system will be a stepping stone for introducing a greater number of species such as *Anona squamosa*, vanilla, pineapple, cocoa, cinnamon, cloves, etc.

Agroforestry Systems with Multipurpose Trees

Other species of multipurpose nature (including medicinal plants) such as Agatti (*Sesbania sesban*), *Morinda tinctoria*, tamarind, cashew, *Acacia auriculiformis*, *Thespesia populnea*, *Adothoda vesica*, *Aloe vera*, *Vinca rosea*, etc. are of greater importance in view of the output with reference to value added products. Greening the islands by adopting home garden strategies with MPTs will be yet another ideal approach (Plate-7). This agroforestry practice is commonly through incorporation of tree species in the already existing coconut plantations after thinning of coconut trees. Recommendations from the Regional Institute of ICAR can be taken for carrying out thinning in the existing coconut groves. In the openings created, suitable MPTs can be introduced to diversify the farms and to sustain the farm income. Growing trees along with crops and livestock is postulated to enhance crop yield, conserve soil and recycle nutrients while producing fuel wood, fodder, fruit and timber.

As an interface between agriculture and forestry, agroforestry is considered to be a promising approach to land use, particularly in small holdings, and as an important part of agricultural development and ecosystem management. Ecologists and environmentalists consider it as a superior land use and land management system that integrates all components of a stable ecosystem combining conservation with production. Foresters tend to look up on it as a potential line of defence against unabated depletion of forest under pressure of population. Planners and donor agencies have seen it as an answer to rural needs for fuel, fodder and timber. However, agroforestry, farm forestry, community forestry and home gardens are the most important terms that have become prominent among those representing tree planting efforts on farms, community land, wasteland, etc. In practice all these refer directly or indirectly to growing and using trees to provide a variety of products and services. By greening the islands, a favourable change in microclimate/environment is also expected which in turn will play a significant role in the conservation of the environment.

As mentioned earlier, since the island ecosystems are peculiar in many aspects designing plantations for environmental protection needs special attention. Multistorey plantations, which will serve as shelterbelt also will be an ideal approach, in addition to what have been already mentioned (agroforestry/home garden, etc.). Windbreak establishment, considered to be a form of farm forestry, is reported to increase crop and productivity. It increases crop development, yield and quality, primarily by their favourable effects on moisture conservation and energy budgets and secondarily by reducing incidence of abrasion by sand particles, canopy damage and negative influence on ecology of pests and disease causing organisms. Hence, not surprisingly, windbreaks have been recognised as a tool to provide shade, shelter and productive microclimate for environmental conservation. Planting of windbreaks is also seen as a way to arrest land degradation while maintaining or even improving agricultural productivity. Suitably designed windbreaks even have the potential to alter mean wind speed, wind duration and turbulence of air flow.

In addition to the direct effects of wind breaks such as reduction in wind erosion, physical damage to vegetative and reproductive tissues due to sand blasting, 'intermittent' effects such as protection against crop lodging in case of severe storm and 'incremental' effects because of decreased evapo-transpiration (ET), and improved water use efficiency (WUE) owing to shelter afforded by windbreaks need to be considered which can result in increased yield economic benefits during a crop growth season.

Since windbreaks present a porous obstacle to approaching airflow, forcing the air to flow over the trees at reduced speed and forcing it to accelerate over the top, deriving maximum benefit from wind breaks is a complex and challenging task. In this context, design of the wind break becomes critically important. Some of the important features that need to be considered have been outlined along with suggestions for deriving maximum benefit from them for enhanced crop productivity. *Casurina equisetifolia* with its particular silvicultural characteristics and fast growth is arguably an ideal species for coastal plantations and has adapted well to the low to medium rainfall areas.

In addition to species of agroforestry importance which have been already listed, some of the economically, ecologically important species which can be tried are *Tounefortia, Pandanus, Calophyllum, Salvadora,* etc. in the fringes of the islands and *neem*, cashew, *Acacia auriculiformis, Thespesia populnea*, bamboo as avenue planting. Other species that may be included are *Aegle marmalos, Saraca ashoka, Emblica officinalis, Azardiracta indica, Terminalia arjuna* and *Terminalia chebula*. Some of the important herbs and shrubs include *Andrographis paaniculata, Cassis ungustifolia, Embelia ribes, Gymnema sylvestre, Withania somnifera, Plantago ovata, Phyllanthus niruri, Asparagus racemosus,* etc. These plants should ideally be taken up for cultivation as an agroforestry component and suitable marketing strategies developed. Agroforestry is an eco-friendly land use system, which ensures biodiversity and mimics the natural ecosystem wherein another eco-friendly economic venture such as bee keeping can be successfully practised. Agroforestry and apiculture are complementary to each other. Tree growing and bee keeping can be easily combined because beekeeping is primarily a forest-based activity. Inclusion of apiculture in agroforestry helps to enhance the productivity, stability and sustainability of the total system. Inclusion of beekeeping paves the way for supplementary income.

Shore Protection

The coastline of the islands of Lakshadweep is subject to erosion and accretion as a natural phenomenon, besides due to human interventions. Protection of the coast is necessary and is, in principle, supported by the provisions of the Coastal Regulations. However, implementation of the CRZ provisions is constrained by practical difficulties in view of the minuscule geographical area of these islands. Therefore, civil construction has continued in the islands well within the 500 metre zone from the high tide mark. This calls for careful and sustained protection of the shores.

The PWD has undertaken shore protection works by placing large boulders or specially designed concrete tetrapods, besides hollow blocks and coir bags.[2] The problem with such works is that they restrict the access to and enjoyment of the beaches and the coastlines. Accessible coastlines are essential for the normal life of these islands, apart from the development of tourism. Therefore, suitable technology needs to be evolved to break the ferocity of the waves away from the coast so that the beaches remain undisturbed as far as possible. Eco-friendly techniques for shore protection such as growth of sea-grass also need to be explored.

The option of placing shore protection devices such as tetrapods on the reef instead of on the shores, may also be studied, as this will enable unhindered access to the shores. The traditional approach of *casurina* plantations on the shores needs to be reviewed as there are concerns that these plantations inhibit turtle nesting, besides causing restrictions for fishermen to access the shores and the sea.

---

2. The PWD has undertaken shore protection works stretching over 50.33 km over the past 10 years, costing, on average, Rs. 15,000 per metre or, Rs. 1.50 crore per km.

The Coral Reef and the Lagoons

The Lakshadweep archipelago consists entirely of coral reefs. The coral diversity of Lakshadweep is second only to that of the Andaman and Nicobar islands. The mucus produced by the coral plays a significant role in the coral ecosystem. These form an important food item for reef invertebrates, fish and shrimps. Coral genera such as *Montipora, Pavona, Porites, Favia, Favites, Goniastrea, Platygyra, Hydnophora* and *Symphillia* are common here. Some subgenera like *Psammocora (Plesioseris)* and *Psammocora (Stephanaria)* are found only in Lakshadweep.

On lagoon shoals and windward and leeward sides of the reefs, genera such as *Pocillopora, Acropora, Porites, Goniastrea* among the *Scleractinians* and the blue coral *Heliopora* are found. In some of the lagoon reefs and shoals (Minicoy, Chetlat) at least 80 per cent of the reef surface and lagoon floor is occupied by blue coral, which makes large hemispherical colonies. *Psammocor* is another common genus found especially in Kadmat and Chetlat. The lagoons of Minicoy show species found in Maldives like *Lobophyllia* and *Diploastria*. A total of 78 species of *Scleractinian* corals divided among 31 genera have so far been reported from Lakshadweep. Out of these, 27 genera with a total of 69 species are hermatypes and the remaining 4 genera with 9 species are ahermatypes.

The Community Structure of Corals

The various habitats in the reefs and lagoons of Lakshadweep show coral association and assemblages which are unique. Three distinct coral communities have been identified:

a. *Porites*: *Porites lutea* and *P. solida* are found in the inner lagoon reef community. Faviids like *Favia, Favites, Platygyra* and *Goniastrea* are found along with *Pocillopora* and *Acropora* species.

b. *Acropora*: Various species of *Acropora* predominate the lagoon coral diversity. This community forms the most ideal habitat for many reef fishes including important live-bait fishes.

c. *Heliopora*: *Heliopora* is a common coral both in lagoon reef and open reef flat. Many fungiids and faviids are also found here. There is a paucity of reef fishes here.

Coral Status Matrix: Based on the above discussions, the coral status matrix of different islands is as below:

Agatti	(+)
Amini	(- -)
Andrott	(++)
Bangaram	(-)
Bitra	(+)
Chetlat	(++)
Kalpeni	(++)
Kavaratti	(- -)
Kadmat	(+)
Kiltan	(- - -)
Minicoy	(- -)
Suheli	(+++)

Satisfactory	(+)
Good	(++)
Very good	(+++)
Unsatisfactory	(-)
Bad	(- -)
Critical	(- - -)

The above account pertains to the state of coral before the 1998 bleaching event. The bleaching episode resulted in the massive mortality of corals, up to 80 per cent in various islands. Continuous monitoring of the recovery since then has shown that the present coral cover is generally between 10 and 20 per cent. Some islands like Kavaratti and Bitra shows a better recovery, up to 35 per cent at certain sites. A list of corals occurring in the Lakshadweep region is given in Annexure A-29. The *Lakshadweep Biodiversity Strategy Action Plan Report* (2002) points out the problems in conservation of coral reefs and the action plan required for their conservation.

The Destruction of the Reef/Coral Death and Diseases

The coral reefs around the Lakshadweep islands have been adversely affected from time to time by global climatic factors like El Nino and the 1998 bleaching affect. Of late, the reefs face threats from the modern development that has brought with it a host of synthetic products such as rubber, plastics, cement and metals. These seem to impede coral growth and lead to crumbling of the coral colony. The collection of corals and shingles from the reef for construction activities and fishing causes destruction to the reef. It is also felt that continuous diving operations lead to disturbance within the coral reef ecosystem. There is also the view that the coral debris, which collects on the shore by a natural process, could be utilised in a controlled manner. If this is not collected and removed, excessive deposition of the coral shingle will adversely affect the fragility of the islands.

Corals, the major denizens of the reef, are deteriorating due to global factors such as climate change including coral bleaching, presence of predators like crown-of-thorns starfish, dredging of the reef to create wider entry points for navigation, pollution (oil spills, sewage), etc. and overexploitation of certain resources for example, the drop in the number of live-bait fishes.

Corals represent the health status of the ecosystem. Any activity in the land, lagoon, reef and sea will have an effect on the population of the corals. Dredging in the lagoons, building jetties, collection of shingles, boulders, sand, movement of boats, will have direct impacts on the coral reefs. The local people are sceptic about use of tetrapods in controlling soil erosion. Disturbance to the corals with the movement of human beings in the reef for gleaning, dragging fishing nets will affect the growth of young corals.

Coral Reef—National and International Initiatives

The world over, island ecosystems are critically threatened. Lakshadweep Islands are characterised by their small size and distance from the mainland shore. Most of these islands have the sea on the east and reef on the west. These islands are built of coral reefs from the late tertiary times. Accumulation of coral is continuing even now. The exposed coral rock erodes into white coral sand and adds to the formation of land.

Coral reefs are among the world's most fragile and endangered ecosystems. Although they cover just about 0.02 per cent of the ocean floor, they are home to a quarter of the known marine plant and animal species. The net benefit from these coral reefs to society is estimated to be around US $ 30 billion. However, 11 per cent of the world's coral reefs have already been lost due to human interference. In 1998, 16 per cent were severely damaged as a result of El Nino and warming of the oceans. It is expected that 32 per cent of the reefs may be lost in the next 30 years if the threats are not reduced. Loss of healthy coral reefs will lead to elimination of primary sources of food, income and employment for millions of people around the world, as well as the extinction of many fascinating and beautiful marine species.

At the global level, many international agencies are working together to protect and conserve the corals. The International Coral Reef Action Network (ICRAN) maintains a database of corals and provides guidelines for monitoring the health of corals. GCRMN—Global Coral Reef Monitoring Network—is a worldwide programme jointly promoted by four international agencies: the Intergovernmental Oceanographic Commission (IOC), the United Nations Environment Program (UNEP), The World Conservation Union (IUCN) and the World Bank.

There are four coral reef regions in India. They are the Gulf of Kutch, the Gulf of Mannar, Andaman & Nicobar Islands and Lakshadweep Islands. To monitor the various aspects of coral reef conservation ICRMN—the Indian Coral Reef Monitoring Network was initiated in 1999 by the Ministry of Environment and Forests, Government of India with active support from the Departments of Science and Technology, Biotechnology, Ocean Development and Space, the Ministry of Agriculture and the University Grants Commission. In order to implement these action plans and to strengthen the conservation of the coral reefs, a Coral Reef Task Force under ICRMN needs to be constituted. This task force can also work out a specific strategy action plan for conservation of the coral reefs of Lakshadweep.

The Lagoons

The lagoon and atolls of Lakshadweep also abound in a variety of marine *macrophyte* or algae. They belong to *Chlorophyta* (Green Algae), *Phaeophyta* (Brown algae) and *Rhodophyta* (Red algae). The sea grass community of the lagoon contributes to the benthic plant biomass of islands. The predominant seaweeds observed are *Enteromorpha, Ulva, Codium, Laminaria, Turbinaria, Sargassum, Padina, Gelidium, Gracilaria, Hypena* and *Ceramium*. There are potentially useful seaweeds. The survey done by CMFRI (1977-1979) collected 82 species of seaweeds. It has been estimated that the agarophyte resource with an abundance of *Gelidiella acerosa* can be utilised for starting an Agar-agar unit. Agatti and Kadmat islands have more agarophytes. *Caulerpa, Dictyota* and *Laurencia* can be used as food in different forms. Seaweed also grows on the coral reef. Blue-green algae like the *Lyngbya majuscula, Anabaena* and *Oscillatoria* species were observed in the lagoon in many islands associated with sea-grasses. The branching coral beds support seaweed growth to a large extent. The lagoon is also home to a wide variety of organisms such as crabs, lobsters, and molluscan fauna including gastropods and bivalves, octopuses, sponges, turtles, surface living *holothurians*, cowries, sea cucumbers and dolphins. A brief description is given in Annexure A-30. There were qualitative assessments about the changes in frequency of sightings and capture of the above species. The general observation is that though there was a sharp decline a while ago, now the population is picking up. There were comments about the size of the tiger cowries and octopus. It was also noted that the increase in the number of turtles in the lagoon has caused a depletion of sea-grasses, which in turn has affected the live-bait fish population. The people are generally aware of the fact that these are protected species but concepts of the population dynamics and reef ecology are not clearly understood.

The lagoon is also susceptible to influences both from the sea and the land. The major threats to the lagoon are sewage and pollution, use of detergents, pesticides and fertilisers which causes eutrophication, excessive use of propeller boats and speed boats which causes turbidity, dumping of plastics and other waste in the lagoon and tourism related damages.

The Department of Science and Technology and the Department of Environment and Forests should enforce the laws[3] that ensure protection of the species. There must be continuous awareness programmes by which people become the real stewards of the reef. Oil spillage in the sea, use of plastics on land, pollution of the reef with sewage, use of pesticides and detergents will indirectly affect the growth of corals.

The Lakshadweep Biodiversity and Strategy Action Plan (2002) identified many strategies; of which the ones relevant to conservation of corals are listed below:

- The Department of Environment and Forests and the Department of Science and Technology have to work together and enforce laws that reduce the reasons for the destruction of the reefs.
- The Building Materials Board has to become more active in supplying building materials at subsidised rates for the public.
- There is no in-depth study about the status of the corals and the lagoons. This has to be initiated by the Department of Environment and Forests and Department of Science and Technology.
- There has to be a strict ban on the disposal of non-biodegradable toxic materials like plastics and batteries.
- There should be a comprehensive plan to enforce stoppage of disposal of pollutants by ships and pollutants from the islands.
- People have to be made aware of the laws which pertain to the protection of corals. There is a popular misconception that coral debris and shingles are dead remains and can anyway be disposed of as these do not contribute to the equilibrium of the coral reef ecosystem. This calls for more intense awareness programmes which the Department of Environment can initiate in every island.
- There have to be constant awareness programmes, which will instil the need for conservation of the reef. Environmental education programmes should be initiated from the primary level onward so that a child grows up sensitive to the island environment.

These steps need to be pursued in a time bound manner.

3. A list of the laws and regulations is placed at Annexure A-31.

Chapter 6

Governance Issues

Economic and Social Database

The sensitiveness of the ecology, the remoteness of the Lakshadweep Islands from the mainland and the scattered nature of its constituent islands make it imperative to bring in a system of database management for the various aspects of economic and social administration.

Database on Economic Sectoral Development

Lakshadweep is one of the very few administrative units of the country for which the Gross/Net State Domestic Product (GSDP/NSDP) data are not published. Thus, a standard indicator required to measure the level of economic development of this Union Territory and to compare it with other units of administration, remains unavailable. Detailed data on savings and investment in various sectors particularly in the household sector and the private sector are not available either. Absence of the estimates of GSDP/NSDP and related information makes it difficult to analyse, among other issues, the pattern of savings and investment as well as the fiscal performance of the administration.

It is further necessary to maintain and update information relating to individual islands, so as to capture the trends of inter-island variations.

Database on Natural Resources

The ground data and the information from remote sensing need to be digitised for effective management of the natural resources of the island. The areas under different vegetation cover, open lands, breeding zones of avifauna and other fauna, distribution of corals, extent of lagoons are some of the zones which have to be identified through remote sensing and brought under GIS.

The application of GIS in biodiversity conservation is a multidisciplinary approach, which requires inputs from various departments namely Environment, Forests, Fisheries, Agriculture and Horticulture. The Indian Institute of Remote Sensing has prepared a document on Biodiversity Characterization at Landscape Level in Andaman and Nicobar Islands using the Satellite Remote Sensing and Geographic Information System (GIS) in 2003. Similar reports on the Lakshadweep islands will help in better management of the resources.

Studies are also required to monitor the rate of inflow of fresh water into the subsurface lens. The approach to harvesting such water sources should be based upon a careful match between the rates of discharge and recharge.

While the available theories strongly recommend against removal of the sand and even the dead corals, there were also suggestions from some local representatives during the two seminars held at Kavaratti (October 2004) and in Delhi (February 2005) to the effect that the dead corals and the white sands are not necessarily exhaustible and that these are recharged, to a certain extent, naturally, if harvested carefully. The proponents of the latter model stated that by not harnessing these materials, considerable economic gains are being missed out. It would, therefore, be worthwhile to conduct studies through institutions such as the National Institute of Oceanography, etc. to find out if the dead corals and the white sands were really replenishable and if so, to what extent and under what conditions.

Funds may be earmarked from the administration's annual budget for conducting such studies leading to the creation and maintenance of such a database from time to time, through specialist institutions. Local educated youth may also be engaged for such studies, as research personnel. The local people may also be associated with such studies and the results/findings discussed with them.

Social and Ecological Database

Any approach to the growth and development of the Lakshadweep Islands has necessarily to keep in view the need to maintain the social, cultural and ecological uniqueness of the area and the people. Interaction with the mainland and also with the rest of the world is necessary, but the capacity of the region and the people to handle the adverse fall out of such interaction appears to be severely limited. Concerns have been expressed in recent times that along with tourism development, diseases such as AIDS are also coming in. The existing pressure on the limited landmass of the islands from the indigenous population is getting compounded by the pressure from the visiting tourist population and the services required to cater to them leading to pollution of the natural resources. This is manifested in the abnormally high level of prevalence of certain communicable diseases such as diarrhoea, respiratory infection, pneumonia, and so on.

There is a strong need to prepare and maintain a database on the status and health of soils, water, coral reefs and other natural resources available in the various islands. Such a database needs to be updated regularly and disseminated to all concerned, including the local people.

Fiscal Management

On the finance side, Lakshadweep being a Union Territory without a Legislature, is part and parcel of the Central Government. All the revenue receipts,[1] tax as well as non-tax, of the Lakshadweep Administration are retained by the Central Government in the Consolidated Fund of India, except for what is collected and allowed to be retained by the local bodies. On the other hand, the entire expenditure needs of the Lakshadweep Administration are provided by the Central Government through releases from the Consolidated Fund of India. There is no nexus between revenue mobilisation and revenue expenditure of the Lakshadweep Administration as the fiscal data for Lakshadweep and other Union Territories without legislatures, given in Table 6.1, will show.[2]

As the size of these UTs vary very significantly, it would be more appropriate to compare their fiscal performance in per capita terms, rather than absolute numbers. The other option of comparing the figures for receipts and expenditure in relation to GSDP is also not viable as the estimates of GSDP are not available for some of the UTs including Lakshadweep.

In respect of per capita revenue receipts from the various tax and non-tax sources, Lakshadweep at Rs. 3,023 stood higher than Andaman & Nicobar (Rs. 2,463), but lower than the other three by considerable margins. However, in respect of per capita non-plan revenue expenditure, Lakshadweep at Rs. 30587 was far above the other four. As a result, the gap between the non-plan revenue receipts and revenue expenditure in Lakshadweep at Rs. 27,564 was far higher than that for the other four, being Rs. 13,103 for Andaman & Nicobar, Rs. 164 for Chandigarh, Rs. 7,845 for Dadra and Nagar Haveli and Rs. 7,181 for Daman & Diu. The very small size of the population of Lakshadweep seems to be the main reason for this extraordinary high level of revenue deficit.

The level of plan expenditure for Lakshadweep, measured in terms of per capita outlay for the Tenth Plan (2002-2007), looks impressive, being as high as Rs. 72,118, while the all-India average is Rs. 5,754 and the average for the UTs is Rs. 17,854 (Table 6.2).

The Plan outlays/expenditure have been dominated by three sectors, namely, Transport (mainly, Ports & Shipping), Agriculture and Allied (mainly Fisheries) and Tourism. Sector-wise details of the outlays/expenditure in respect of the Eighth, Ninth and the Tenth Five-year Plans is placed at Annexure A-37.

Panchayati Raj Institutions

Structure

There are no municipalities in Lakshadweep and the local body set up is in the form of two-tier Panchayati Raj Institutions. Lakshadweep used to have Island Councils set up in 1990-91 in each of the 10 inhabited islands and a Pradesh Council at the district level. These were governed by the Island Councils Regulation 1988. With the introduction of the 73rd and 74th Constitutional Amendments, suitable legislative changes were introduced by the Government of India in

1. A time series of data for revenue receipts of Lakshadweep is placed at Annexure A-32, while detailed itemised receipts are in Annexure A-33. A comparative picture of revenue collections by the various Union Territories is placed at Annexures A-34 and A-35.

2. A comparative picture of receipts and expenditure of Lakshadweep Administration on the revenue accounts is placed at Annexure A-36.

TABLE 6.1

Revenue Receipts, Revenue Expenditure and Revenue Deficit of Lakshadweep and other Union Territories (without Legislature) for 2002-03 (R.E.)

	Unit	*A & N Islands*	*Chandigarh*	*D & N Haveli*	*Daman & Diu*	*Lakshadweep*
A. Revenue Receipts (Tax+Non-Tax)	('000 Rs.)	877370	7166500	1323384	1024800	183185
B. Total Revenue Expenditure (Plan+Non-Plan)	('000 Rs.)	7514300	8121900	3279500	2292190	2155500
C. Non-Plan Revenue Expenditure	('000 Rs.)	5545400	7314600	3052800	2159800	1853400
D. Gross Revenue Deficit (Plan+Non-Plan) (B-A)	('000 Rs.)	6636930	955400	1956116	1267390	1972315
E. Non-Plan Revenue Deficit (C-A)	('000 Rs.)	4668030	148100	1729416	1135000	1670215
F. Population (2001 Census)	(Persons)	356265	900914	220451	158059	60595
G. Per Capita Revenue Receipts (A/F)	(Rs.)	2463	7955	6003	6484	3023
H. Per Capita Total Revenue Expenditure (B/F)	(Rs.)	21092	9015	14876	14502	35572
I. Per Capita Non-Plan Revenue Expenditure (C/F)	(Rs.)	15565	8119	13848	13665	30587
J. Per Capita Total Revenue Deficit (D/F)	(Rs.)	18629	1060	8873	8018	32549
K. Per Capita Non-Plan Revenue Deficit (E/F)	(Rs.)	13103	164	7845	7181	27564
L. Ratio of Non-Plan Rev. Exp. to Total Rev. Exp. (C/B)	(%)	73.80	90.06	93.09	94.22	85.98
M. Ratio of Total Rev. Exp. to Rev. Receipts (B/A)	(%)	8.56	1.13	2.48	2.24	11.77
N. Ratio of Non-Plan Rev. Exp. to Rev. Receipts (C/A)	(%)	6.32	1.02	2.31	2.11	10.12

Source: Budget of M/o Home Affairs.

respect of Lakshadweep. Under the Lakshadweep Panchayats Regulation 1994, 1 District *Panchayat* and 10 Village (*Dweep*) *Panchayats* were constituted, to replace the Pradesh Council and the Island Councils, respectively. Under the new arrangements, the first set of general elections were held for these bodies on 14.12.1997 and the 10 Village (*Dweep*) *Panchayats* were brought into being on 19.12.1997 while the District *Panchayat*, on 23.1.1998. After the expiry of the term of the first set of the *panchayats*, the second round of general elections was held and the *Dweep Panchayats* and the District *Panchayat* were established in December 2002 and January 2003, respectively.

The District *Panchayat* has 33 members "21 male and 12 female. Of these 33 seats of members, 22 are filled in by direct elections, 10 by way of exofficio membership to the chairpersons of the Village (*Dweep*) *Panchayats* and 1, by way of *ex officio* membership to the Member of Parliament representing Lakshadweep. Of the 22 seats for elected membership of the District *Panchayat*, 20 are reserved for the Scheduled Tribe, including 7 for Scheduled Tribe women. Details about the number of seats for the *panchayats* and reservations for the Scheduled Tribe and women, are placed in Annexure A-38

The ten Village (*Dweep*) *Panchayats* have in all 79 members which includes 49 seats for male members and 30 for female. All these seats are filled in through direct elections, as per the constitutional requirement. Of the 10 *Dweep Panchayats*, 4 have women chairpersons, all belonging to the Scheduled Tribe.

As of February 2004, 25 major schemes have been transferred to the District Panchayats and 24 to the *Dweep Panchayats*, along with the staff. Transfer of staff to the *panchayats* is in the nature of deputation. The elected representatives of the *panchayats* preferred having full control over their staff. However, keeping in view the smallness of the island and its administration, the existing arrangements in terms of deputation could be continued for some more time.

TABLE 6.2

Total and Per Capita Outlay for the Tenth Plan for all States and UTs

States/UTs	*Tenth Plan Outlay (Rs. in Lakhs)*	*Population 2001 No. of Persons*	*Per Capita Outlay (Rs.)*
Non Special Category States			
1. Andhra Pradesh	4,661,400	75,727,541	6,155
2. Bihar	2,100,000	82,878,796	2,534
3. Chhattisgarh	1,100,000	20,795,956	5,289
4. Goa	320,000	1,343,998	23,810
5. Gujarat	4,000,700	50,596,992	7,907
6. Haryana	1,028,500	21,082,989	4,878
7. Jharkhand	1,463,274	26,909,428	5,438
8. Karnataka	4,355,823	52,733,958	8,260
9. Kerala	2,400,000	31,838,619	7,538
10. Madhya Pradesh	2,618,993	60,385,118	4,337
11. Maharashtra	6,663,200	96,752,247	6,887
12. Orissa	1,900,000	36,706,920	5,176
13. Punjab	1,865,700	24,289,296	7,681
14. Rajasthan	2,731,800	56,473,122	4,837
15. Tamil Nadu	4,000,000	62,110,839	6,440
16. Uttar Pradesh	5,970,800	166,052,859	3,596
17. West Bengal	2,864,100	80,221,171	3,570
Total-Non-Spl. Cat. States	**50,044,290**	**946,899,849**	**5,285**
Special Category States			
1. Arunachal Pradesh	388,832	1,091,117	35,636
2. Assam	831,524	26,638,407	3,122
3. Manipur	280,400	2,388,634	11,739
4. Meghalaya	300,900	2,306,069	13,048
5. Mizoram	230,001	891,058	25,812
6. Nagaland	222,765	1,988,636	11,202
7. Sikkim	165,574	540,493	30,634
8. Tripura	450,000	3,191,168	14,101
9. Himachal Pradesh	1,030,000	6,077,248	16,948
10. Jammu & Kashmir	1,450,000	10,069,917	14,399
11. Uttaranchal	763,000	8,479,562	8,998
Total-Spl. Cat. States	**6,112,996**	**63,662,309**	**9,602**
Union Territories			
1. A & N Islands	248,300	356,265	69,695
2. Chandigarh	100,000	900,914	11,100
3. Dadra & Nagar Haveli	30,400	220,451	13,790
4. Daman & Diu	24,500	158,059	15,501
5. Delhi	2,300,000	13,782,976	16,687
6. Lakshadweep	**43,700**	**60,650**	**72,118**
7. Pondicherry	190,649	973,829	19,577
Total-UTs	**2,937,549**	**16,453,089**	**17,854**
Grand Total-All States & UTs	**59,094,835**	**1,027,015,247**	**5,754**

Source: *Tenth Five Year Plan (2002-2007) Document*, Planning Commission.

Relationship between the District Panchayat and the V(D)Ps

Each Chairperson of the Village (*Dweep*) *Panchayat* is *ex officio* member of the District *Panchayat* and has a right to vote in the meetings of the District *Panchayat* (including the election of the President and Vice President of the District *Panchayat*). As per the Lakshadweep Panchayat (Finance and Accounts) Rules 1997, the budget of the Village (*Dweep*) *Panchayat* after having been passed by the Village (*Dweep*) *Panchayats* shall be placed before the District *Panchayat* and the District *Panchayat* with or without modification, approves the budget proposals of the Village (*Dweep*) *Panchayats*.

However, apart from the above two provisions, the District *Panchayat* and the Village (*Dweep*) *Panchayats* are constituted as separate entities and the Village (*Dweep*) *Panchayats* function independent of the District *Panchayats*. The funds to the Village (*Dweep*) *Panchayats* are transferred by the concerned departments, directly without routing through the District *Panchayat*. The utilisation accounts of the funds are submitted by the Village (*Dweep*) *Panchayats* directly to the departments of the administration and not through the District *Panchayat*.

District Panchayats as well as the Village (*Dweep*) *Panchayats* maintain their separate establishments leading to the duplication of efforts and at times sub optimal implementation of the schemes. The Village (*Dweep*) *Panchayats* and the District *Panchayats* are not administratively linked. It appears that if the Village (*Dweep*) *Panchayats* and District *Panchayats* are linked in a functional chain, the Village (*Dweep*) *Panchayats* can articulate their requirements and priorities in a more forceful manner through the District *Panchayat*, that is, together they can constitute a strong pressure group. Technical staff like engineers cannot be made available to each Village (*Dweep*) *Panchayat* as there are a limited number of posts available in the administration and even these posts have a lot of vacancies. Functional linkage can provide a large pool of officers and staff whose services can be properly utilised by a coordinated deployment and inter-*panchayat* transfers. In such a linked setup the schemes and programmes of the District *Panchayat* can also be implemented by the Village (*Dweep*) *Panchayats*.

Despite large variations in the population and area of the various islands, each island has got one V(D)P which leads to uneven distribution of the workload on the staff of the V(D)Ps. Further, equal amount of funds are given to each V(D)P, which means that the larger V(D)Ps get the same amount as the smaller ones, leading to uneven benefit being made available to the people. In the island conditions, it may not be convenient to club together two or three islands to constitute one Village (*Dweep*) *Panchayat* but the larger islands such as Andrott, Kavaratti, Minicoy and Amini can be subdivided to have more than one Village (*Dweep*) *Panchayat* in each.

Transfer of Functions and Resources to the Panchayats

Transfer of the various developmental schemes to the *panchayats* was achieved in Lakshadweep in two stages, by way of the UT Administrator's Orders dated 17.7.1998 and 9.4.2001, respectively. As of February 2004, 25 major schemes have been transferred to the District *Panchayat* and 24 to the *Dweep Panchayats* along with the personnel numbering 799 and 249, respectively. Schemes transferred to the District *Panchayats* relate to the Departments of Agriculture, Education, Fisheries, Industries and Social Welfare, whereas those transferred to the *Dweep Panchayats* relate to the Departments of Agriculture, Animal Husbandry, Cooperation and Civil Supplies, Electricity, Environment and Forests, Labour and Employment, Medical and Health Services, Public Works and Social Justice and Empowerment, etc. (Lists of the transferred schemes and staff are at Annexures A-39, A-40.A and A-40.B).

Funds released by the various departments to the *panchayats* and the expenditure incurred by the *panchayats* during 2002-03, are given in Table 6.3.

In addition to the scheme based transfers, *panchayats* are provided with untied grants-in-aid. Year-wise details of allocation and utilisation of funds allotted to the panchayati Raj Institutions is presented in Table 6.4.

A perusal of the schemes and staff transferred to the *panchayats* shows that more than one-third of the regular staff (including officers) of the administration have been transferred to the *panchayats*. In the education sector, the number of employees transferred is very large because the number includes teaching as well as non-teaching staff up to Class VII. The Lakshadweep Panchayat Regulation stipulates that the staff on deputation who complete three years in the *panchayats* will be deemed to be the staff of the *panchayats*. The present deputationists are not willing to be absorbed in the *panchayats* and they cannot be absorbed against their will. *Panchayat* representatives feel that they have inadequate control over the

TABLE 6.3

Funds Released to the *Panchayats* during 2002-03 and the Expenditure Incurred

Rs. in Lakh

Department	*Amount Released*		*Expenditure*	
	V(D)P	*DP*	*V(D)P*	*DP*
1. Agriculture	107.01	10.85	106.43	7.41
2. Animal Husbandry	23.35	2.35	22.72	1.29
3. Fisheries	36.02	21.10	35.93	17.75
4. Industries	0	5.30	0	4.35
5. Medical & Health	30.00	0	33.67	0.00
6. Education	0	1089.57	0.00	854.48
7. Social Justice & Empowerment	14.95	76.26	14.66	62.56
8. Labour & Employment	15.42	0	15.12	0
9. Panchayats & Rural Devt.	102.72	29.42	49.71	2.88
10. Environ. & Forests	13.63	37.05	13.10	34.34
11. Public Works	16.03	0	15.40	0
Total	**359.13**	**1271.90**	**306.74**	**985.06**

Note: DP= District *Panchayat*; V(D)P= Village (*Dweep*) *Panchayats*.

Source: Lakshadweep Administration.

deputationist cadres. It is necessary to provide adequate staff to the *panchayats* with suitable control mechanisms.

The regulations stipulate that the Administrator shall consult the President-cum-Chief Counsellor and the Vice Chairman-cum-Counsellor on matters of the territory. The version of the administration is that this has been done regularly in the islands on every major issue concerning the islands, whether the issue or subject pertains to the schemes/activities transferred to the *panchayats* or not. However, the *panchayat* representatives feel that much more needs to be done in this respect. A more specific structural arrangement of interface between the elected representatives of the *panchayats* and the administration is called for.

The elected representatives of the *panchayats* feel that some streamlining of the administrative arrangements in respect of the transferred schemes/staff is required. A system of periodic review of the transferred schemes and staff seems appropriate.

Revenue Mobilisation by the Panchayats

Section 51 of the Lakshadweep Panchayats Regulation 1994 enlists the taxes, which the Village (*Dweep*) *Panchayats* and the District *Panchayat* may impose. The upper limit for the rates of various taxes is to be prescribed by the Administrator. The Administrator had notified in November 2001 the upper limits of taxes/fees to be levied by the District *Panchayat* and the *Dweep Panchayats*. For the District *Panchayat*, the notified levies are Professional (Employment) tax, surcharge on stamp duties on transfer of immovable properties and fees for registration of motorised vehicles and mechanised boats and sailing vessels. In respect of

TABLE 6.4

Allocation of Funds to the Panchayati Raj Institutions and Utilisation

Rs. in Lakh

Year	*Village (Dweep) Panchayat*			*District Panchayat*		
	Allotted	*Utilised*	*Per cent*	*Allotted*	*Utilised*	*Per cent*
1999-00	290.52	233.08	80	1068.81	861.13	81
2000-01	341.90	241.61	70	1153.63	934.36	81
2001-02	353.41	291.8	83	1249.17	959.35	71
2002-03	359.13	306.74	85	1271.92	985.06	77

Source: Lakshadweep Administration.

TABLE 6.5

Revenue Collection by the *Panchayats* in Lakshadweep

Rs. in Lakh

Panchayat	*1997-98*	*1998-99*	*1999-00*	*2000-01*	*2001-02*	*2002-03*
District Panchayat	Nil	Nil	Nil	Nil	Nil	5.26
Dweep Panchayats#	1.62	3.01	4.23	6.75	10.35	13.39

Note: #: All the 10 Village (*Dweep*) *Panchayats* put together.

Source: Lakshadweep Administration.

the *Dweep Panchayats*, the notified limits relate to tax on buildings rented out, tax on boats and octroi. The revenue actually collected by the *panchayats* is presented in Table 6.5.

Strengthening the Panchayats

Panchayats in Lakshadweep are far closer to the people than those in rest of the country, owing to the smallness of the area and population. Such proximity enhances the levels of expectation of the people, while the smallness of the population makes it difficult for the *panchayats* to raise much higher level of resources by way of taxes, etc. from the residents, though some improvement does appear possible in both respects.

Scope of Additional Resource Mobilisation by the Panchayats

The tax base of the *panchayats* needs to be broadened and they need to be motivated to increase resource mobilisation through their own plan and non-plan resources. Analysis of the taxes currently allowed to be imposed by the *panchayats* indicates the scope for review on the following lines:

Property taxes: At present, *Dweep Panchayats* levy building tax only on rented buildings. Building tax needs to be imposed on non-rented buildings including residential buildings and shops, etc. too. Further, vacant lands also need to be brought into the property tax net.

The procedure for levy of building tax on rented buildings, which currently is linked to the amount of rent received, needs to be reviewed, as is the trend in the rest of the country. A standard rate of building tax for different types of construction and localities will enable introduction of a rationalised and buoyant system of property taxation that will also be amenable to self-assessment.

Profession Tax: While the Profession Tax has been introduced in the form of Employment Tax and is linked to the gross yearly income, it is likely to omit self-employed professionals. A review in this regard is desirable with a view to widen the tax base. The rate of tax, which is pegged at the maximum of Rs. 300 per annum per person, also needs to be reviewed.

Other new taxes: The following tax options appear appropriate to be explored for imposition as new levies:

- Tax on visitors/tourists.
- Entertainment Tax on cable TV connections.

In addition, some kind of levy on fish catch may also be considered.

Functional Involvement of Panchayats

The *panchayats* at both the tiers have already been assigned various functional responsibilities along with a fair share of the staff. The representatives of the *panchayats* fell that the transfer of staff should be on a permanent basis and not on deputation. This demand need not be a high priority as the small size of the *panchayats* may make the cadre management difficult. The existing staff, transferred to the PRIs on deputation, may be give suitable orientation training to work effectively for and under the *panchayats*. Secondly, several functions have been transferred to the PRIs recently. The administration needs to interact closely with the *panchayats* to ensure that the transferred schemes are implemented effectively and efficiently. On their part, the *panchayats* need to create a database of the schemes being implemented through them and modernise their arrangements for programme monitoring and review.

Disaster Management

Storms and cyclones are the main natural hazards occurring in Lakshadweep. Fortunately, in the last hundred years, it has not faced loss of human life due to natural disasters. However, effective disaster mitigation efforts are of prime importance considering predictions on global climate change and rising sea levels. A glimpse into the recorded history of disasters in Lakshadweep shows that some islands like Andrott and Kalpeni have been frequented by cyclones causing considerable damage (See Annexure A-41). Infrastructure and economic activities being located near the coast, they become highly vulnerable to cyclones and sea-level fluctuations. Low-lying islands are at greater risk from sea-level rise. Andrott, Kalpeni and Minicoy lie in a cyclone belt. The remaining islands are subject to the fury of the Southwest and Northeast monsoons causing heavy damages to coconut crops, seashore land, sheds and dwelling houses that are not able to withstand cyclonic winds or in areas subject to flooding. Were the December 26, 2004 tsunami that hit East Asia including the Andaman and Nicobar Islands and the eastern coast of India to hit Lakshadweep with the same severity, it would almost annihilate the islands, as the land surface is hardly 1–3 metres above sea level.

To avoid chaotic sets of actions alerted during a disaster response, the suggested model for disaster management in Lakshadweep is the expand-contract model wherein prevention, preparedness, relief and rehabilitation are carried out as a continuous process in a parallel series of activities although with varying degrees of emphasis with respect to the time of disaster occurrence. Specific budgetary provisions should be earmarked every year for disaster mitigation efforts and disaster response. Disaster mitigation efforts should be seen as cost-effective over disaster management. It is emphasised that disaster mitigation activities be built into the overall developmental scheme of Lakshadweep rather than being seen as isolated activities.

Development projects may consciously force a choice between reducing disaster vulnerability and economic vulnerability. The awareness amongst the local people and the administration, of the direct link between the survival of the coral ecosystem and the survival of the Islands is essential to prevent inconsiderate development and consequent disasters. An integrated approach of sustainable development and management of coral ecosystems is therefore of importance. Community based disaster management (CBDM) models have to be preferred over centralised and top-down approach to turn disaster into an opportunity for development and empowerment. This however, requires awareness creation through educational institutions and government departments, imparting of training programmes to representatives from all the government institutions, *panchayat* heads, *mullahs* and other leaders. This also requires availability of information on all aspects of government procedures and rules on development and disaster related initiatives on the internet. Tapping potential at the individual level, with government institutions playing a key supporting role in socioeconomic and political empowerment and by providing adequate know-how, training and resources will effect a cascade of activities related to the overall development and disaster mitigation efforts. Toward this end, collaborative ventures with national institutes for increased awareness, sustenance, research, development and disaster mitigation in Lakshadweep are suggested.

A National Institute for Coral Ecosystem, to undertake research and monitor the health of the coral ecosystem, is a priority. The coral forming polyps are critical components in a small island environment supporting a unique ecosystem and forming important protective barriers against natural hazards such as sea ingress during high tide or cyclones. Environment impact assessment of development projects, appropriate waste management systems, suitable mechanisms to deal with major oil spills have to be put in place to prevent coral bleaching and death of corals. Adequate enforcement of fisheries management regulations and increased awareness are necessary to curb over-fishing and destructive fishing. Strategies for providing adequate water resources are necessary for mitigating epidemic and drought associated disasters. Provision should be made for safe storage of aviation fuel.

Many Research and Development organisations and other Central Government institutions have been mandated to work on disaster related studies, directly or indirectly (See Annexure A-42). All such organisations should be involved in disaster management and prevention efforts. For instance, the Indian Council of Forestry Research and Education should be involved in developing strategies for shelterbelt plantations and ecological restoration of soils—a limited resource in Lakshadweep. Shelterbelt plantations can play a crucial role in the disaster mitigation efforts of Lakshadweep. The India Meteorological Department is engaged in prediction and monitoring of natural disasters such as droughts and floods and for the study of district level droughts, using long series of meteorological data. A National Centre for Disaster Management (NCDM) has been set up at the Indian Institute of Public Administration. NCDM is the nodal agency for coordinating relief and rehabilitation work during natural calamities and for human resource development in the area of disaster management. Coordinated efforts of these institutions will go a long way in timely prediction of natural disasters and also in the management efforts, once the disasters do occur.

A sub-centre of National Centre for Disaster Management (NCDM) with a strong wing for extension activities may be set up at Lakshadweep to develop, disseminate and implement strategies for disaster mitigation and management. NCDM has to be involved in refining organisational and procedural measures for disaster mitigation and disaster response and for human resource development in the area of disaster management.

To ensure proper coordination between personnel in disaster management committees, departments, and financial authorities, and for clear delineation of roles and responsibilities, mock drills should be conducted at least once a year and weak links in the sequence of response action addressed to ensure swift response action. All the information pertaining to the committees involved, the roles and responsibilities should be disseminated through the Lakshadweep website, *panchayats* and extension wings of government departments. Adequate training to personnel from each department may be considered mandatory. In addition, school children may be trained in disaster response as they form the most vulnerable group during disasters. The committees should meet in April and August to assess the disaster preparedness activities. Representatives of the committees should be regularly deputed for disaster mitigation works in other disaster prone regions of the country. The committees should have links to disaster management committees in the mainland. Mechanisms for swift external response for disaster management from the mainland should be put in place as disasters can upset the most well laid out plans in small islands.

Disaster forecasting, the immediate percolation of early warning disaster signals to the people, and preparedness of the people are critical in disaster reduction. Provision of mobile communication sets to *panchayats* for use by fishermen can help in rescue and warning efforts. Mapping vulnerable areas based on surveys and demographic census are prerequisites for effective disaster response. The relationship between economic status of communities and their vulnerabilities are increasingly being recognised. Demographic information for Lakshadweep has to be compiled according to the format provided by the UNDP. A disaster management plan has to be prepared similar to the database of the District Disaster Management Plan prepared by the District Collectorate, Puri. Cyclone shelters should be identified or built outside the High Risk Areas. Kavaratti, Minicoy, Kadmat, Agatti and Bitra have been identified as less prone to inundation by sea. The local people should be made aware regarding where and when to take refuge. Concrete steps have been proposed for disaster preparedness and management

Cyclone Shelters

Vulnerability maps for cyclones should be prepared and cyclone shelters identified or built outside High Risk Areas. Emergency supplies, such as food, drinking water, basic first aid, medical supplies, ORS packages, blankets, etc. should be housed in flood-proof structures.

Shelterbelt and Windbreak Plantation

The protective works to control erosion of shorelines as being applied now are a continuing drain on resources. Shelterbelt planting of wind resistant tree species like Casurina along coastal tracts can help in binding soil, reduce cyclone damage, and limit the erosive effects of wave action. Planting of trees under a social forestry component to improve cyclone protection and stabilise embankments will have ancillary benefits in poverty alleviation, environmental improvement, and increased production of wood and other forest products. Agriculture management is crucial to disaster management.

Waste (including Sewage) Disposal

Lack of appropriate facilities for safe disposal of human waste results in serious pollution of coastal waters around beaches, reefs and lagoons. The influence of the market economy has resulted in the increased use of non-degradable plastics, bottles and metal-based equipment and industrial effluents/oil spills resulting in problems associated with disposing of them when they become unusable. These wastes can result in serious health and pollution problems choking the ecosystem. Appropriate waste management systems have to be established to prevent coral bleaching and death of corals.

Overfishing and Over-harvesting of Marine Invertebrates

Modern boats and destructive fishing practices, targeting of spawning aggregation sites, and the over-harvesting of target species cause adverse impacts on the region's marine biodiversity resulting in steady reduction in the productive potential of coastal fisheries, one of the most important subsistence sources of protein. Adequate enforcement of fisheries management regulations and increased awareness are necessary to curb overfishing and destructive fishing.

Protection of Coral Reefs

Coral reef ecosystems are under increasing pressure primarily from human interactions. The reefs are also damaged by heavy wave action during frequent tropical cyclones, and outbreaks of coral-eating crown-of-thorns sea stars, but these are natural phenomena. The main preventable cause is the rapid population growth that has led to associated problems of sanitation, overexploitation and degradation of natural resources, which adversely impact the coral reefs. Control of illegal trade in coral and regulated tourism are advocated to minimise further damage by human interventions. Coral reefs are also destroyed by construction or dredging, pollution and siltation. These activities need to be regulated.

Mitigating Epidemic and Drought Associated Disasters

Major epidemics threatening the islands of Lakshadweep are waterborne diseases such as gastroenteritis and cholera. Malaria and pneumonia have also been reported in Lakshadweep. These diseases point towards the most widespread environmental problem namely, the lack of sanitation facilities posing grave risks to human health. Facilities are still rudimentary or entirely lacking. During cyclones and droughts, these constraints can cause havoc to the island population causing more damage than the disaster itself. Serious efforts are required to improve sanitation facilities.

Water Supply and Conservation

Strategies for providing adequate water resources include improved storage and distribution systems; development of underutilised or alternative sources, better management of water supply and infrastructure; increased water conservation programmes; construction of ground water recharge basins for runoff; more effective use of satellite forecast information; efficient sanitation facilities and application of new technology, such as desalinisation.

Safe Storage Facilities for Petro-products

Open storage of oils used for aviation and electricity generation can cause serious risk to the local population. Immediate steps are needed for constructing proper storage facilities.

Disaster Forecasting and Dissemination

Disaster forecasting is important for a rapid disaster response. The organisations involved in disaster warning are: (i) the Indian Meteorological Department which looks at drought, rainfall, cyclone and crop position; (ii) the Department of Space which deals with satellite monitoring of drought and floods; and (iii) the Ministry of Water Resources which studies riparian floods. The Meteorological Department has a coastal network of 10 cyclone detection radars, but the main instrument is the INSAT-IB that enables satellite imageries and remote sensing for cyclone forecasting.

Dissemination of Disaster Warning

Cyclone warning to Lakshadweep is provided from the Area Cyclone Warning Centres at Chennai and Trivandrum. A monitoring Cell functions at the Collectorate Headquarter at Kavaratti, which immediately transmits such messages to all islands. The TV network also plays a vital role. The communication network of BSNL, Naval detachment, Interstate Police Wireless, Lakshadweep Police Wireless, India Reserve Battalion Wireless, NIC, etc. can be fully utilised for warning and for communication. Provision of mobile communication sets to *panchayats* for use by fishermen can help in rescue and warning efforts.

Disaster should be seen as an opportunity for development and empowerment. Involving local communities in the design and implementation of post-disaster plans and programmes is important. After a disaster, rehabilitation should be given equal priority as relief and reconstruction. Systematic and sustained efforts are needed to tackle the long-term needs of survivors. The psychosocial need is an essential aspect of overall rehabilitation and reconstruction efforts. All the steps suggested in this respect need to be codified in the form of a Disaster Management Plan, which should be prepared by the administration in consultation with the related government departments, people's representatives, NGOs involved with the issue and the various expert bodies. The Plan should be periodically reviewed and updated.

Modernisation of Administration

The scattered nature of the landmass and the difficult means of inter-island communication in Lakshadweep call for innovative administrative arrangements. The administration has experimented with success videoconferencing systems for holding public meetings as also for departmental reviews. The same system has been refined to extend telemedical facilities wherein super-specialists sitting in the mainland hospitals examine the patients of the islands through satellite based on-line communication. Such arrangements are no doubt costly to provide, but definitely need to be extended. VSAT based connectivity to provide a fast and effective communication interlink among the islands and the islanders would facilitate these requirements.

Use of computers in stand alone as well as in networked environment too is imperative. The unit offices of various departments are scattered in the islands and compilation of the progress reports and other information by the District Heads faces frequent difficulties. These obstacles need to be tackled through intensive computerisation of the various offices and their inter-networking.

Ecological monitoring of the various natural assets, on shore as well as in the sea, is yet another necessity for Lakshadweep. The fact that the entire islands are based on corals, which are highly susceptible to ecological disturbances and environmental pollution, makes it necessary to monitor the ecological parameters of the region regularly. A suitable administrative arrangement for this purpose, which involves the subject matter specialists, local officers as well as people's representatives, needs to be created.

Fisheries, the mainstay of the economy of these islands, needs to be accorded higher attention. Illegal fishing by mainland boats poses serious economic and ecological hazards. This needs to be addressed quickly.

It is also necessary to equip the local administration to undertake adequate techno-economic and environmental feasibility studies for the various projects mooted for the islands. This is necessary as many of the centrally sponsored schemes under implementation elsewhere in the country, if implemented as they are in Lakshadweep, could play havoc with its ecology. This holds good for the projects in all the sectors including the economic as well as the social sectors. At the same time, project monitoring mechanism also needs to be strengthened.

Sensitising the People

Creating awareness among the masses about their rights and responsibilities under various general and special laws and schemes is essential. To an extent, this is achievable through the system of representative local bodies. However, there are instances of serious shortcomings in the matter of public awareness. The large-scale ignorance about waterborne diseases, emanating largely out of the pollution caused by the residents in their own backyards, is a case in point. Similarly, the danger to the soils, the lagoons, the corals and to the very existence of these islands, on account of natural as well as man-made distaters is very real. It is necessary to make innovative efforts on a sustained basis, to bring about awareness among the people in respect of various important issues of health, social and legal rights, gender issues, environmental matters, etc.

E-Governance

Creation of Database of Residents of Lakshadweep and Issue of Citizen Identity Cards

With a population of over 60,650 Lakshadweep is a Union Territory having the lowest population in the country. The islands are restricted territory and access to educational and health facilities, employment opportunities and poverty alleviation programmes is limited to the *bona fide* residents of Lakshadweep. Even in the shipping sector, it may be required by the residents to prove that they are *bona fide* resident of the islands. With the use of IT we may create database of each and every citizen in Lakshadweep with their up-to-date details and it may be made mandatory to have the resident identity card to avail any facilities in the islands. The Government Employees from other parts of the country working in Lakshadweep, permit holders coming to Lakshadweep for various works, etc. can also be included in the database with restricted access to the facilities.

Implementation of State Wide Area Network (SWAN)

The major bottleneck in the development of Lakshadweep is the geographical isolation from the mainland and also between islands. With the development in IT it is now possible to virtually connect the islands. A proposal for a state wide area network for Lakshadweep islands is already submitted and this envisages Internet connectivity to each and every offices and cybercafes/CIC's in the islands.

Establishment of Videoconferencing Facilities in All the Islands in Lakshadweep

The SWAN will provide virtual connectivity to the islands. However, for face-to-face communications, high-tech video-conferencing studios may be established in all the islands. This facility is already available at Kavaratti, Minicoy and Chetlat islands. To maintain the quality of the conference, an exclusive network with Multi Conferencing Unit (MCU) may be established.

Lakshadweep Government Portal Providing all Citizen Services with a Slogan "If it is not there then it is nowhere"

The Lakshadweep administration is having a web site with static information. It is essential to develop a Lakshadweep Portal similar to and as a part of the India Government Portal with the slogan "If it is not there then it is nowhere." This will be the one point most reliable information resource about Lakshadweep and also for availing any citizen services.

Web-enabled Employment Registration System

The UT of Lakshadweep is having only one Employment Exchange at Kavaratti and the live register of the Employment Exchange is maintained there. Even though the upgradation in the live register can be done in the islands through authorised officers, it is reflected in the live register only when the details are physically reached at Kavaratti. In order to keep the live register up-to-date, faster and improve transparency in the system, a web-enabled employment exchange registration system may be introduced.

E-literacy Programme

In this IT era, when nobody can afford to remain away from using IT tools, it is essential to impart basic training in information technology to at least one member in every family. The basic infrastructure like Information Technology Training Centre may be created in each island and this work may be outsourced to the private entrepreneurs. The training content in Malayalam and Mahl may be made available for this training programme. This also generates employment opportunities in the islands.

IT@everyhome.lakshdweep

The information technology is changing the way we work, we do business and it is becoming part of our daily life. The problems in the geographic isolation of the islands can be reduced to a great extent by providing virtual connectivity. Information Technology is becoming part of our life and it may be essential to have a PC with Internet access at every home in Lakshadweep. A scheme may be drawn up for the same. The costs of PCs are coming down and the connectivity is becoming cheaper and it may be possible to get a PC at less than Rs. 10,000 a piece and will cost only around Rs. 10 crores to provide PCs in the 10,000 odd homes in Lakshadweep.

Dweep Vidya Project

The Education Department is the largest department in the territory with more than 1,000 teachers and 10,000 students. However, there is no regular interaction between the teachers and students in various islands. With the limited communication and manpower, it is always difficult to compile the information from the islands.

The "Dweep Vidya Project" envisages the creation of single window portal for the Department of Education where each and every student, teacher and parent will have access to the up-to-date information they want at any instance. Each and every teacher will be provided with access to this portal to update the details of the students at any time. News, events, discussions groups, knowledge bank, chatting, instant messenger, e-mail, etc. also will be available in this portal.

Modernization of Administration

With the developments in Information Technology and introduction of computers is changing the faces of the offices. It is essential to re-engineer the offices and modernise and Information Technology may be used as a catalyst to create modern e-offices. The Kerala model experimented at 'Palakkad' district and is being replicated in all the districts in Kerala, may be taken as an example for this process.

In the first phase we may experiment the same in the sub-divisional offices and may replicate the same to all offices in the territory.

Digital Library Project

Knowledge is power and the availability of right resources at right time is essential. It is essential to create a digital library with latest CDs on various topic may be made available through the net. It is also required to automate the activities of libraries in all the islands. The E-Granthalaya Project may be revived and implemented on a time bound manner.

Lakshadweep Administration Net

The idea behind this network is to connect all the offices in Lakshdweep. Computer systems and Internet connectivity will be provided to all the offices. Once this network is operational, all the sanction orders, bills, etc. will be generated using a web-enabled software. The details of the bills updated by the Pay and Accounts Offices, Banks, etc. and the details of funds available, expenditure incurred, etc. will be available from anywhere at anytime.

Web-enabled Integrated Personnel Information System for the Administration

This project envisages the creation and maintenance of a single database for the entire employees of Lakshadweep Administration. All the offices and employees will have access to this database. The details of the employee will be updated by the respective offices and will be available to any authority at any instant of time. The payroll details also will be maintained and the pay bill can be generated by the respective offices.

E-Post

E-Post Service is launched by Department of Posts nationwide a year ago. E-Post service enables people to send and receive messages or scanned images through e-mail in all 1,56,000 post offices in the country. For the first time in the country, people who would not normally have access to internet would be able to send and receive e-mail messages without possessing an e-mail id thereby bridging the digital divide in the arena of public communication systems.

The facility is not introduced to any of the post offices in the Lakshadweep islands so far. It is essential to introduce this facility in the islands at the earliest.

E-Hospital

The state-of-the-art information and communication technology tools may be used to manage the ever-expanding volume of health information and for harnessing the benefits of Information Technology for the benefits of patients, doctors, nurses, paramedical personnel and other professional, administrators.

A health card system may be introduced for every resident of the territory and information systems for real time access to patient records, medical records managements, and medical inventory management may be introduced.

E-Commerce Project for LCMF

The Lakshadweep Cooperative Marketing Federation, LCMF, the prime agency for the supply of essential commodities in the islands is still using traditional communication methods like surface mail, telegrams, etc. for the sending indent requests, invoices, etc. It is essential to modernise the Lakshadweep Cooperative Marketing Federation and the Cooperative Supply and Marketing Societies for sending the essential commodities to the islands based on the indents received. An Integrated Management Information System may be developed and for inventory management system and public distribution system.

Cargo Management System

A large number of cargo is being transported to the islands from mainland every day in various ships. There is no mechanism available to monitor the movement of this cargo. It is essential to implement a system to monitor the movement of the cargo and generate various reports. The details of each and every item may be captured and bar coded at mainland before transportation.

Lakshadweep Times Portal

A portal for collecting and disseminating the news from all the islands may be developed. The authorised officials will update the portal from various locations and the same will be reviewed and published by the Chief Editor. *The Lakshadweep Times* may be made available on the net and the same may be printed from all the islands.

Television News Broadcasting Service

A television news service can be started for Lakshadweep by recording a news capsule of 30 minutes every day and transmitting the same through video-conferencing facilities in the islands and further transmitting the same through the cable network in the respective island.

The administration is also working on introducing Lakshadweep Multi-Purpose Citizen Identity Card in line with national initiative of Multi-purpose National Identity Card (MINC). It will be a smart card which will store various information such as name, place of birth, residence, age, medical history, economic status, etc. and serve not only as an Identity Card/Voter Card/ Driving License but also Health Card, Ration Card, etc. This is being done by interdepartmental group consisting of Collectorate, NIC, IT Department with the close assistance of all other departments.

Chapter 7

Summary, Conclusion and Recommendations

Lakshadweep, the tiniest member in the fraternity of the 28 States and 7 Union Territories that comprise India, is a land full of promise for growth and development. Yet, the perspective plan for development of Lakshadweep offers a set of challenges too. The complexities in working out a strategy for this island territory emanate largely from the peculiarities of its social, economic and ecological dimensions. The key issues arising out of the detailed analysis of the various dimensions for an all round and sustainable development of Lakshadweep and the recommendations presented in the various chapters can be summarised as has been done in the succeeding paragraphs.

The overall health indicators give a mixed picture—the longevity, IMR and gender ratios are favourable, but the prevalence of waterborne diseases is severe and alarming. The local bodies are in the nascent stage and need to be nurtured to play a greater role in the development and growth of the island. Economic activities are still predominantly in the hands of the government. While non-government investments in the economic activities of the island need to be pursued, that need not delay the investment by the government in essential sectors of education, medical and healthcare, water supply and sanitation, besides in economic sectors too, such as in agriculture, environmental conservation, fisheries, tourism, etc. The strategic and ecological sensitive character of Lakshadweep calls for continued involvement of government in its all round development.

The strategic location of the islands of this Union Territory in terms of the defence of the country cannot be overemphasised. These islands can be the natural sentinels of the west coast of India. They also provide outposts capable of monitoring international maritime traffic and also for surveillance of the economically important western coast of India. Therefore, quicker access by air to the defence services would also be undoubtedly advantageous.

Development Paradigm

The paradigm of development for Lakshadweep ought to be a vision of the goals which the society wishes to pursue, the direction in which various sectors of the economy should proceed to subserve them, the anticipated externalities that may emerge in the process and the manner in which they will be dealt with. Otherwise the growth process in various parts may fall apart, or work at cross purposes throwing up dissonance and even conflict between what people had expected as its outcome and what it ended up achieving.

As the decisions in respect of these complex matters may be neither easy nor always based on social consensus, it is essential that such decisions are taken by the affected community fully conscious of various pros and cons of each measure. This will, however, require equipping the local community with necessary information and demystified substantive technical knowledge regarding the kind of choices involved and how they can impact them. The finesse and the vigour with which this effort is pursued would alone determine the paradigm of development which is people-centred—a model where development is for the people and not *vice versa*.

Goals of Development

The paradigm of development perception could focus on the following objectives:

- Raise the living standard of people: (1) through enhancement of income, (2) raising employment opportunities for youth, particularly the educated youth.

- Enhance the quality of life, particularly in respect of improving drinking water supply, primary and secondary healthcare, sanitation amenities and providing swift inter-island and islands-mainland connectivity.
- Promoting small family norm.
- Ecological protection.
- Preserving the existing social structure, vibrant community life and cultural values.
- Preventing migration from the mainland.
- Check against growth of social and economic inequalities, inter-island and intra-island.
- Strengthen democratic decision making with widest level of participation.
- Provide sustainable development programmes.

Constraints and Strengths

While Lakshadweep islands possess a set of helping features, any strategy for their development faces certain constraints as well. The constraints include the limited landmass, typology of the soil that restricts the choice of crops, lack of fresh water sources, pressure of population, vulnerability of the islands to natural disasters, flat and sandy terrain leading to problems relating to sanitation and drainage, high level of unemployment, lack of entrepreneurship characteristics and technological skills among the people, isolation and remoteness of the islands leading to high cost of transportation of goods and the people, absence of raw materials for most of the traditional and popular economic activities, and ecological sensitivity and fragility of the islands.

As against such limitations, there are supportive factors as well. These are, principally, relatively egalitarian and homogeneous society, high level of awareness among the people, absence of problems of acute vulnerability to food insecurity, malnutrition, acute poverty, severe exploitation and social disharmony, near absence of crime and law and order related problems and the strong social solidarity, culture and moral values among the people.

Agrarian and Social Structure

Land tenure from the beginning of colonisation has been intertwined with the caste system prevalent in Kerala society. The high caste group among the earlier settlers managed to appropriate all lands that could be brought under cultivation and became *Jenmis* (landlords) as per the prevailing practice in Kerala and created a variety of tenancy arrangements. After the implementation of land reforms, the landholding pattern now exhibits preponderance of small holdings. Nearly 87.35 per cent of the total holdings have an area of less than 0.5 hectare each. A small 8.16 per cent are in the size-class of 0.50 to 1.00 hectare group.

The social character of the population now represents a unique hybrid-mix of the Hindu tradition of the Kerala coast with an Islamic superstructure. A majority of the people in all the islands belong to the Shafi School of the Sunni sect. In terms of religious differentiation even within Islam, Agatti also has a large number of Wahabi while Kalpeni has people following the Ahamadiya sect. The Hindu-Muslim influence is also characterised by the coexistence of matriliny of Kerala Hindu society along with the patriliny structure of Islam, something which is rare in a single social formation. However, Minicoy stands apart from other groups of islands in this respect and shares greater affinity with Maldives islands in the language spoken and the culture practised. Kavaratti islanders are most progressive where women's education is concerned. It was first started here. Bangaram and Tinnakara are also very fertile islands with dense coconut trees. Minicoy is the most prosperous island. Kadmat is economically the most backward island. Thus, each island has its own unique social and economic characteristics.

Status of the Economy

The islands also represent a variety of skill endowment in human resources. Agatti and Minicoy islanders are expert sailors. Amini and Chetlat islands produce the best local craftsmen. Put together, these islands possess a variety of economic skills, though these may not be technologically very advanced.

The cropping pattern in Lakshadweep comprises mainly coconut which does not require intensive labour support for crop management. The other major economic activity, fisheries, is limited by the surrounding lagoons which prevent landing of larger ships on the island harbours. The poverty levels, vary among the islands. Kiltan and Chetlat have more than 50 per cent of their population below the poverty line with a consumer expenditure of Rs. 15 per person for a month at 1960-61 rural prices; but other islands are much better off. However, according to the BPL Survey

2002 (Provisional figures), the maximum poverty level in the UT of Lakshadweep is around 31 per cent. The per capita consumption expenditure in Lakshadweep is Rs. 967 per month as against the all-India average of Rs. 591.

As for the household economic pattern, almost three-fourths of the houses have cement flooring *pucca* construction and tiled roofs, only 19 per cent are thatched and 95 per cent of the houses are electrified. As many as 65 per cent have at least one salaried working member while remittances from a member account for at least 53 per cent of the households. This is based on the study conducted in 1987, the situation has definitely improved since then.

Despite the overall appearance of a better economy, inter-island disparity existing which is not merely related to resource endowment but also in terms of human resource development. This feature is broadly similar to the kind of regional imbalances which are noticed in larger mainland states.

Various development initiatives particularly for augmenting incomes, building up infrastructure and processing and marketing of agricultural and industrial produce undertaken in Lakshadweep earlier have at times fallen through on account of lack of foresight and professional rigour in planning and project appraisal and management. The development framework for Lakshadweep needs to take care of the inter-island disparities as well as of the ecological sensitivities of the islands in future also.

Economic Issues

The economic activities in Lakshadweep depend primarily on the land as well as on the surrounding water bodies, the lagoons, coral reefs and the ocean. The landmass is very limited and the soil has unique characteristics. The scope for industrial development has severe limitations in view of the ecological and cost related factors. The prospects for economic activities have to focus mainly on agriculture and allied activities, fisheries and tourism and the supplementary activities in the sectors of animal husbandry and small scale and cottage industries.

Agriculture

Landholdings in Lakshadweep are predominantly small and marginal, 87 per cent of the operational holdings were of the size of 0.5 hectare or less (2000-2001). The other striking feature is that almost the entire cultivable lands are planted with coconut, with intercropping in some. These factors, coupled with lack of irrigation facilities, have generally limited the availability of employment from the agriculture sector. The yield of coconuts in terms of numbers is very high, but the size of the nuts is very small. There is also a wide variation in the yield of the nuts among the various islands of Lakshadweep. There is scope for improving the cropping practices with a view to obtain better size of coconuts and higher yield. Efforts are also required to increase the area under intercropping of the coconut fields with various fruits and vegetable crops, as also for crop diversification. Keeping in view the sensitive ecology of the islands, the administration has taken measures to discourage the use of chemical fertilisers and pesticides, which has proved to be a right decision. A soil nutrient management strategy based on organic manures and pest control is recommended eliminating the need of chemical fertilisers and pesticides altogether. Lastly, the forward and backward linkages for crop production activities, that would include inputs/loans, marketing and agro-industries, etc. should be pursued. Projects for bringing about value addition to coconut and its by-products including the palmwood, coir, husk, coconut-honey, tender nut, desiccated coconut powder, coconut milk, etc. need to be encouraged in a bigger way.

Animal Husbandry

In Lakshadweep commercial livestock farming is neither feasible nor advisable. Keeping small units of cows and goats under stall-feeding should be an ideal model to meet the requirement of livestock products and for supplemental income. Poultry offers a viable commercial proposition and farmers could be encouraged to establish large units. For better production and adaptability, new strains of poultry suitable to the island conditions may be developed in consultation with various poultry institutes/universities.

Animals required for both milk and meat for the islands are brought from coastal cities like Calicut and Mangalore. It is necessary to establish a quarantine unit to ensure prevention of diseases from the mainland.

The requirements of fodder, feed and other support infrastructure required for animal husbandry are currently met largely by way of imports from the mainland, which is a costly proposition, in view of transportation costs and uneconomical volumes. It is desirable to make the islands self-sufficient in respect of fodder and feed. The local people can also be trained to provide basic veterinary care.

Soil and Water Conservation

In the whole of Lakshadweep, the small size of the islands, the near table like flatness of the terrain, the highly porous sandy soil and absence of any significant source of fresh water except for some shallow layers of rainwater collection floating on the thicker seawater in all the islands, make water conservation one of the most critical issues, not only for agriculture, but even for the sustainability of human activities. To meet the inadequacy of sweet water for various purposes including drinking and agriculture, schemes for rain-water harvesting, and soil conservation need to be pursued.

The usual issue of soil runoff because of flow of rainwater is not very prominent in Lakshadweep as the rainwater velocity is broken by the thick canopy of coconut palms that cover nearly the entire area. However, the quality of the soil is prone to damage due to excessive watering, inadequate drainage, and indiscriminate application of chemical fertilisers and pesticides. Therefore, for agriculture, drip and sprinkler irrigation should be encouraged. Also, instead of chemical fertilisers and pesticides, organic substitutes should be used.

Fisheries and Ocean Development

The extensive exclusive economic zone of 4 lakh sq km that surrounds Lakshadweep provides ample opportunity for exploiting the fishery resources from the vast oceanic spread and depths. The present level of fish catch, which is of the order of 15,000 metric tonnes per annum, largely tuna, is almost negligible compared to the available potential, which is estimated to be between 50,000 to 1,00,000 tonnes per annum. A well thought out strategy to periodically monitor the movement of the various varieties of fishes, prawns, shrimps, etc. needs to be developed. Simultaneously, sophisticated vessels to enable the catch, store it in cold conditions on the high seas, and to handle at the shore such as packaging, etc. needs to be worked out. The details will include introduction of a system of mother/collector vessels networked to a set of smaller fishing boats, mechanical splashers and GPS system in the boats, new generation pole and line fishing vessels with multi-day fishing ability, experimental fishing by purse seines and satellite-based monitoring of the tuna environment. Attention is also required to increase the facilities for storage, processing, marketing and export of the various types of fishes including the ornamental varieties as well as tuna/fish products. The current fishing activities generate about 2,000 tonnes of waste, which is not only non-utilised but also becomes a health hazard. Arrangements should be introduced to utilise such waste for production of fishmeal. Shelter for the island fishermen and warehouses for their fish, etc. are required on the mainland in areas such as Mangalore, Kochi and Calicut.

Besides fisheries, Lakshadweep with its vast exclusive economic zone, offers considerable scope for ocean related economic development activities in a variety of ways. These include pearl culture, for which Bangaram Island has been found more suitable, culture of seaweeds, which are useful for human food, animal food, and pharmaceutical purposes, establishment of artificial reefs to provide habitat for many types of fishes and other aquatic life, culture and sea ranching of the threatened fin fish (groupers and sea horse) and of shellfish including the pearl oyster. These activities will not only promote the livelihood status of the community but also help preserve the flora, fauna including the coral reef ecosystem. Seaweed cultivation again needs to be promoted, as it is useful for industrial and mariculture purposes.

It is also suggested that an Ocean Development Authority on the lines of the existing Island Development Authority be set up and empowered to achieve the task of optimal and efficient exploitation of the economic wealth lying within the exclusive economic zone of Lakshadweep.

Tourism

Lakshadweep, nestled in the Arabian Sea, away from the usual hustle and bustle, offers tremendous scope for development and promotion of tourism, but subject to the constraints of ecological considerations on the one hand and national security concerns, on the other. Keeping such limitations in mind, a perspective for tourism development of Lakshadweep needs to be worked out. Suggestions would include upgradation of the aqua sports centre in Kadmat, development of aqua sports facilities in Minicoy, theme park and beach resort in Andrott Island, fun and entertainment complex in Cheriyam Island on the lines of Sentosa Island of Singapore, projection of the historical significance of Amini besides developing it as a resort complex, improvement of the infrastructure in Kavaratti in view of its status as the UT Headquarters, etc. In all such efforts, the concept of 'Back to Nature' can be highlighted as the essence of Lakshadweep. The experience of tourism promotion efforts in Mauritius and Maldives can also be made use of.

The strength of Lakshadweep for growth as a tourism centre lies in its location, the scenic beauty, nature and climate, the blue water lagoons, the coral reefs, the unspoilt virgin beaches, the calm waters ideal for water sports such as diving, snorkelling, windsurfing and parasailing. Add to this the many rare species of marine life and perhaps the biggest natural underwater zoo in the world that the islands and the adjoining biodiversity offer. These factors are further helped by the low crime rate of the islands and the helpful and friendly attitude of the local people.

Tourist arrivals have been hovering around 4,000 in the recent years. There has, in fact, been a small decline, more noticeable in the case of foreigners. Inadequate communication facilities and restrictions on the visitors are the main reasons behind the low level of tourism activities in these islands. A recent study report has projected significant growth in tourist arrivals in the coming years, reaching the level of close to 38,000 by 2020-21. However, careless growth of tourism is likely to harm the fragile ecosystem of the region. The example of the Maldives needs to be studied carefully and modified appropriately to work out a model for appropriate growth and development of tourism in Lakshadweep. Cruise-based tourism, wherein the visitors spend their days in the islands but retire to their ships for the night, appears to be a suitable model for Lakshadweep.

The approach to the growth and development of tourism in this territory should keep in focus the need to maintain and nurture, besides the ecology, the local culture and traditions. This is particularly important as the very small size of the local population and the rather rudimentary level of the local economy makes them vulnerable to external influences that come along with modernity. Analysis of the strengths, weaknesses, opportunities and threats of the tourism potential in Lakshadweep Islands gives a useful insight into the possible approaches. The tourism policy should enable the economic benefits to reach the people of the islands.

Industries

Industrial activity in Lakshadweep centres around coir and fish. Though the territory abounds in corals, picking them is prohibited on ecological grounds, thus leaving no scope for harnessing them for any economic activity. Though a large amount of fish is captured and vast unexploited potential exists in the islands, present processing facilities are not adequate. Fish-based industries such as canning, oil extraction and pickle production may be geared up. Value addition by processing, minimising spoilage and avoiding glut in the market will certainly increase returns to the fishing families. However, the ecological parameters may be taken into account before initiating any industry.

Ecological and environment considerations prevent the setting up of large-scale industrial units in these islands as has been done for the mainland states. The strategy for industrialisation of Lakshadweep will have to focus on fisheries and agro-based units of medium and small-scales.

Savings and Investments

Detailed data on savings and investment in various sectors particularly in the household sector and the private sector are not available. The available information indicates that private sector capital investments are low and the bulk of investment is in the government/public sector. Investments from the banking and insurance sectors in Lakshadweep is also low. It is possible that the more affluent individuals and institutions keep their investments in the main land based institutions. As for the government budgetary expenditure, more than 70 per cent is in terms of revenue expenditure, leaving a small amount for capital investment. The strategy for economic growth of the region lies in tapping the savings of the private sector and also in attracting private sector investment. Tourism, shipping, air services, industry, fishery etc. offer ample scope for the purpose.

Infrastructure

The island territory of Lakshadweep is connected with the mainland primarily through the seaways, which are also the principal means of inter-island connectivity. Air services are also available, but largely as a privileged and contingency service. The study found the internal road network in the islands to be reasonably good. However, special attention seems to be warranted in respect of shipping and air services. The study has also brought out the need for special attention to the power, public health, sanitation, medical care and telecommunication sectors.

Energy

The entire requirement for electricity in Lakshadweep is generated locally, in view of the distance of the islands from the mainland. The existing power generation capacity of 9720 kW falls short of the requirement of 12410 kW. About five per cent of the power supplies are met through solar powered generation systems and the rest, through diesel based systems. The latter type of system offers an ecologically preferable solution as the need to burn diesel is obviated. It is desirable to set up more systems for power generation through alternative sources such as solar, wind and oceanic currents, which have proved successful in trial/pilot efforts. As the solar energy based power generation systems require large and uncovered areas, such plants can be set up in the lagoons. Biomass based generation, including through coir residues, also need to be explored. The option of bio-diesel, which has proved to be far more eco-friendly, needs to be popularised.

At the household level, arrangements for smokeless and fuel efficient *chullas*, energy efficient stoves and pressure cookers should be popularised, to bring about savings in energy consumption, besides offering a healthier alternative system for cooking.

Shipping Services

The principal means of communication between the islands of Lakshadweep and the mainland as well as among the various islands of Lakshadweep, for passenger and cargo services, is the shipping services. Passenger services are operated entirely by the government, whereas the cargo services are by private operators (85 per cent) and by government (15 per cent). As against a population of 60,650 of Lakshadweep (2001), the annual passenger traffic stood at about 1.56 lakh and cargo traffic, at 1.86 lakh metric tonnes (2002-03) and the projected traffic for 2014-15 is placed at about 3 lakh and 3.9 lakh MT, respectively. A committee was set up in February 2000 to examine the projected demands on the shipping services and to suggest suitable measures to meet them. The committee recommended acquisition of three passenger ships for island-mainland services and three high speed ferries for inter-island services, improvement in landing and embarkation/disembarkation facilities, procurement of oil barge and LPG ship etc. These recommendations need to be implemented in a time bound manner. Dry-dock facilities are required, but there is no land available for the purpose. Hence, the scope for setting up a dry-dock in the lagoons, subject to ecological impact studies.

Roads

Intra-island movement of humans and goods is heavily dependent on roads. Additionally, good roads are essential for promotion of tourism too. All the islands of Lakshadweep are serviced by all weather cement concrete roads providing at least the main connectivity within the respective islands. Each island is serviced by a main road and branch routes. The situation in this regard seems satisfactory. Road construction and maintenance is handled by the administration as well as by the District *Panchayat*.[1]

More attention is required for maintenance of the roads than construction of fresh ones, as the main roads are largely in place. Some interior roads are required, which would include those along the wharfs, coastal ring roads and other linking roads. Arrangement for public transport could also be considered, to facilitate the movement of the people as well as goods. Use of electricity and natural gas based transport vehicles needs to be considered, as diesel and petrol pose environmental hazards in terms of transportation, storage and handling. This will, however, call for studies regarding transportation, storage and handling of gas including compressed natural gas (CNG).

Telecommunication

The existing facilities for telephone and telegraph services, including mobile telephony, are in general adequate. However, some of these facilities could be augmented, such as internet PCOs and extension of WLL system. Some islands have reported waitlists for new telephone connections, which too may be addressed. The high level of literacy among the islanders will enable implementation of extensive Internet connectivity among the islands.

Civil Aviation

The airways connectivity between Lakshadweep and the mainland is through a small (15-seater) airplane operated by the Indian Airlines between Agatti and Cochin/Goa. Lakshadweep Administration operates a helicopter service mainly for emergency evacuation purposes. These facilities have turned out to be inadequate as well as costly. It is necessary to introduce a 50-seater aircraft between the mainland and Lakshadweep and also rationalise the fare structure so as to make it not only affordable but attractive too. Side by side, the main airstrip in Agatti should be developed and other (bigger) islands also provided with connectivity with 5-6 seater Beach Islander aircraft. These will facilitate normal passenger traffic and also encourage tourism activities.

---

1. Details of construction of rural roads under the Eighth, Ninth and Tenth Plans is placed at Annexure A-18.

Managing Human Development

Population Density

The population of Lakshadweep as per the 2001 Census is 60,650 giving a density of 1,894 per sq km that is far higher than the average for India (324). The decadal growth rate during the recent years (1971-2001) has been in the range of 17 to 32 per cent. It may be difficult for Lakshadweep to sustain such high population density and growth in terms of infrastructure and ecological balance. Any plans for economic development of Lakshadweep should take note of this factor.

Gender Ratio

The gender ratio in the overall population as well as for the population in the age group of 0 to 4, as per the 2001 Census, stood at 947 and 974 per 1000 male, the corresponding figures for India as a whole being 933 and 927, respectively. Despite the gender ratio being better than the all-India average, there is still scope for improving it further.

Literacy and Education

The population of Lakshadweep has a very high rate of literacy (87.52 per cent), which should provide hopes for accelerated development of the region. There are also claims that most of the remaining illiterates are, in fact, capable of reading and writing non-Eighth Schedule local languages such as Arabic or Mahl.

There are no institutions of professional/higher level of education. In 2005-06, the administration has set up degree level University Centres of Calicut University in the three islands of Kadmat, Andrott and Kavaratti. It appears infeasible as of now to set up such institutions on full-fledged scale, owing to the small population of the territory. Facilities to support the island students pursuing higher studies in mainland institutions need to be extended. This includes provision of hostel facilities, besides the existing schemes for providing reserved seats as well as financial support

Public Health and Medical Care

In respect of public health, Lakshadweep faces a very high rate of prevalence of certain types of communicable diseases such as acute respiratory infection, acute diarrhoeal disease and pneumonia. Some of these arise owing to lack of adequate systems for supply of safe drinking water and disposal of sewage. In the absence of proper arrangements for both, households have made individual arrangements of open wells to store drinking water and pits for disposal of household waste. The sandy and porous nature of the soil, and the close proximity of households have led to frequent contamination of the sources of drinking water, resulting in the large-scale prevalence of waterborne diseases. Therefore, supply of safe water for drinking, arrangements for adequate disposal of municipal waste and a proper study of the causes and solutions for the high prevalence of acute respiratory infection, deserves serious attention. Simultaneously, special efforts needs to be launched to bring about greater awareness among the general population on the need and scope for preventive measures against such infectious diseases.

Infrastructure for medical and healthcare for the general public is entirely in the folds of the government in Lakshadweep. There are, by and large, adequate facilities for general medical care. However, there is an acute shortage of specialist medical personnel. The island administration has launched telemedicine facilities in collaboration with a Cochin based hospital. This arrangement needs to be strengthened and extended to all the islands.

While it may be difficult to provide for the availability of various medical super-specialists in all the specialised disciplines, yet arrangements are required to ensure that specialist medical personnel in the key disciplines such as those dealing with gastronomy, respiratory diseases, radiology and pathology, are available in the islands on some days of the month regularly, on a visiting basis.

Drinking Water and Sanitation

The islands face acute shortage of potable water supply. The available sources are almost invariably unprotected open wells, which get contaminated by the adjoining soak pits due to the porous soil and unscientific construction of the soak pits. This has led to large-scale prevalence of communicable diseases such as diarrhoea and pneumonia. There is an urgent need for provision of safe drinking water to the people. Various options for providing safe drinking water in Lakshadweep have been examined and recommended. The desalination technology, tried and tested on a pilot basis by the NIOT in Chennai, for converting saline water into potable water, has been introduced in Kavaratti too. Based on the experience of this plant, such plants should be set up in other islands as well. There is also a case for making rainwater harvesting system mandatory for all buildings. It would be worthwhile to extend budgetary subsidies for such construction. The quality of drinking water being consumed from various sources also needs to be regularly monitored.

Employment Generation

The level of unemployment in Lakshadweep is significant, as indicated by the Work Participation Rate of 25.33 per cent as against the all-India average of 39.26 (2001 Census). The classification pattern of workers indicates that about 6 per cent are in household industries, none in agriculture or industries and 94 per cent in "Other" sectors. This skewed distribution of the work force is surprising. As against a population of 60,650 (2001), the number of registered job seekers as on 1.12.2003 was as high as 10,946. It is also observed that the unemployment rate for females was higher than that for males, for the urban as well as rural areas. There are, however, claims that many of the persons registered as unemployed are actually employed in the private sector but still report themselves as unemployed in pursuit of government jobs. A careful review of the live register is, therefore, called for.

The strategy for employment generation needs to focus on fisheries, tourism, fisheries and coconut/coir based industries and agro-processing. The high level of literacy and education prevalent among the islanders should be utilised to bring in job opportunities based on IT and call centres. While these activities will remain in the hands of the private sector, Government should facilitate the process.

Poverty and Inequality

Over the 20 year period, that is, 1981 to 2000, the poverty ratio for the country declined by about 41 per cent whereas in the case of Lakshadweep, it declined by 63 per cent. The most recent poverty ratio of Lakshadweep at 15.60 per cent compares very favourably with the all-India figure of 26.10. The pattern of distribution of the expenditure of the households indicates that the inequalities in Lakshadweep are not only among the lowest in the country, but have also declined during the last decade.

Biodiversity and Environment Protection

Current Status and Challenges

The ecology of Lakshadweep islands comprise not merely the landmass, but the continuum of the ocean, the reef, lagoons and shores. The deep seas are host to an innumerable variety of flora and fauna, like most other oceans. The reef and the lagoons, however, offer uniqueness to the ecology of these islands, primarily due to the corals and the inhabiting polyps. The vegetation of the reef and the lagoons comprises mainly the strand corals, of 78 enumerated species of which the blue coral 'heliophora' comprise about 80 per cent. The available (listed) fauna include sponges (41 species), turtles (4 species), fishes (601 species), birds (101 species) and echinoderms (10 species). The landmass is practically covered fully by coconut palms in the inhabited as well as uninhabited islands.

The islanders draw resources from the land, the lagoon, reefs and the deep sea. The reefs and lagoons provide them with their basic energy needs. These include construction materials, food and cash income. Fishing and coconut cultivation are the mainstay of the economy and are important source of protein. Scuba diving tourism is an emerging industry. Fisheries comprise commercial fishing in the deep sea and subsistence fishing in the lagoon using a variety of traditional methods. The island households use all the ecosystems within their vicinity but they put nothing back in terms of management of these free natural resources. The problems of managing these resources emanate primarily because of the rapid growth of the island population and the incidental factors. The human population which was 13,882 in 1901 rose to 31,810 in 1971 and to 60,650 in 2001. The increase in population has created an ecosystem of its own in these islands. This man-made ecosystem has to depend on the natural ecosystem involving land, lagoon and sea for meeting its livelihood.

The biodiversity of the Lakshadweep Islands faces many kinds of pressures and challenges from various quarters. These include the pollution of the oceans due to the discharge of waste and fumes from the navigating shipping vessels, while the reefs and the lagoons face a similar onslaught from the ferryboats. Overexploitation of the fishery resources in the adjoining reaches and poaching by foreign vessels add to these problems. The land, which is a thin strip of coral sand, faces multifaceted problems. These include collection of jelly (accretion deposits of coral sand/boulders) for construction, loss of natural vegetation including the stragglers like *Mulli* (*Spinifex*) and *Ipomoea* which prevent erosion, monoculture of coconut which takes away all the nutrients, use of pesticides and chemicals which causes toxicity of the soil and the fragile ground water, construction activities which bring more land under concrete, and erosion of the beach. The availability of sweet water bodies in these islands too is being subject to a variety of stresses. Some of these have been identified as the non-regeneration of water lens, highly extractive usage of ground water with pumps and tanks, pollution with diesel from the electricity generating units, concretisation of land which reduces the area available for rainwater to percolate, wastage of water and mixing of sewage with freshwater lens.

Fortunately, such threats can be mitigated through concerted efforts. But for this, there has to be complete rethinking and an honest and critical dialogue between planners, the people, scientists and other groups interested in the survival of the islands.

Afforestation Measures

Existing information reveals that there are no forestry resources available for the well-being of the local community. Further, on the basis of per capita requirements, the expected demand for fuel wood could be around 1,75,000 tonnes and for fodder it could be approximately 70,000 tonnes. The supply of fuel wood is expected to be only 20-30 per cent or even less, particularly from the agricultural residues including the supply of fuel materials from coconut plantations. Similarly, only 15-20 per cent of fodder requirement can be met from the existing biological sources. However, introduction of forestry components having potential of fuel wood, small timber, medicinal value, biofuel, etc. can be envisaged for sustainable development in this island ecosystem. The main islands are covered with green vegetation mainly comprising coconut and this green cover is up to 80 to 86 per cent. As such, practically no land is available for forestry operations. However, trees of forestry/agroforestry values such as casurina, moringa, sesbania, jatropha, cashew and such others are important in the context of greening the islands of Lakshadweep and environment protection.

Traditional forestry activities are not feasible in Lakshadweep as most of the landmass is already covered with coconut plantations. However, there is adequate scope for agro and farm forestry. The suggested species are *casurina equisetopholia* (for fuel, poles and pulpwood), medicinal plants such as *emblica* (*amla*), *sesbania*, *gloriosa*, etc.

Shore Protection

The problem of coastal erosion, which is quite widespread in Lakshadweep, is currently being tackled through laying a mesh of concrete tetrapods, which restricts access to and enjoyment of the beaches, besides looking ugly. A more appropriate solution recommended is through cultivation of seaweed and through coastal forestry. Afforestation measures recommended for Lakshadweep include, besides coastal forestry, farm forestry, agroforestry and home gardens. The option of placing shore protection devices such as tetrapods on the reefs instead of on the shores, may also be studied, as this would enable unhindered access to the shores. The side effects of casurina plantations on turtle nesting and other natural phenomena may also be carefully studied.

Protection of the Coral Reef and the Lagoons

The lagoons and atolls of Lakshadweep are home to a wide variety of organisms including crabs, lobsters, sponges, echinoderm, turtles, tuna and other fishes and birds. These are in a delicate equilibrium with the human beings and their related activities. Any plan for development of these islands needs to take into account the fall out on the biodiversity too. The strategy for this purpose would consist mainly of protection of corals and documenting their diversity and the impact of any developmental activities on the corals, listing of all bio-resources, which include flora and fauna, and recording of their diversity, frequency and density, protecting the habitat of migratory birds, educating the local people about the importance of ecological issues and enlisting their support in conservation activities, and encouraging the indigenous system of medicine and developing an action plan for growing medicinal plants for local use. The creation of a Bio-resource Board for Lakshadweep and its planning and monitoring is suggested.

Protection of the coral reef too deserves high priority in Lakshadweep. Coral reefs along with fringes of mangrove and the sea-grass bed environment constitute the natural protective mechanism for the ecosystem of these islands. Above all, coral reefs provide Lakshadweep its unique identity. The threat to the coral reef ecosystem comes from natural as well as man-made phenomena. It is necessary to develop a monitoring mechanism for the former and, for the latter, preventive measures in relation to sewerage discharge, solid waste disposal, chemical pollution and overexploitation of sea life including fish and marine invertebrates.

Governance Issues

As a centrally administered territory, Lakshadweep does not have its own legislative bodies, though it does have local bodies in the form of *panchayats*. The entire range of governance related issues is handled by the bureaucracy led by the Administrator who is appointed under Article 239 of the Constitution, along with the two-tier PRI set up. The PRI representatives need to be consulted on various policy issues that affect the economy and life of the islands and the inhabitants. The study points out the scope and need for improvements in certain key areas relating to development of an economic database, functioning of the *Panchayati Raj* bodies and disaster management issues.

Economic and Social Database

Lakshadweep is one of the few units of administration in the country for which a proper database leading to construction of the Gross and the Net State Domestic Product is not available. This makes it difficult to examine certain critical dimensions of the economic activities in the territory within a short time frame. The first and foremost requirement is to set up full fledged Department of Economics and Statitistics (DES) so as to build up a proper database for construction of the Gross and the Net State Domestic Product for Lakshadweep. This will enable preparation of a suitable strategy for development of the territory with a comparative picture of other States and Union Territories in the background.

It is necessary to strengthen the arrangements for protection of the biodiversity of the region. This would require augmenting the monitoring mechanism and periodic updating of the database relating to the ecology of the region. Involvement of the people in these efforts by way of awareness building measures and by giving suitable powers and responsibilities, to the local bodies, may also be considered.

The island economy depends to a considerable extent on marine fisheries. However, the fishermen do not have access to scientifically derived information on the movement of fish schools and are thus not able to go in for optimal fishing operations. It is possible and highly desirable to make arrangements for monitoring the availability of fish schools in different reaches of the ocean, by using satellite imagery, SONAR system, etc.

There is a strong need to prepare and maintain database on the status and health of the soils, water, coral reefs and other natural resources available in the various islands. Such a database needs to be updated regularly and disseminated to all concerned, including the local people.

Funds may be earmarked from the administration's annual budget for conducting such studies leading to creation and maintenance of such a database from time to time, through specialist institutions. Local educated youth may also be engaged for such studies as research personnel.

Fiscal Management

The per capita outlay for the Tenth Plan for Lakshadweep is Rs. 72,118 which is the highest among all States and UTs. The dominant sectors for plan outlay are Transport (mainly, Ports and Shipping), Fisheries and Tourism. While these sectors deserve the kind of attention that they receive now in the Five Year Plans, certain other issues namely of unemployment and of public health—drinking water supply, sanitation and specialist healthcare—need greater attention.

The revenue expenditure of the Lakshadweep Administration is about 12 times the revenue receipts. For instance, in 2002-03 (R.E.), its revenue expenditure was Rs. 215.55 crore, whereas revenue receipts were only Rs. 18.32 crore. Of the total budgetary expenditure, capital expenditure forms just about 20 to 25 per cent and the rest is expended on revenue account. There is a strong case to review the trends in the budgetary expenditure in Lakshadweep to bring about greater share for capital expenditure. Also, certain common taxes such as sales tax and tourist tax may be introduced to bring in greater self-reliance in public expenditure.

Panchayati Raj Institutions

The entire area of Lakshadweep is classified as rural and, therefore, it has no urban local bodies but only Panchayati Raj Institutions (PRIs) in a two-tier setup. There is 1 District *Panchayat* for the whole of the territory and 10 Village (*Dweep*) *Panchayats*, one for each inhabited island. Many functions have been transferred to these bodies along with funds and staff. There is, however, a need to review the effectiveness of such transfers. It is also appropriate to work out a functional linkage mechanism between the V(D)Ps and the DP, to bring about synergy of efforts and resources.

Panchayats have been empowered to levy taxes, but they are yet to exploit these powers fully to mobilise financial resources. It is also possible for the *panchayats* to levy some more taxes to raise resources for implementing developmental activities.

The PRIs can be fruitfully associated with many more developmental activities, such as watershed management, development and propagation of bio-manures and biogas plants, social forestry, systematic conservation and exploitation of the biodiversity resources including minor forest produce, fuel and fodder development, dredging and cleaning of water bodies, waste water collection and disposal, development of non-conventional energy sources and various schemes for technological advancement of the village communities.

Disaster Management

Lakshadweep has been identified as susceptible to a variety of natural disasters. These include sudden but predictable hazards such as cyclones and floods, slow and predictable hazards such as drought and coral bleaching, sudden but unpredictable hazards such as earthquakes and tsunamis, besides other disasters such as storms, epidemics, oil spills, fires, explosions, etc. Some of these, including cyclones, storms and epidemics such as malaria, gastroenteritis and diarrhoea, have occurred in the past. The severity of damage to life and property in these islands gets accentuated owing to their relatively unique features such as high density of population, proximity of economic activities to the shore, and poor sanitation arrangements. The suggested model for disaster management in Lakshadweep is the expand-contract model wherein prevention, preparedness, relief and rehabilitation are carried on as a continuous process with provision for varying the relative degrees of emphasis in case of actual occurrence of a disaster. The possible adverse impact of development projects on the ecological balance of the territory, leading to occurrence of a disaster, should be continuously observed and monitored. A sub-centre of the National Centre for Disaster Management may be set up in Lakshadweep. The Administration should prepare a Disaster Management Plan, in consultation with the related government departments, people's representatives, NGOs involved with the issue and the various expert bodies. The Plan should be periodically reviewed and updated.

Modernisation of Administration

The scattered nature of the islands and the difficult means of inter-island communication in Lakshadweep call for innovative administrative arrangements. The interaction of departmental heads with the inhabitants of the various islands needs to be arranged through videoconferencing systems on a regular basis. Government offices themselves need to be completely computerised and interconnected through inter-networking. Complete e-Governance should be promoted.

Ecological monitoring of the various natural assets, on shore as well as in the sea, is yet another necessity for Lakshadweep. The fact that the entire islands are based on corals, which are highly susceptible to ecological disturbances and environmental pollution, makes it necessary to monitor the ecological parameters of the region regularly. A suitable administrative arrangement for this purpose, which involves subject matter specialists, local officers as well as people's representatives, needs to be created.

The Lakshadweep Administration needs to be better equipped to undertake techno-economic and environmental appraisal of various developmental and welfare projects, with a view to ensure their suitability for the islands.

Creating awareness among the masses about their rights and responsibilities under various general and special laws and schemes is essential. To an extent, this is achievable through the system of representative local bodies. However, there are instances of serious shortcomings in the matter of public awareness. Large-scale ignorance about waterborne diseases, emanating mostly out of the pollution caused by the residents in their own backyards, is a case in point. It is necessary to make innovative efforts on a sustainable basis, to bring about awareness among the people in respect of various important issues of health, social and legal rights, gender issues and environmental matters.

Bibliography

Abraham, John (1987). *Lakshadweep: Economy and Society*, Inter India Publications.

Administration of the Union Territory of Lakshadweep, *Framework of Disaster Management Plan in Lakshadweep.*

———. *Lakshadweep and Its People 2002-2003.*

———. *Lakshadweep Development Report.*

———. (various years). *Lakshadweep Administration Annual Reports*, 1999-00, 2001-02, 2002-03, Kavaratti.

———. (1990). *Report of the Economic Census.*

Ahmed, M.F. (1997). "Asia-Pacific Forestry Sector Outlay Study: In-Depth Country Study India", *Working Paper No.* APFS/OS/WP/26, FAO, Rome.

Banerjee, U. (1996). "A Study in Forestry Extension", in G.L Ray, K. Bhattacharya and S.K. Maity (eds.), Calcutta: Naya Prokash.

Bharat Sanchar Nigam Ltd. *Brief for the Study Group II of Estimates Committee of Lok Sabha Lakshadweep 2003*, Kerala Telecommunications.

Bhargava, B.S. and Avinash Samal (2001). *Lakshadweep–Towards Decentralized Governance*, New Delhi: Kanishka Publishers, Distributors.

Bhargava, P. and V.J. Nair (1999). "Lakshadweep: Floristic Diversity and Conservation Strategies in India-In the Context of States and Union Territories, Vol. III, *Botanical Survey of India.*

Census Commissioner of India (2001). "Tables on Houses, Household Amenities and Assets", Census.

Census of India (2001). *Provisional Population Totals: Series-1.*

———. (2001). *Series 32: Lakshadweep, Provisional Population Totals*, Paper 3.

Chandra, Satish, B. Arunachalam and V. Suryanarayan (eds.) (1993). *The Indian Ocean and its Islands*, Sage Publication.

Datta, S.K. and M. Roy (1996). "Government Forest Service Training in India - Recommendation for Change", *Unasylva No.* 184: Special Issue–Forestry Extension.

Department of Economics & Statistics (various years). *Lakshadweep: Basic Statistics 1987-88, 1993-94, 2001-2002*,. Lakshadweep Administration.

Department of Environment and Forests (2002). *Lakshadweep Biodiversity Strategy and Action Plan Report*, UT of Lakshadweep, May, Kavaratti.

Department of Science, Technology & Environment, *Lakshadweep Environment Impact Assessment of Ninth Five Year Plan 1997-2002.*

———. *Environment Impact Assessment of Tenth Five Year Plan 2002-2007*, Lakshadweep, in collaboration with the Centre for Earth Science Studies, Thiruvananthapuram.

Development Commissioner for Small Scale Industries (1993). *Report of the Expert Group on Prospects of Rubber, Coir and Boat Building Industries*, Government of India, New Delhi.

District Collectorate. *Database of District Disaster Management Plan, 2002-2003*, Puri.

Forest Survey of India (1997). *State of Forests: Report 1997*, Dehradun.

George, Alex (1993). "Traditional Navigation and Trade in Lakshadweep, 1850-1950" in Satish Chandra, B. Arunachalam, V. Suryanarayan (eds.), *The Indian Ocean and its Islands*, Sage Publication.

Government of India (GoI) (various issues). *Economic Survey.*

———. (various years). *Draft Five Year Plans*: Seventh to Tenth, of the Union Territory of Lakshadweep.

———. (1990). *Energy Studies of Island Communities with an Emphasis on Time/Energy Availability for Women's Need*, Vol. 31, Sponsored by the Department of Science & Technology, August, New Delhi.

———. (2003), *Selected Educational Statistics 2001-2002*, Plan Monitoring & Statistics Division, Department of Secondary & Higher Education, Ministry of Human Resource Development, New Delhi, 2003.

———. (2003). *India 2002*, Publications Division, New Delhi.

Gowda, Srinivasa (ed.) (1997). *Infrastructure and Economic Growth*, New Delhi: Deep & Deep Publication.

The Hindustan Times, December 25, 2003.

Hoon, Vineeta (2002). *Socio-Economic Assessment and Monitoring of Coral Reefs of Agatti Island–UT of Lakshadweep*, Chennai: Centre for Action Research on Environment Science and Society.

Joseph, A. (2003). "Learning from Latur", in *The Hindu*, October 26.

Joshi, B.M. (1990). *Infrastructure and Economic Development in India*, Ashish Publishing House, New Delhi.

Karanim, R. and B. Arunachalam (1993). "Traditions of Shipbuilding in Lakshadweep and Minicoy" in Satish Chandra, B. Arunachalam, V. Suryanarayan (eds.), *The Indian Ocean and its Islands*, Sage Publication.

Madras Naturalists Society (1991). *Pitti Island Lakshadweep–An Ornithological Study.*

Maragos, J. (1998). "Status of Coral Reefs of the Southwest and East Pacific: Melanesia and Polynesia", in Clive Wilkinson (ed.), *Status of Coral Reefs of the World: 1998*, Australian Institute of Marine Science, pp. 79-88.

Maragos, J., Charles Birkland and Gregor Hodgson (1998). "Status of Coral Reefs in the Northwest Pacific Ocean: Micronesia and East Asia", in Clive Wilkinson (ed.), *Status of Coral Reefs of the World: 1998*, Australian Institute of Marine Science, pp.89-108.

Ministry of Environment of Forests (1988). *National Forestry Policy 1988*, Government of India, New Delhi.

Ministry of Health & Family Welfare (various issues). *Health Information of India*, Central Bureau of Health Intelligence, Government of India.

Ministry of Home Affairs (various years). *Demands for Grants*, 1999-2000 to 2003-04, Government of India.

Ministry of Shipping. *Master Plan on Harbour Facilities Required for Lakshadweep upto 2025 A.D.*, Lakshadweep Harbour Works, GoI, Kavaratti.

Ministry of Statistics and Programme Implementation (2001). *Statistical Abstract of India 2001*, Government of India.

Ministry of Works & Housing (1983). *National Master Plan–India, International Drinking Water Supply and Sanitation Decade 1981-1990*, Government of India, July, New Delhi.

Mukerji, Sarit Kumar (1992). *Islands of India*, Publications Division, Ministry of Information and Broadcasting, Government of India.

Murkot, Ramunny (1999). "India's Coral Islands in the Arabian Sea-Lakshadweep", Lakshadweep Socio Cultural Research Commission.

National Bureau of Soil Survey and Land Use Planning (1997). *Soils of Lakshadweep for Land Use Planning*, Publ. 70, Bangalore: ICAR Regional Centre.

NEERI (1996). *Development of Comprehensive Waste Management System for Lakshadweep Islands*, October, Nagpur.

Negi, S.S. (1996). "Transfer of Forestry Research Results to Users. An Analysis Pertaining to India", *Van Vigyan*, Vol. 34(3), pp.119-123.

Planning Commission (2001). *Report on the Task Force on Panchayati Raj Institutions*, December, New Delhi.

———. (2002). *National Human Development Report 2001*.

———. (2002). *Tenth Five-Year Plan (2002-2007)*.

———. (2002). *Report of the Steering Committee on Drinking Water Supply & Sanitation (Rural & Urban) for the Tenth Five Year Plan*, Government of India, February, New Delhi, downloaded from the Internet

Reserve Bank of India. *Annual Report 2002-03*, Mumbai.

S.J. College of Engineering (1999). *A Comprehensive Design of Wastewater Treatment System for Kavaratti Island, U. T. of Lakshadweep*, Final Report, Mysore.

Saigal, Omesh (1990). *Lakshadweep*, National Book Trust, New Delhi. The author had worked as Administrator of Lakshadweep during 1982-85.

Saxena, N.C. (1992). "Farm Forestry and Land Use in India: Some Policy", *Ambio*, Vol. 21, pp.420-425.

Saldanha C.J. (1989). *Andaman, Nicobar and Lakshadweep–An Environment Impact Assessment*.

Tata Services Ltd. (2003). *Statistical Outline of India 2002-2003*, Department of Economics and Statistics, Mumbai.

UNDP (1992). *An Overview of Disaster Management*, 2nd Edition, Disaster Management Training Programme.

UT of Lakshadweep, "Water Supply and Sanitation Sector document", *Eighth Five Year Plan (1992-1997)*.

———. "Water Supply and Sanitation Sector document", *Tenth Five Year Plan (2002-2007)*.

Vadivelu *et al.* (1993). "Soils of Lakshadweep Islands", *Research Bulletin* No.9, Central Agricultural Research Institute, Port Blair, Andamans.

Victoria, L. (2002). *Impact Assessment Study of the Orissa Disaster Management Project*, Prepared for the Asian Disaster Preparedness Centre, Thailand. *http://www.adpc.ait.ac.th/infores/adpc-documents/orissaeval.pdf*.

Report of the First Finance Commission for the Union Territories, August 1998.

Webliography

http://mospi.gov.in/cso_test1.htm: Central Statistical Organisation Website.

http://www.adpc.ait.ac.th/infores/adpc-documents/orissaeval.pdf: Victoria, L. (2002). Impact Assessment Study of the Orissa Disaster Management Project, Prepared for the Asian Disaster Preparedness Centre, Thailand.

http://www.education.nic.in/htmlweb/edusta_pt3.htm: The website of the Department of Secondary & Higher Education, of HRD, GoI.

http://cbhidghs.nic.in: The website of the Central Bureau of Health Intelligence, Ministry of H&FW, GoI.

http://coralreef.gov: U.S. Coral Reef Task Force, South Pacific Region-Executive Summary.

http://www.coralreef.org: the website of the International Coral Reef Information Network (ICRIN).

http://envfor.nic.in/unccd/chap-6-ii.pdf: Measures to Combat Desertification and Mitigate the Effects of Drought. Planning, Programmes and Institutional Framework.

http://www.gcrmn.org: The website of the International Global Coral Reef Monitoring Network.

http://www.grif.umontreal.ca/pages/i-rec%20papers/nehal.PDF: Karim, Nehal. *Options for Cyclone protection: Bangladesh Context*.

http://www.icran.org: The website of the International Coral Reef Action Network (ICRAN).

www.indiadisasters.org: "Cyclones: Trapped in a Spin Cycle", *India Disaster Report*, pp.181-190.

http://www.iucn.org: The website of the International Conservation Union.

http://lakshadweep.nic.in: The website of the Lakshadweep Administration.

http://ioc.unesco.org/iocweb/index.php: The website of the International Oceanographic Commission of the UNESCO.

http://www.usgcrp.gov: National Assessment Synthesis Team (2000). "Overview: Islands in the Caribbean and the Pacific", in *Climate Change Impacts on the United States: The Potential Consequences of Climate Variability andCchange*, US Global Change Research Program.

http://www.local.gov.za/DCD/dcdlibrary/dmg/dmgindex.html: Disaster Management Guidelines for Municipalities.

Annexures

ANNEXURE A-1

A Note on the Different Types of Tenancy Arrangements Prevalent in Lakshadweep Islands Prior to British Rule

Nadapu Tenancy

Nadapu tenancy was prevalent in Agatti, Amini, Andrott and Kavaratti islands. Under this system of tenancy, in some islands there were two categories of tenants: one which enjoyed protection from eviction and the other which could be evicted at will. Under this system, the tenant was bound to provide some customary services also, such as working as a crew on the boats, thatching of the boat shed of the *Themi*, repairing his boat and rendering services on occasions of birth, marriage and death in the *Jenmi* house. In return, he was granted a certain number of coconut trees. About 30–40 trees constituted a *Nadapu* where the tenant had a right to plant coconut trees. He was required to pay annual rent in terms of *copra* or cash to the landlord though these terms varied between the islands. The tenant was also completely dependent on the landlord for obtaining from the mainland various goods and articles for daily consumption and for carrying his produce of coconut trees for sale to the mainland markets. Customary tradition mandated that only *Jenmis* could own a sailing boat. The tenant was not paid any remuneration in cash or kind for serving as a sailor on *Jenmi's* boats. The tenant was also charged very high freight, almost double of what was charged from others for carrying his produce to the mainland markets and for bringing his household goods. Thus, the arrangement represented a dual form of exploitation by *Jenmis*—both as landowners as well as *odam* owners. Not only this, as *odam* owners, *Jenmis* also cheated the *Kudiyans* in terms of price realised from sale of *copra* and the consumer goods brought for him. This multilayered web of exploitation led to perpetual indebtedness of the tenant to the *Jenmis* which spanned generations almost on the pattern of bonded labourers of the mainland. It is a different matter that the *odam* owners may also have been cheated by the middlemen in the mainland which resulted in their indebtedness to them and disposal of their produce on terms dictated by their lenders year after year. Perhaps, the *odam* owners squeezed the tenants to compensate for their loss. As happens elsewhere, when the tenants had no means of subsistence, they were forced to borrow stocks of provisions from their landlords. In return, they had to pawn their coconut trees for 10 or 12 years. This implied that the yield from these trees also went to the landlords. Eventually, the tenants would lease the entire coconut trees to the *Jenmis* (landowners) for their inability to pay back the debt. In this manner, the tenants lived a completely dependent existence. As the landlords also never allowed the tenants to work for other land/boat owners, the latter had no scope to earn from any other source.

The lower caste tenants—*Melacheris*—were also subjected to certain forms of social inequalities, such as mandating them to carry out menial jobs, not being allowed to wear shirts or slippers or use umbrellas, being prevented from singing during weddings or other functions, their women not being permitted to wear gold jewellery or silk. With *Jenmis* in complete command of the justice administration system, there was little possibility of any redress of these grievances. *Jenmis* also practised another fraudulent mechanism to exploit the tenants who were able to carry out cultivation successfully since it carried the potential of his economic freedom. The landlord would execute a document handing over the tenant land to somebody else without the knowledge of the former. This obviously led to acrimony and quarrels, ending with the disputes being settled by the elders of the community according to a predetermined strategy. A compromise would be announced as terms of settlement under which some trees were handed over to the person in whose name the document was made. It was in this background that prolonged struggles by *Melacheris* for social equality and economic rights were witnessed in the islands. Only the land reforms carried out by the Lakshadweep Administration closed this sordid chapter of control over land and labour.

In the design of the land reforms carried out, the *Nadapu* tenancy was abolished in 1963 with an agreement between the tenants and *Jenmis*, according to which the latter agreed to transfer ownership of three-fourths of the land and trees to the tenants and the tenants agreed to renounce their rights on the remaining one-fourth of the tenanted lands in favour of the *Jenmis*. This arrangement virtually conferred ownership rights for all practical purposes and can be compared to the purchase of ownership rights by tenants from landowners in various states of the mainland. The property was then subsequently demarcated by the administration and entered into the land records.

Pattom Tenancy

Pattom tenancy represented a temporary arrangement in the form of a contract between the parties under which the tenant had to pay rent but did not render any mandatory service to the landlord. Still he was obliged to carry out some customary functions, like helping the landowner to thatch his house and provide services on occasions of social functions. The landlord, however, had the right to terminate such tenancy at will but was expected to give compensation for the improvements made on the land. There was obviously no security of tenure for the tenant under this arrangement as well though the 'debt bondage' character of agrarian relationship did not seem to operate here.

House Site Tenancy

The House Site tenancy was almost on the pattern of *Kudikidappu* system of Kerala prior to 1970 under which a tenant could build a house on the plot which belonged to the landlord. No rent was charged from the tenant but he was required to render some customary services to the landlord. In case the house was dismantled, the site reverted to the landlord.

Pandaram Lands

Pandaram lands consisted of uncultivated lands in the inhabited islands and the entire area of uninhabited islands was considered by Ali Raja as their private property. These lands were managed by some inhabitants on their behalf. The cultivation was carried out by people of lower castes and there were different patterns of tenancy systems operating in various islands.

After the British took over the Laccadive group of islands in 1875 for failure of Ali Raja to pay annual rent, all *Pandaram* lands were converted into full-fledged government lands. The British divided these lands into plots and leased them out to individuals for making improvements on them subject to payment of tree tax. This was known as the "*Cowle* system". This is how the land in Andrott and Kalpeni were cleared of the jungles and trees were planted. They were auctioned for five years on the specific condition that the lessee would plant a stipulated number of trees. This also carried a condition that in case government ejected the lessee, compensation would be paid for all the trees planted by him. If it was observed that the sufficient number of trees had not been planted on these lands, the lease was cancelled and given to some other eligible lessee. Despite the specific term lease, the arrangement carried for all practical purposes security of tenure. Over a period of time, the system degenerated, as in *Zamindari* areas, and the *Cowledars* started giving lands to subtenants, almost carrying the same terms on which *Jenmi* landlords had imposed lands allotted by them to their tenants. After the land reforms of 1965, occupancy rights with permanent heritable and transferable rights were conferred on the occupants of *Pandaram* lands. Earlier, the annual tree tax charged from *Cowledars* varied and differed between different islands and sometimes within the same island. After the land survey was carried out in 1976, a uniform rate for trees was fixed.

In Minicoy Island, the agrarian structure had a different character. This island had two types of lands, one occupied by villages with a small area near them and the other consisted of *Pandaram* property. The small area near the occupied villages in the first category of land was owned by people belonging to the upper strata of society under an arrangement called "*Valiya Pattom*". The people also were permitted to cultivate the land on the seashore on payment of rent per tree. This was known as "*Athiri Pattom*". The bigger chunk of the landowner was *Pandaram* which was classified as 'common land' carrying communal rights.

The British divided the islands into nine blocks and granted *Cowles* for the village *Pandaram* land and lands held under *Valiya Pattom*. But the people strongly resisted any attempt to permit individualisation of their communal property and, therefore, the area of the South *Pandaram* lands was never leased out. Under a compromise arrangement, people agreed to the arrangement under which these lands were given to the local inhabitants as common property on payment of annual rent. In 1971, as a part of the land reforms programme, these South *Pandaram* lands were subdivided and allotted to nine village chiefs for the collective enjoyment of the people belonging to each village as well as individual families who opted to have lands for themselves. Standardised *pattas* were distributed to these village chiefs and individual families on payment of annual fees. However, new sets of rules specifically for South *Pandaram* lands in Minicoy were enacted with the consent of all the villagers and the village chiefs of two villages where *Pandaram* lands set apart for these two villages were subdivided and allotted to individual families and a registered lease deed of allotment was given to them in 1979. These rules carried the stipulation that this arrangement could be replicated in case of other villages wherever individual families came forward to claim individual allotments.

ANNEXURE A-2

A Note on the Administrative Status of Lakshadweep

At the time of Independence, the northern group of islands (Amindivis) and the southern group (the Laccadives and Minicoy) were under the administration of the Collectors of South Canara and Malabar, respectively. This arrangement continued even after Independence and till the year 1956, when the two administrative units were merged into a single Union Territory and called the Laccadive, Minicoy and Amindivi Islands. The headquarters of the unified territory was initially retained at Cochin and was shifted to Kavaratti in April 1964. The name was changed to 'Lakshadweep' in 1973.

While under British Rule, these islands were declared as a Scheduled District under the Scheduled Districts Act of 1874 and accorded special protection. Under the provisions of this Act, the area so declared was to remain outside the purview of the written laws prevalent in other areas unless any such law was specifically extended to any such area under the relevant clause of this Act. The British Government had held that there was no need to extend sophisticated laws to the comparatively simple society that existed in the Territory. In the year 1912, the judicial administration of these islands was codified in the form of the Laccadive Islands and Minicoy Regulation of 1912. The Scheduled Districts Act of 1874 was repealed by the Government of India Act of 1919, but the special legal protection to these group of islands was continued by declaring these as 'Backward tract' under section 52-A of the Act. The same protection was continued under the Government of India Act of 1935 by declaring these as 'Excluded areas'.

The British Government had imposed restrictions on the entry of outsiders to these islands, under section 38 of the Laccadive Islands and Minicoy Regulation of 1912. Such restrictions have continued to date even after replacement of the Regulation of 1912 by the Lakshadweep (Laws) Regulation 1965.

ANNEXURE A-3

Geographical Area and Population of States and Union Territories in India

	States	*Area ('000 sq km)*	*Population ('000)*			*Population Density (persons/sq km)*		
			2001	*1991*	*1981*	*2001*	*1991*	*1981*
1	Andhra Pradesh	275	75728	66508	53551	275	242	195
2	Arunachal Pradesh	84	1091	865	632	13	10	8
3	Assam	78	26638	22414	18041	342	287	231
4	Bihar	174	82879	86374	69915	476	496	402
5	Goa	4	1344	1170	1008	336	293	252
6	Gujarat	196	50597	41310	34086	258	211	174
7	Haryana	44	21083	16464	12922	479	374	294
8	Himachal Pradesh	56	6077	5171	4281	109	92	76
9	Jammu & Kashmir	101	10070	7719	5987	100	76	59
10	Karnataka	192	52734	44977	37136	275	234	193
11	Kerala	39	31839	29099	25454	816	746	653
12	Madhya Pradesh	443	60385	66181	52179	136	149	118
13	Maharashtra	308	96752	78937	62783	314	256	204
14	Manipur	22	2389	1837	1421	109	84	65
15	Meghalaya	22	2306	1775	1336	105	81	61
16	Mizoram	21	891	690	494	42	33	24
17	Nagaland	17	1989	1210	775	117	71	46
18	Orissa	156	36707	31660	26370	235	203	169
19	Punjab	50	24289	20282	16789	486	406	336
20	Rajasthan	342	56473	44006	34262	165	129	100
21	Sikkim	7	541	406	316	77	58	45
22	Tamil Nadu	130	62111	55859	48408	478	430	372
23	Tripura	10	3191	2757	2053	319	276	205
24	Uttar Pradesh	294	166053	139112	110863	565	473	377
25	West Bengal	89	80221	68078	54581	901	765	613
	Union Territories							
1	A & N Islands	8.0	356	281	189	45	35	24
2	Chandigarh	0.1	901	642	452	9010	6420	4520
3	D & N Haveli	0.5	220	138	104	440	276	208
4	Daman & Diu	0.1	158	102	79	1580	1020	790
5	Delhi	1.5	13783	9421	6220	9189	6281	4147
6	**Lakshadweep**	**0.03**	**61**	**52**	**40**	**1894**	**1625**	**1250**
7	Pondicherry	0.5	974	808	604	1948	1616	1208
	All-India	3166	1027015	846303	683329	324	267	216

Note: (1) The 1981 Census could not be held in Assam. Total population for 1981 has been worked out by interpolation.

(2) The 1991 Census could not be held in Jammu & Kashmir. Total population for J&K as projected by Standing Committee of Experts on Population Projection (October 1989).

Source: Statistical Outline of India 2002-2003, Department of Economics and Statistics, Tata Services Ltd., Mumbai.

ANNEXURE A-4

A. Operational Holdings and Area Operated in Lakshadweep: 1990-1991

Size Class	*No. of Holdings*			*Area Operated*		
Hectare	*No.*	*% to Total*	*Cum. %*	*Hectare*	*% to Total*	*Cum. %*
<0.5	4,475	71.99	71.99	800	30.19	30.19
0.5 to 1.0	1,197	19.26	91.25	773	29.17	59.36
1.0 to 2.0	369	5.94	97.18	489	18.45	77.81
2.0 to 3.0	94	1.51	98.70	216	8.15	85.96
3.0 to 4.0	39	0.63	99.32	128	4.83	90.79
4.0 to 5.0	24	0.39	99.71	101	3.81	94.60
5.0 to 10.0	16	0.26	99.97	98	3.70	98.30
>10.0	2	0.03	100.00	45	1.70	100.00
Total	**6,216**	**100**		**2,650**	**100**	

Source: Lakshadweep: Basic Statistics 2003-04, Table 3 (pp.26), Lakshadweep Administration.

B. Operational Holdings and Area Operated in Lakshadweep: 2000-01 (Provisional)

Size Class	*No. of Holdings*			*Area Operated*		
Hectare	*No.*	*% to Total*	*Cum. %*	*Hectare*	*% to Total*	*Cum. %*
<0.5	8,918	87.35	87.35	1276	46.23	46.23
0.5 to 1.0	833	8.16	95.51	526	19.06	65.29
1.0 to 2.0	323	3.16	98.68	411	14.89	80.18
2.0 to 3.0	71	0.70	99.37	154	5.58	85.76
3.0 to 4.0	28	0.27	99.65	96	3.48	89.24
4.0 to 5.0	19	0.19	99.83	85	3.08	92.32
5.0 to 10.0	15	0.15	99.98	130	4.71	97.03
>10.0	2	0.02	100.00	82	2.97	100.00
Total	**10,209**	**100**		**2,760**	**100**	

Source: *Lakshadweep: Basic Statistics 2003-04,* Table 4 (pp.26), Lakshadweep Administration.

ANNEXURE A-5

Island-wise Brief Description of Soils

A. Minicoy Soils

(i) *Morphological Characteristics:* The soils are moderately deep to very deep with the depth ranging between 80 and 140 cm. The depth of the soil is limited by the water table in the western part and by hard pan in the eastern part of the island. The texture of surface soils is sand in the west and it turns to sandy loam in the east through a transitional central zone with loamy sand texture. The subsoils are loamy sand to sandy. The structure is single grained and develops weak subangular blocks in the surface of pedons situated closer to the eastern coast. All the morphological characteristics show the sign of soil development from west to east.

(ii) *Physical Characteristics:* Generally, the clay content is less than 10 per cent and the percentage of sand is above 90 per cent. The percentage of clay increases up to 16 per cent in the eastern pedons owing to increase in organic matter. The interesting feature is the distribution of sand fractions. The fine and medium sand fractions are higher and the coarse sand is lower in the pedons near the western coast. The situation reverses towards east. The percentage of coarse sand and very coarse sand increases at the cost of fine and medium sand. This may be due to cementation of finer sand to coarse sand particles indicating development with time.

(iii) *Water Retention:* The percentage of water held at 33 kPa ranges between 3 per cent and 16 per cent. The lowest water retention value is recorded in the pedon situated at the western beach and the values increase gradually in the soils situated eastward. This increase in water retention is due to their higher clay and organic matter contents. The overall condition of water retention, however, is very poor and therefore the major part of the rainfall reaches the ground water rapidly through the porous sandy soils. The water held at 1500 kPa ranges between 1 and 6 per cent indicating a very poor water retaining quality of these soils.

(iv) *Physico-chemical Characteristics:* The pH of the soils ranges from 7.90 to 8.70. The lower pH of the surface soils is due to the acids released during decomposition of accumulated organic matter. The electrical conductivity (EC) of the soils is very low and measures less than 0.23 dS/m in 1:2 soil-water suspension. The cations exchange capacity (CEC) is generally low, the surface soils having 3.8 to 8.4 cmol(+)kg^{-1} and the subsoils having 2.5 to 6.8 cmol(+)kg^{-1}. Calcium is dominant among the cations. The notable feature is the very low content of exchangeable potassium ranging between 0.01 and 0.045 cmol(+)kg^{-1}.

(v) *Fertility Status:* The content of calcium carbonate is above 90 per cent. It is almost 100 per cent in the western beach soils and decreases to 91 per cent towards the east indicating soil development. The organic carbon content of the soils is, generally, high ranging between 0.20 and 2.01 per cent. It increases in the pedons from west to east. The organic carbon content, generally, decreases with depth but some of the subsoil horizons also have high organic carbon owing to accumulation of roots biomass. Total nitrogen and total phosphorus are generally high in the soils ranging from 0.04 to 0.45 per cent and from 0.05 to 0.22 per cent, respectively. The total as well as the available potassium are low ranging from 37 to 134 ppm and 4 to 18 ppm, respectively. The available nitrogen and phosphorus are, generally, medium to high in the surface soils ranging from 73 to 270 ppm and from 10 to 16 ppm, respectively. All the nutrients (N,P,K), generally, decrease with depth in association with organic carbon. Organic carbon and the nutrients increase in soils from west to eastward showing soil development.

(vi) *Micronutrients:* These nutrients play an important role in realising high productivity. The content of the DTPA extractable micronutrients is, generally, low in the soils. The surface soils recorded higher content of micronutrients than the subsoils in accordance with organic carbon. Iron, manganese and copper in surface soils ranged from 1.74 to 12.12 ppm, 0.36 to 7.60 ppm and 0.48 to 4.46 ppm, respectively. The content of zinc is very low and ranges from 0.02 to 0.34 ppm. In general, the micronutrients also increase in pedons from west to east and it leads to a belief that accumulation of micronutrients in these soils of 'single mineral-parent material' can be taken as one of the soil forming processes.

(vii) *Microbiological Characteristics:* The population of bacteria, fungi and actinomycetes is high in all the soils. The notable feature is the very high population of actinomycetes ranging from 4.5 to 8.5 lakh CFU/g soil. The high population of actinomycetes indicates the suitability for planting casurina trees and reduced incidence of root rots.

B. Kavaratti Island Soils

(i) *Morphological Characteristics:* The soils are deep to very deep, excessively drained and occur on nearly level to gently sloping land. The depth of the soils is limited by either water table or hard pan. In pedons having hard pan, the cementation occurs just above the water table. The texture, in general, is sandy and ranges up to sandy loam in the surface layers of pedons situated in the central part of the island. The structure of the parent material is single grained, but it develops into fine weak subangular blocky in the surface soils with accumulation of organic matter indicating active soil development. The consistence is loose. Root growth is observed throughout the pedon up to the water table or hard pan which limits the roots. The morphological characteristics such as darkening of soil colour and subsoil hard pan suggest the development of soils in the central and eastern parts of the islands compared to the west where the coral sands are just heaped.

(ii) *Physical Characteristics:* The clay content is low and ranges between 1.5 and 16.7 per cent. It is higher in the surface soils than the subsoil horizons indicating alteration of coarser particles to finer particles, possibly, by the organic acids released during the decomposition of organic matter. The clay content is also higher in pedons situated at the centre of the island than in pedons situated near both the coasts. Consequently, the sand content is lower (77 to 97 per cent) in pedons situated at the centre of the island than in pedons near the coasts (96 to 98.5 per cent). It indicates that the process of weathering is active in the centre of the island than at the fringes. It is also supported by the increase of coarse and very coarse sand in the subsoil horizons at the cost of fine and medium sand. It is interesting to note that a process of disintegration of coral sand goes on in the surface layers whereas a process of aggregation is active in the subsoil layers.

(iii) *Water Retention:* Though the water retention capacity of the soils is very low, the surface soils hold more water than the subsoil layers. The water held at 33 kPa ranges between 13.77 and 20.32 per cent in the surface soils except the soils situated at the western beach which hold only 1.94 per cent water. The water retained in the subsoils ranges between 7.32 and 14.12 per cent. The water held at 1500 kPa is as low as 0.24 per cent in the soils of western beach and in other soils ranges between 2.66 and 3.61 per cent. All these data indicate that the water retention capacity of the soils is very low and therefore, rainwater received through monsoon storms reaches the pool of ground water through the rapidly permeable medium of coral sands.

(iv) *Physico-chemical Characteristics:* The pH of the soils ranges from 7.95 to 8.95. It is lower (7.95 to 8.28) in the surface than in the subsoils (8.50 to 8.95) possibly due to accumulation of organic matter and its decomposition on the surface. The electrical conductivity (in 1:2 soil-water ratio) is less than 0.24 dS/m though the water table is just below one metre. The CEC is, generally, low. It is less than 5 cmol(+)kg^{-1} and shows minor variation as a function of depth in the western beach. The CEC of soils in the centre and near the east coast of the island is comparatively higher ranging from 6.0 to 14.6 cmol(+)kg^{-1} and decreases with depth. The higher CEC in surface soils is due to accumulation of organic matter. Calcium is the dominant ion in the exchange complex. Sodium is also present in significant quantities but the adverse effects of sodium is not noticed due to very low percentage of clay in the soils. Exchangeable potassium is low in quantity ranging from 0.015 to 0.180 cmol(+)kg^{-1}.

(v) *Fertility Status:* The content of calcium carbonate is above 90 per cent. It seems to decrease with increasing organic carbon content due to the dissolution of calcium carbonate by the organic acids released during decomposition of organic matter. Content of organic carbon is high, the surface soils having 0.71 to 2.46 per cent and the subsoils having 0.34 to 1.05 per cent. It, generally, decreases with depth; however, in horizons of root accumulation particularly above hard pan or water table it increases. The available nitrogen (155 to 215 ppm) contents are high in surface soils of all the pedons except those in the western part and decrease with depth. The available phosphorus varies from 10 to 47 ppm respectively in the surface and decrease, generally with depth. The available potassium contents are low and range 14 to 70 ppm in the surface soils and decrease with depth. The content of organic carbon and major nutrients (N,P,K) increases showing soil development in the central and eastern parts of the island.

(vi) *Micronutrients:* DTPA extractable iron content varies from 4.90 to 10.00 ppm in the surface soils of pedons situated in the central and eastern parts of the island and decreases with depth. It is low with very little difference in depth wise distribution in western Kavaratti. The content of other micronutrients *viz.*, Mn, Cu and Zn are also low in western Kavaratti. In the other four pedons situated in the central and eastern parts of the island, the content of Mn, Cu and Zn vary from 4.80 to 7.16 ppm, 0.30 to 3.04 ppm and 2.14 to 5.50 ppm respectively. The distribution of micronutrients, generally, follows the pattern of distribution of organic carbon.

(vii) *Microbiological Characteristics:* The microbial population seems to be very high in these soils. The bacterial population ranges from 135 to 220 million CFU/g soil, the fungi from 7.5 to 12.0 lakh CFU/g soil and actinomycetes from 7.5 to 11.5 lakh CFU/g soil. In Kavaratti also the population of actinomycetes is quite high suggesting suitability for casuarina plantations and reduced incidence of root rots.

C. Kalpeni Island Soils

(i) *Morphological Characteristics:* The soils are moderately deep to deep, excessively to imperfectly drained. The depth of the soils is limited by the water table in the western part and by hard pan in the central and eastern parts. In the south-eastern truncated part also the depth is limited by ground water. The texture of the soils, in general, is loamy sand varying up to sandy clay loam. The soils occurring at the central part of the island have sandy loam or sandy clay loam texture in the surface and loamy sand or sandy texture in the subsoils. Comparatively heavier textures of sandy loam and sandy clay loam soils of the central and eastern parts of the island may be due to higher accumulation of organic matter. The structure is, generally, single grained but formation of weak subangular blocks is noticed in the surface soils. The consistence of the soils is loose. All these morphological characteristics show increasing soil development from the western part towards the east in the island.

(ii) *Physical Characteristics:* The clay content of these soils is higher at the surface (9.4 to 21.5 per cent) and decreases through depth in all the pedons. It also increases in soils from west to east indicating soil development. The content of sand varies from 72.7 to 88.7 per cent in the surface soils and increases with depth indicating pedogenic development in the surface. Fine, medium and coarse sands contribute most to the total sand percentage. Coarse sand fractions increase with depth at the cost of fine and medium sand showing aggregation of sand particles in subsoil horizons. Very fine and very coarse sands are less than 10 per cent in these soils.

(iii) *Water Retention:* The water retained at 33 kPa ranges from 12.78 to 20.30 per cent indicating poor water retention quality of the soils. Therefore, most of the rainfall will reach the ground water through the rapidly permeable sandy soils. The water held at 1500 kPa ranges from 2.05 to 3.91 per cent.

(iv) *Physico-chemical Characteristics:* The pH of the soils ranges from 7.44 to 8.10 in the surface and from 7.75 to 8.60 in the subsoil horizons. It decreases with increasing organic carbon content. Electrical conductivity of the soils is low and ranges from 0.012 to 0.642 dS/m. It is higher in soils situated in the western coast (Kalpeni-1) and south-eastern part indicating the saturation of soils with seawater during high tides, but low (< 0.2 dS/m) in the central part of the island (Kalpeni-2 and 3) indicating that this part has the least influence of fluctuations in sea level. Cation exchange capacity is higher (8.1 to 12.0 cmol(+)kg^{-1}) in surface soils than in subsoils (3.8 to 8.8 cmol(+)kg^{-1}) and seems to increase with increasing organic matter. Among the exchangeable cations calcium is predominant. Significant amount of sodium is also present to the tune of more than 15 per cent exchangeable sodium percentage (ESP). Adverse effects of high sodium are not noticed due to the high percentage of sand and very low percentage of clay. Exchangeable potassium is very low and ranges from 0.015 to 0.050 cmol(+)kg^{-1}.

(v) *Fertility Status:* Calcium carbonate content ranges from 86.9 to 95.0 per cent in the surface soils and in the subsoils from 91.3 to 99.9 per cent. The loss of calcium carbonate is due to dissolution of decomposing organic matter. Organic carbon content is high in the soils of Kalpeni. In the surface soils it ranges from 1.59 to 2.25 per cent and then decreases with depth except in horizons of root accumulation above the cemented horizon. Available nitrogen was also high with 161 to 228 ppm in surface soils and decreased generally, with depth. The total and available phosphorus are also high. Available phosphorus ranged from 10 to 65 ppm. Phosphorus content in soils depends on the phosphorus content of the parent material and also organic carbon content. Available potassium contents in the soils are very low and ranged from 16 to 31 ppm. The data show that decrease of calcium carbonate and increase of organic carbon, indicating active processes of soil development.

(vi) *Micronutrients:* The DTPA extractable micronutrients contents of these soils are higher in the surface and decreased through depth. But they are distinctly higher and do not follow any trend in Kalpeni-5 profile taken in the low-lying agricultural farm. Waterlogging and accumulation of organic matter seem to increase the micronutrients (Fe, Mn, Cu, Zn) in the soils. Available iron in the surface soils ranges from 9.40 to 27.16 ppm and in subsoils from 1.58 to 27.40 ppm. Available manganese is, generally, low and it ranges from 2.74 to 6.56 ppm in the surface soils decreasing with depth to 0.28 ppm. Copper and zinc also are present in very low quantities. Copper in surface soils ranges from 1.22 to 5.86 ppm and decreases through depth to 0.44 to 0.22 ppm. Zinc content ranges from 0.52 to 4.50 ppm in the surface soils and traces to 3.52 ppm in the subsoils. Micronutrients seem to increase with increasing organic carbon in these soils.

D. Kadmat Island Soils

(i) *Morphological Characteristics:* The soils occur on nearly level to gently sloping land with excessive drainage. The soils are moderately deep to very deep in the island. The texture of the surface soils is sandy loam and that of the subsoils is mostly sand and at some places loamy sand. On the western coast the surface is sandy up to a depth of 15 cm and then sandy loam up to 40 cm. The sudden change in texture indicates that the 15 cm thick sandy surface is a recent accumulation. The structure is weak subangular blocky in the surface and single grain thereafter through the depth. The consistence is generally loose but moderate cementation is noticed below 50 cm depth along the eastern coast. Roots are distributed throughout the profile and an accumulation of roots is observed above the cemented horizons.

(ii) *Physical Characteristics:* The soils have very low clay and very high sand content. Generally, the surface soils have slightly higher clay percentage (4.9 to 10.2) than the subsoils which have 2.9 to 7.9 per cent clay. But for the layer of sand accumulation in the western coast all these pedons have about 10 per cent clay in the surface indicating that they are in the same stage of development. The sand content in the surface ranges from 83 to 88 per cent and increases downwards except on the west coast. The sand fractions do not follow a definite trend indicating that the soils seem to be at the same stage of development.

(iii) *Water Retention:* The water retained at 33 kPa is very low in these soils and ranges from 12 to 14.54 per cent in the surface except the west coast. The percentage of water retained in the soils decreases with depth. As the water retention capacity of the soils at 33 kPa is very low, major part of rainfall reaches the ground water through the porous sandy soils. The water retained by these soils at 1500 kPa is less than 4 per cent and in some horizons as low as 0.92 per cent. It is because these soils become absolutely dry at 1500 kPa.

(iv) *Physio-chemical Characteristics:* The pH of the soils in the surface ranges from 7.95 to 8.25 and in the subsoil horizons from 8.15 to 8.85. The lower pH of the surface soils is due to higher organic matter content. The electrical conductivity of the soils is less than 0.1 dS/m. The CEC is low in the soils. It varies from 8.0 to 9.2 cmol(+)kg^{-1} in the surface soils except in the west coast and decreases downwards to a low of 3.0 cmol(+)kg^{-1}. Calcium is dominant among the cations. Exchangeable potassium is very low in the soils ranging from 0.015 to 0.080 cmol(+)/kg.

(v) *Fertility Status:* The calcium carbonate content is very high in the soils and ranges from 78.3 to 88.6 per cent in the surface soils and 91.8 to 99.9 per cent in the subsoils. It increases through depth, generally. The organic carbon content is high ranging from 1.22 to 1.84 per cent in the surface soils and decreases through depth except in horizons of root accumulation. Higher content of organic carbon corresponds to decrease in the content of $CaCO_3$ owing to its dissolution by organic acids. The total and available nitrogen contents are high in these soils in accordance with organic carbon. Available nitrogen ranges from 144 to 221 ppm in the surface soils and follows the trend of total nitrogen. The available phosphorus contents range, in the surface soils, from 7 to 23 ppm respectively. Available phosphorus increases with increasing organic carbon content. Total and available potassium contents are low in the soils. Total potassium ranges from 78 to 288 ppm and available potassium from 14 to 23 ppm in the surface soils. They, generally, decrease with depth.

(vi) *Micronutrients:* The DTPA extractable iron ranges from 7.46 to 9.68 ppm in the surface soils and decreases with depth to 1.04–1.30 ppm. Available manganese content ranges from 3.70 to 3.98 ppm in the surface and decreases with depth to 0.26 ppm. Available copper and zinc are low in the soils ranging from 3.98 to 0.02 ppm and 1.50 ppm to traces, respectively. The content of all these micronutrients corresponds to organic carbon content suggesting their origin through addition of organic matter.

(vii) *Microbiological Characteristics:* The population of bacteria, fungi and actinomycetes is very high in the soils. Bacterial population ranges from 95 to 165 million CFU/g. The population of fungi and actinomycetes ranges from 3.0 to 13.5 lakh CFU/g and 5.0 to 13.5 lakh CFU/g, respectively. It is interesting to note that actinomycetes are higher than the fungal population suggesting suitability for casuarinas and reduced incidence of root rots.

E. Amini Island Soils

(i) *Morphological Characteristics:* The soils occur on nearly level to gently sloping land. They are very deep and excessively drained along the western and eastern coasts, but in the central part of the island they are moderately deep to the hard pan and imperfectly drained owing to the water table at 85 cm depth. The texture of the soil is loamy sand in the surface and sand in the subsoil horizons of pedons situated in the western and eastern parts of the island. The pedon situated in the central part of the island has sandy loam texture up to a depth of 62 cm and sand thereafter up to the hard pan. The structure is mostly single grain in coastal pedons and weak subangular blocks in the centrally located pedon showing development of soil. The structural development may be due to prolonged wetness and accumulation of organic matter. The consistence is loose in both dry and moist conditions with lack of or unstable aggregation in the soils. Roots are distributed, almost, throughout the profile.

(ii) *Physical Characteristics:* The clay content is higher in the central pedon than in the coastal pedons. The surface soils of the central pedon have a clay content of 15.1 per cent which decreases through depth. The surface soils of the coastal pedons have a clay content ranging from 7 to 8 per cent which decreases through depth. The higher clay content corresponds to higher organic matter content explaining the genesis of clay size particles through break down of calcium carbonate by organic matter. The content of sand is higher (>88 per cent) in the coastal pedons and lower (72 to 73 per cent) in the central pedon. The sand content increases through depth. Medium and coarse sands are the dominant sand fractions. Very coarse sand content is higher in the central pedon showing aggregation of sand fractions particularly in the subsoils. There is no distinct difference in sand fractions of the west and the east coast in contrast to the situation in other islands where sand fractions differ in distribution and indicate that the soil development proceeds from west to east.

(iii) *Water Retention:* The water retained at 33 kPa works out to 10 per cent in the west coast and east coast pedons whereas it is about 20 per cent in the central pedon. As the water retention is low in these soils most of the rainfall reaches the ground water. The water retained at 1500 kPa is as low as 3 to 1 per cent.

(iv) *Physico-chemical Characteristics:* The pH of the soils ranges from 7.80 to 8.25 in the surface and 8.12 to 8.78 in subsoil horizons. The lower pH of the surface soils is due to organic matter accumulation. The electrical conductivity is less than 0.12 dS/m in the west coast and east coast pedons whereas it is 0.5 to 0.8 dS/m in the central pedon due to high ground water and prolonged wetness of the soils. Even though the ground water is very close to the surface these soils do not become salt affected because of very high sand and very low clay contents. The CEC is also low. The CEC ranges from 4 to 6 cmol(+)kg^{-1} in the west and east coast pedons whereas it is slightly higher (8.2 cmol(+)kg^{-1}) in the central island. The higher CEC corresponds to higher clay and organic carbon contents. Calcium is the dominant ion in the exchange complex. The important feature in view of plant nutrition is that the soils contain very low exchangeable potassium of 0.010 to 0.060 cmol(+)kg^{-1}.

(v) *Fertility Status:* The distribution of calcium carbonate in the soils of the island is interesting. Calcium carbonate content in the coastal pedons varies from 81.5 to 97.7 per cent whereas it drops to 68 to 69 per cent in the central pedon. This drop may be due to parent material composition and organic matter accumulation arising out of intensive cultivation and prolonged wetness. The organic carbon content in the coastal pedons ranges from 0.39 to 1.06 per cent and decreases through depth. In the central pedon the organic carbon content is slightly higher at levels of 1.97 to 0.96 per cent. Available nitrogen contents vary from 32 to 140 ppm in the coastal pedons. In the central pedon they range from 74 to 162 ppm. Total and available phosphorus contents are high in the soils of Amini. In the coastal pedons, total and available phosphorus range from 0.11 to 0.14 per cent and 18 to 43 ppm respectively in the surface and thereafter decrease through depth. In the central pedon total and available phosphorus contents are very high to the extent of 1.10 per cent and 133 ppm respectively and then decrease through depth. The total and available potassium contents are low in the soils ranging from 72 to 144 ppm and 4 to 23 ppm respectively. The potassium content also decreases through depth. The content of the major nutrients (N,P,K) in the soils, generally, corresponds to the content of organic carbon.

(vi) *Micronutrients:* The DTPA extractable micronutrients are distinctly higher in the central pedon than the coastal pedons. In the central pedon iron ranges from 2.12 to 24.80 ppm; manganese from 0.52 to 6.04 ppm; copper from 0.40 to 2.48 ppm and zinc from 0.84 to 3.00 ppm. In the coastal pedons micronutrients are lower than in the central pedon, iron ranging from 1.06 to 4.48 ppm, manganese from 0.38 to 2.22 ppm, copper from 0.20 to 2.82 ppm. The content of micronutrients depends on organic matter content.

(vii) *Microbiological Characteristics:* It is high in the soils, bacteria ranging from 110 to 165 million CFU/g, fungi from 6.0 to 12.5 lakh CFU/g and actinomycetes from 5.0 to 10.0 lakh CFU/g. The population of actinomycetes is quite high also in the soils of Amini indicating the suitability for casuarinas and reduced incidence of root rots.

F. Andrott, Agatti, Kiltan, Chetlat, Bitra

Soil morphological, physical, water retention, physico-chemical and fertility characteristics of these islands are very similar to those described previously. They are not described in detail so as to avoid repetition. If anyone is still interested in more details he can refer to "Soils of Lakshadweep for Optimising Land Use", NBSS Publ. 70 of NBSS&LUP, Nagpur–440 010, Maharashtra.

Annexure A-6

Rainfall, Temperature and Potential Evapo-transpiration of Selected Lakshadweep Islands

Month	*Minicoy*			*Amini*		*Agatti*		*Andrott*	
	Rainfall (mm)	**PET (mm)*	*Mean Temp. (°C)*	*Rainfall (mm)*	*Mean Temp. (°C)*	*Rainfall (mm)*	*Mean Temp. (°C)*	*Rainfall (mm)*	*Mean Temp. (°C)*
Jan	13.5	119.8	26.5	1.6	27.0	1.4	27.2	5.3	27.1
Feb	17.2	119.7	26.8	13.0	27.7	6.7	27.8	4.3	27.9
Mar	21.1	144.9	27.8	1.1	28.4	0.4	28.2	0.8	29.0
Apr	68.6	141.1	28.8	29.4	29.5	24.5	29.6	8.5	29.5
May	203.6	132.5	28.4	181.8	29.5	154.4	29.2	186.3	29.0
June	258.6	110.8	27.8	389.1	27.9	260.8	27.7	445.2	27.3
July	273.1	120.0	27.2	348.6	27.2	261.6	27.2	511.0	27.0
Aug	252.1	120.7	27.0	257.2	27.2	240.5	27.4	246.0	27.0
Sept	209.2	124.9	27.2	176.2	27.0	145.0	27.5	109.8	27.3
Oct	166.6	123.4	27.2	122.2	27.8	95.8	27.4	251.7	27.1
Nov	161.1	107.9	27.0	169.9	27.4	57.2	27.7	156.5	27.0
Dec	83.6	114.7	25.8	24.8	27.2	6.8	27.6	8.4	26.8
Annual	**1728.3**	**1480.4**	**27.3**	**1714.9**	**27.8**	**1255.1**	**27.9**	**1933.8**	**27.7**

Note: *: PET (Potential Evapo-transpiration) data available only for Minicoy.

Source: Basic Statistics, Dept. of Planning & Statistics, Kauaratti.

ANNEXURE A-7

A. Livestock Population over the Years

Species	*1972*	*1987*	*1992*	*1997*	*2002*	*Growth Rate (%) Over 1997*	*Annual Growth Rate (%)*
Cattle	1311	2728	2519	3399	4206	23.74	4.75
Goat	3817	15343	16886	25521	46333	81.55	16.31
Poultry	25410	50156	61240	76191	130651	71.48	14.30

Source: Basic Statistics 2003-04, Table 1 (pp.29), Lakshadweep Administration

B. Projected Livestock Population in Lakshadweep for the Year 2002

Islands	*Cattle*	*Goat*	*Poultry*
Bitra	-	158	227
Chetlat	52	1321	4644
Kiltan	106	4367	6920
Kadmat	189	4825	8256
Amini	533	3821	16747
Agatti	151	8189	20900
Kavaratti	458	7910	19255
Andrott	2165	8625	25960
Kalpeni	425	1307	6517
Minicoy	165	4733	17574
Lakshadweep	**4244**	**45,256**	**1,27,000**

Source: Lakshadweep Administration.

ANNEXURE A-8

Some of the Common Fish Landing in the Lakshadweep Islands

Scientific Name	*English Name*	*Vernacular Name*
Katsuwonus pelamis	Skipjack	*Mass Choora*
Neothunnus macropterus	Yellowfin	*Poovanchoora*
Auxis thazard	Frigate mackerel	*Ragundi*
Euthynnus alleteratus	Little tunny	*Letti*
Sphyraena sp.	Barracuda	*Thiruthakkadian*
Acanthocybium solandri	Seer fish	*Ayakura*
Coryphaena hippurus	Dolphin fish	*Avunose*
Istiophorus gladius	Sailfish	*Olameen*
Exocoetus volitans	Flying fish	*Parava*
Hemiramphus far	Halfbeak	*Kudukka*
Belone annulata	Garfish	*Karuthonamkunhi*
Elegatis bipinhulatus	Rainbow runner	*Chameen*
Kyphosus vaigensis	Chub	*Phunji*
Lutianus bohar	Red snapper	*Pulariam*
Lutianus gibbus	Red snapper	*Chemmali*
Lutjanus argentimaculatus	Grey snapper	*Metti*
Thalassoma sp.	Rainbow fish	*Choolam*
Gomphosus coeruleus	Rainbow fish	*Irachi choolam*
Echeneis naucrates	Shark sucker	*Keesakam*
Ostracion lentginosum	Boxfish	*Thombu*
Diodin hystrix	Porcupine fish	*Mullaka*
Myrichthys columbrians		*Malanji*
Caranx stellatus	Kingfish	*Kuluval*
Pelatas quadrilineatus	Croaker	*Manhan*
Holocentrus rubrum	Soldier-fish	*Lattam*
Cephalopolis argus	Rock cod	*Chemmum*
Cheilodepterus quinquilineatus	Cardinalfish	*Phootham*
Caranx cruminophthalmus	Kingfish	*Bangada*
Chaetodon falcula	Butterfly fish	*Fakkikadia*
Chanetodon auriga	Butterfly fish	*Fakkikadia*
Chanetodon citrenellus	Butterfly fish	*Fakkikadia*
Acanthus triostegus	Lancet fish	*Kurichi*
Acanthurus lineatus	Surgeon fish	*Varipad*
Acanthurus lineolatus	Surgeon fish	*Neythala*
Acanthurus leucosternon	Surgeon fish	*Chettipetii*
Naso brevirostris	Unicorn fish	*Karukkan*
Naso unicornis	Unicorn fish	*Mudiyan*
Gerrus punctatus		*Prachi*
Aprion vivescens	Streaker	*Chavadukallan*
Chromis caeruleus	Coral fish	*Panchachala*
Halichoeres centriquadrus	Rainbow fish	*Payathalayan*
Callydon sordidus	Parrot fish	*Pacha pheesam*
Leptoscarus coeruleopunctatus	Parrot fish	*Pheesam*
Siganus rivulatus	Rabbit fish	*Kalloran*
Odonus nigger	Trigger fish	*Kappuvalan karatti*
Balistapus undulatus	Trigger fish	*Balappallam karatti*
Rhinocanthus aculeatus	Trigger fish	*Vella karatti*
Chaetodon xanthocephalus	Butterfly fish	*Fakkikadia*

ANNEXURE A-9

Proposed Action Plan for Fisheries Development in Lakshadweep

Based on the analysis of the status of the fishery resource, the extent of present exploitation through traditional methods, potentials for future growth, emerging needs, development opportunities, practices, cultures and aspirations of the people identified during the presentations and discussions held in the Lakshadweep on 12-13 October, the following strategies are recommended for implementation.

Strategy 1 **Increasing the Yield from Capture Fisheries**

Target	Action	Outputs	Linkages	Time Frame
1. Increased yields from diversified fishing methods.	Diversification of fishing methods by introducing dory fishing, gill net fishing and long line fishing to capture fishes which currently cannot be caught by existing gear.	Higher yields. New species hitherto unexplored. Increased opportunities for fishers, processors.	UT Dept. of Fisheries with Central Institute of Fisheries Technology, Fishery Survey of India, Central Institute of Fisheries Nautical Engineering & Technology, entrepreneurs, financial institutions.	3-4 years
2. Increased yields from new types of fishing crafts and multi-day fishing.	Introduction of deep-sea gill-netters, long liners, oceanic purse seines. Introduction of mother ship with storage and processing facilities.	Many fold increase in the yields from oceanic waters which are yet to be exploited.	Ministry of Agriculture for licence, deep-sea vessel operators at Mumbai, Vishakhapatnam, Fishery Survey of India.	5-7 years
3. Increased yield in near-shore fisheries.	Installation of fish attracting devices (FADs) in the near-shore areas.	Increased yield of tuna and a number of other species which are now not exploited.	CMFRI, NIOT, UT Fisheries department centrally sponsored schemes of DAH&D.	3 years
4. Increased yield from present pole and line fishing.	Provision of water jet/sprinklers in all boats. Provision for collection, holding and transport of live-bait.	Higher yields from the present pole and and line fishing.	UT Fisheries Department.	2 years
5. Providing satellite imageries on Potential Fishing Zones to fishers regularly.	Installation of FAX machines in all fishing islands and making the details on the migration of tuna shoals available to fishers.	Better, faster, easier and higher fish catch especially straddling stocks like tuna.	UT Department of Fisheries and Space application Centre, Ahmedabad, and INCOIS, Hyderabad.	1 year

Strategy 2 **Increasing the Value of Fish and Fish Products**

Target	Action	Outputs	Linkages	Time Frame
1. Easy availability of ice to fishers.	Provision for transport of ice from the present ice plant to all islands and storage in chilled rooms or creation of mini ice plants in major fishing islands.	Storage of fish catch without deterioration so as to fetch better price and markets.	UT Department of Fisheries.	4 years
2. Providing chilled storage facilities on land.	Construction of chilled storage rooms in major fish landing islands.	Better storage and better quality and price of fish.	UT Department of Fisheries.	2 years
3. Providing refrigerated storage in ships for transport of chilled/frozen fish.	Alteration in the ships to provide a chilled storage room for fish and frozen fishery products for transport to mainland.	Easy and unspoiled transport of the highly perishable fish to the mainland resulting in better quality, price and market demand.	UT Administration & Ministry of Shipping and Surface Transport.	2 years

4. Target	Action	Outputs	Linkages	Time Frame
Providing post-harvest processing.	Creation of better and adequate processing facilities for fish. There is only one canning factory, one ice plant and one tunnel freezer.	Better, easier and faster processing of fish into processed products for storage and marketing later.	Private investments in the islands for post-harvest processing. UT administration.	5 years
5. Target	**Action**	**Outputs**	**Linkages**	**Time Frame**
Developing value added products.	Numerous value added products from tuna, fish and shellfish have been developed. Private investment needed.	Branded products from Lakshadweep, many of them with organic labelling to attract international demand and market.	Private investments, Central Institute of Fisheries Technology, Integrated Fisheries Project.	5-7 years
6. Target	**Action**	**Outputs**	**Linkages**	**Time Frame**
Providing a direct market channel to fishers for their products in the mainland.	Eliminate middlemen, develop direct market linkage with traders in the mainland.	Better value and profits to the fishers.	Fisheries development Corporations of the Kerala and Karnataka States, Matsyafed of Kerala.	1 year
7. Target	**Action**	**Outputs**	**Linkages**	**Time Frame**
Providing export linkages.	Creation of separate agency for marketing of fish and fishery products with linkages with Marine Export Development Authority of the Ministry of Commerce.	Organised and value added export of fish and fishery commodities for high-end customers in export market.	Marine Products Export Development Authority (MPEDA), Seafood Exporters Association, Export Inspection Agency.	1 year
8. Target	**Action**	**Outputs**	**Linkages**	**Time Frame**
Providing access to credit.	Promote private investment, entrepreneurship in fisheries.	Creation of development, investment and employment opportunities, increased GNP.	NABARD, Commercial Banks.	1 year

Strategy 3 **Increasing Employment Opportunities in Fisheries**

1. Target	Action	Outputs	Linkages	Time Fframe
Better fishing related employment.	Creation of opportunities in multi-day fishing vessels, larger vessels, mother ship.	Skilled job opportunities in fisheries.	UT Department of fisheries, CIFNET, CIFT.	3 years
2. Target	**Action**	**Outputs**	**Linkages**	**Time Frame**
Better fish processing related employment.	Creation of additional fish processing facilities through private participation.	Increased employment for skilled local personnel.	Training through CIFNET, CIFT.	4-7 years
3. Target	**Action**	**Outputs**	**Linkages**	**Time Frame**
Creating employment through frozen fish transport.	Provide needed infrastructure for frozen fish which will lead to creation of opportunities for local people to take up transport of frozen fish to mainland and export of high value *Sishmi*.	More self-employment opportunities. Development of trade. Other indirect benefits.	UT Department of Fisheries, Matsyafed, Cold Chain of maritime states, MPEDA.	5 years
4. Target	**Action**	**Outputs**	**Linkages**	**Time Frame**
Creating employment through transport of live ornamental fish, crabs, lobsters to mainland.	Creation of fish hatchery, necessary quarantine and holding facility.	Tapping of huge potential for ornamental fish export. Income, employment generation. Entrepreneurship development.	CMFRI, BNFGR, MPEDA, DAH&D (MoA).	4 years

5. Target	Action	Outputs	Linkages	Time Frame
Creating employment through mariculture.	Creation of infrastructure and legal framework for mariculture in the islands through private investment.	High self-employment potential for skilled and semiskilled people. Increased fish production.	CMFRI, NABARD, MPEDA Entrepreneurs.	5 years
6. Target	Action	Outputs	Linkages	Time Frame
Creating employment through organised collection of high value products (e.g., Tuna eye balls).	Awareness of potentials. Creation of minimum common facilities, Development of linkages, NGO involvement.	Employment and income options.	Industry, Exporters, MPEDA.	1 year
7. Target	Action	Outputs	Linkages	Time Frame
Creating employment through sport fishery.	Initiatives by Water Sports agency for creation of infrastructure, facilities, equipment hire. Training for youth.	Creation of added employment opportunities for youth.	Fishing equipment importers, Tourism hospitality industry.	2 years
8. Target	Action	Outputs	Linkages	Time Frame
Creating employment through aqua-tourism.	Training for youth. (HRD for tourism). Preparation of publicity materials.	Self-employment.	Hospitality and Tourism industry.	1 year
9. Target	Action	Outputs	Linkages	Time Frame
Creating employment through fishery related services.	Skill and capacity development, (HRD) awareness, credit for infrastructure.	Employment generation for educated youth sand skilled personnel.	Fishery related information technology (Internet, mobile phones, satellite imageries, cyclone warnings, PFZ advisories).	1 year
Strategy 4	**Increasing Income Generation from Fisheries Related Activities**			
1. Target	Action	Outputs	Linkages	Time Frame
Self-employment through fishery supplies.	Awareness, orientation to youth. Support for initiation into business.	Business development, employment.	Traders, suppliers, UT Department of Fisheries, ATIC of Central Fisheries Institutes.	2 years
2. Target	Action	Outputs	Linkages	Time Frame
Self-employment through repair of engines, outboard engines, boat repair.	Skill development through training at CIFNET, CIFT.	Business and employment generation.	CIFNET, CIFT.	2 years
3. Target	Action	Outputs	Linkages	Time Frame
Self-employment by providing chilled storage, ice supply.	Infrastructure and skill development.	Business development, self employment.	Financial institutions, CIFT for skill development.	2 years
4. Target	Action	Outputs	Linkages	Time Frame
Self-employment through information kiosks on potential fishing zone advisories, trade/ market demand, prices, other information like exporters, suppliers, credits.	Awareness and initiation of a few youth in to self-employment in each of the island for operation of fishery information kiosks.	Self-employment.	INCOIS, BSNL, NRSA.	1 year
6. Target	Action	Outputs	Linkages	Time Frame
Self-employment as middle man with large mainland buyers of fish/fishery products trade.	Awareness and initiation of a few youth into self-employment in each of the islands.	Business mode of trade practices leading to better efficiency and returns. Employment, income.	Traders of the mainland. UT Dept. of Fisheries.	1 year

Strategy 5	Developing Market Linkages for Creating an Established Trade			
1. Target	Action	Outputs	Linkages	Time Frame
Establish a live fish trade.	Creation of a single window mechanism for trade of fish and fishery products. Skill development, market guidance and linkages.	A well set trade for live fish.	CMFRI, MPEDA, traders, exporters.	2 years
2. Target	Action	Outputs	Linkages	Time Frame
Establish a frozen fish trade.	Creation of a single window agency for trade of fish and fishery products. Skill development, market and linkages.	A well-established trade for frozen fish.	Seafood export association, exporters, CIFT, MPEDA.	2-4 years
3. Target	Action	Outputs	Linkages	Time Frame
Establish a high value item trade for tuna eyes, ambergris, canned products.	Awareness, trade linkages, basic infrastructure.	Self-employment.	Traders, exporters.	Less than 1 year
Strategy 6	**Creating Employment and Entrepreneurship through Mariculture**			
1. Target	Action	Outputs	Linkages	Time Frame
Mariculture of ornamental fish.	Establishment of hatchery. Training and skill development. Trade linkages. packaging and transport.	Business development, employment and income to skilled and semiskilled people.	CMFRI, MPEDA, traders.	2-4 years
2. Target	Action	Outputs	Linkages	Time Frame
Mariculture of seaweeds.	Setting up of open seaweed farm. Promotion of private investment.	Business development, employment and income to skilled and semiskilled people.	CMFRI, seaweed traders, processors.	2 years
3. Target	Action	Outputs	Linkages	Time Frame
Mariculture of lobsters.	Setting up of hatchery and nursery, cage culture units.	Business development for for high value item.	CMFRI,MPEDA, seafood industry, hotels and hospitality industry.	2-3 years
4. Target	Action	Outputs	Linkages	Time Frame
Mariculture of sea cucumbers.	Setting up of hatchery, infrastructure for grow out, legal framework, private investments.	Development of high value trade.	CMFRI, MPEDA.	2 Years
5. Target	Action	Outputs	Linkages	Time Frame
Mariculture of fish in open sea cages.	Infrastructure of open sea cages, capture based mariculture activities.	Development of high value trade, private investment.	CMFRI,	2 years
6. Target	Action	Outputs	Linkages	Time Frame
Mariculture of pearl oysters.	Setting up of a grow out farm, hatchery and nucleus implantation facility, grow out rafts.	Development of high value trade, private investment.	CMFRI, jewellery makers, exports.	2 years
7. Target	Action	Outputs	Linkages	Time Frame
Mariculture of octopus, squids, cuttlefish.	Setting up of small culture units in the islands, training.	Small-scale business development, employment generation.	CMFRI, MPEDA.	2 years

Strategy 7 — **Creating Employment and Entrepreneurship through Live Fish Trade**

1. Target	Action	Outputs	Linkages	Time Frame
Trade of Live Ornamentals.	Skill development for eco-friendly selective fishing, handling, storage, transport.	Small business development, employment.	Traders, aquarium industry, Dept. of Fisheries, CMFRI.	1 year

2. Target	Action	Outputs	Linkages	Time Frame
Trade of Live Table Fish.	Skill development in capture, handling and transport.	Small business development.	Tourism industry, hospitality industry, trades, exporters.	1-2 years

Strategy 8 — **Developing Fisheries Related Tourism (Aqua-Tourism)**

1. Target	Action	Outputs	Linkages	Time Frame
Realising the full potential of aqua-tourism in the islands.	Training in scuba diving, identification of corals and other underwater fauna and flora, conservation measures.	Well-developed aqua-tourism. Self-employment, professional tourist guides, services.	CMFRI for scuba training, biodiversity identification and conservation.	2 years

Strategy 9 — **Establishment of Marine Parks**

1. Target	Action	Outputs	Linkages	Time Frame
Sustainability and conservation of the Lakshadweep ecosystem.	Training, awareness, skill development in tourist guidance to marine parks, restoration of biodiversity, conservation.	Well-regulated, healthy environment and protected areas. Prevention of adverse impacts of tourism and anthropogenic activities, employment.	MoEF, CMFRI, WWF, National Biodiversity Council.	10 years

ANNEXURE A-10

Projected Tourists Arrivals from 2002-03 to 2020-21

Year	*Number of Tourists*
2002-03	4450
2003-04	4776
2004-05	5128
2005-06	5506
2006-07	11414
2007-08	12449
2008-09	13581
2009-10	14818
2010-11	16171
2011-12	23395
2012-13	25591
2013-14	27985
2014-15	30619
2015-16	31574
2016-17	32624
2017-18	33780
2018-19	35050
2019-20	36448
2020-21	37985

Source: *Lakshadweep Development Report–Tourism.*

ANNEXURE A-11

Estimates of GSDP/NSDP of Lakshadweep from Supra-regional Sectors at Constant (1993-94) Prices

(Rs. Lakh)

Sl. No.	*Sectors*	*1997-98*		*1998-99*		*1999-2000*		*2000-01(P)*		*2002-03(Q)*	
		GSDP	*NSDP*	*GSDP*	*NSDP*	*GSDP*	*NSDP*	*GSDP*	*NSDP*	*GSDP*	*NSDP*
1.	Railways	-	-	-	-	-	-	-	-	-	-
2.	Communication (Public Sector)	138	109	174	143	221	187	273	235	335	296
3.	Banking & Insurance	94	91	128	124	118	113	144	139	149	139
4.	Central Government Administration	4150	3743	4285	3891	5086	4652	5010	4585	4833	4432

Note: P-Provisional; Q-Quick estimates.

Source: *Basic Statistics Table* 2 (p.158), Lakshadweep Administration, Dept. of Planning & Statistics Kauaratti.

ANNEXURE A-12

Recent Trends in Bank Deposits and Budgetary Capital Expenditure by Lakshadweep Administration (LDA) in Lakshadweep

Year	*Bank Deposits (as on 31st March)*		*Capital Exp. by LDA (During the year)*	
	Rs. Lakh	*Annual Growth (%)*	*Rs. Lakh*	*Annual Growth (%)*
1997-98	3836		1708	
1998-99	5355	39.60	2348	37.49
1999-00	6271	17.11	2383	1.48
2000-01	5553	-11.45	6042	153.54
2001-02	6791	22.29	7986	32.18
2002-03	11077	63.11	6285	-21.30

Source: For Bank Data, *Basic Statistics of Lakshadweep 2003-04*, Lakshadweep Administration and for Budgetary Data, *Demands for Grants of MHA*.

ANNEXURE A-13

A. Monthly Island-wise Solar Energy Generation Potential (kWh)

	Lakshadweep	*Chetlat*	*Kiltan*	*Kadmat*	*Amini*	*Agatti*	*Kavaratti*	*Andrott*	*Kalpeni*	*Minicoy*	*Bitra*	*Bangaram*
Area (Ha)	3200	114	163	312	259	388	422	484	279	439	10	58
Area assumed to be available for SPV (Ha)	13.9	0.54	0.77	1.48	1.23	1.84	2.00	2.29	1.32	2.08	0.05	0.27

B. Global Solar Radiation (kWh/M2/day)

J	5.127	727826.0	28337.5	40517.6	77555.2	64380.8	96446.9	104898.4	120310.0	69352.3	109124.2	2485.7	14417.3
F	5.765	818396.1	31863.8	45559.6	87206.1	72392.3	108448.7	117951.9	135281.3	77982.4	122703.5	2795.1	16211.4
M	6.270	890085.6	34655.0	49550.5	94845.2	78733.7	117948.5	128284.2	147131.6	84813.5	133452.0	3039.9	17631.5
A	6.043	857860.8	33400.3	47756.6	91411.4	75883.2	113678.3	123639.8	141804.9	81742.9	128620.5	2929.9	16993.1
M	4.984	707525.8	27547.1	39387.5	75392.1	62585.1	93756.8	101972.6	116954.4	67417.9	106080.5	2416.4	14015.2
J	3.926	557332.7	21699.4	31026.4	59387.9	49299.6	73854.2	80326.0	92127.4	53106.5	83561.8	1903.5	11040.1
J	3.779	536464.7	20886.9	29864.7	57164.3	47453.7	71088.9	77318.3	88677.9	51118.0	80433.1	1832.2	10626.7
A	4.268	605882.9	23589.7	33729.1	64561.3	53594.1	80287.8	87323.3	100152.8	57732.7	90841.0	2069.3	12001.8
S	4.946	702131.3	27337.1	39087.2	74817.3	62107.9	93042.0	101195.2	116062.7	66903.9	105271.7	2398.0	13908.3
O	4.682	664654.1	25877.9	37000.9	70823.8	58792.8	88075.7	95793.7	109867.7	63332.8	99652.7	2270.0	13166.0
N	4.727	671042.2	26126.6	37356.5	71504.5	59357.9	88922.3	96714.4	110923.6	63941.5	100610.5	2291.8	13292.5
D	4.672	663234.5	25822.7	36921.9	70672.5	58667.3	87887.6	95589.1	109633.0	63197.5	99439.9	2265.1	13137.8
		8402436.8	327144.1	800047.5	895341.6	743248.3	1113437.7	1211006.9	1388927.4	800642.0	1259791.6	28696.8	166441.7

Note: The area of solar panels is assumed to cover only 50 per cent of the total area available for SPV installation. A solar panel efficiency of 11 per cent has been used to calculate the power generation potential and further, a factor of 0.6 has also been used to take into account the effective number of sunshine hours, dust, cloud cover, etc.

Source: Lakshadweep Administration, Dept. of Planning & Statistics.

ANNEXURE A-14

Wind Resources Assessment in Lakshadweep

A. Wind Resources in Agatti Island–20m height

	J	*F*	*M*	*A*	*M*	*J*	*J*	*A*	*S*	*O*	*N*	*D*	*Annual*
Mean Wind Speed (m/s)	3.4	3.7	3.2	3.9	4.3	8.9	8.9	8.4	5.9	3.7	3.4	3.1	5.1
Weibull Parameter'k'	1.2	3.2	2.4	3.5	2.1	3.3	4.9	4.6	3.0	2.0	1.7	2.6	2.9

Source: Mani, A. and S. Rangarajan, *Wind Resource Survey in India, Vol.3.*

B. Wind Resources in Minicoy Island–20m height

	J	*F*	*M*	*A*	*M*	*J*	*J*	*A*	*S*	*O*	*N*	*D*	*Annual*
Mean Wind Speed (m/s)	2.89	3.29	2.95	2.96	5.06	8.15	7.94	7.02	6.01	4.07	3.66	2.77	4.73
Prevailing Wind Direction	NE	N	N/NE	NW/NE	NW/NE	W/NE	W/E	W/NE	W/NE	W/NE	NW/N	NE/N	
Weibull Parameter'k'	2.0	2.3	2.4	2.1	1.8	2.9	3.0	2.8	2.8	2.0	1.9	1.8	2.31
Weibull Parameter 'c' in m/s	2.92	3.44	2.97	3.08	5.00	8.39	4.14	7.31	6.08	4.61	3.78	2.67	4.53
Air Density (g/cum)	1178	1175	1171	1165	1164	1168	1170	1171	1171	1172	1175	1176	1171.33

Source: Mani, A. and S. Rangarajan, *Wind Resource Survey in India, Vol.3.*

	Latitude	*Longitude*	*Height of Mast (m)*	*Mean Annual Wind Speed (m/s)*		*Mean Annual Wind Power Density (W/m2)*	
				At Mast	*At 30m*	*At Mast*	*At 30m*
Agatti	10°51'	72°11'	20	5.11	5.42	178.70	207.70
Amini	11°07'	72°44'	20	4.83	-	140.00	-
Bitra	11°35'	72°12'	20	4.58	5.36	173.00	258.00
Chetlat	11°43'	72°43'	20	5.28	5.57	172.00	205.00
Kadmat	11°13'	72°47'	20	5.00	5.39	168.60	211.40
Kalpeni	10°05'	73°39'	20	4.50	5.25	125.40	181.70
Kavaratti	10°33'	72°38'	20	5.00	5.44	160.60	205.50
Minicoy	08°17'	73°04'	20	4.83	>4.83	161.50	>161.50

Note: It has been assumed that the wind characteristics are the same in all the islands and the low wind speeds at Minicoy have been used for the assessment of the wind power potential in these islands for conservative estimates.

Source: Mani, A. and S. Rangarajan, *Wind Resource Survey in India,* Vol.3.

ANNEXURE A-15

Passenger and Cargo Capacity of LDA Ships, as on 31.12.2005

A. Ships in Operation, as on 31.3.2003

Sl. No	*Name of the Ship*	*Passenger Capacity*	*Cargo Capacity*	*Year of Acquisition*
1	M.V. BHARAT SEEMA	380	160 MT	1982
2	M.V. TIPU SULTAN	658	NIL	1988
3	M.V. DWEEP SETU	150	25 MT	1988
4	M.V. KADEEJA BEEVI	100	NIL	1991
5	M.V. HAMEEDATH BEEVI	100	NIL	1991
6	M.V. UBAIDULLA	NIL	550 MT	1991
7	M.V. THINNAKARA	NIL	550 MT	1993
8	M.V. LACCADIVES	NIL	550 MT	1995
9	M.V. CHERIYAM	NIL	550 MT	1997
10	M.V. AMINDIVI	150	25 MT	2001
11	M.V. MINICOY	150	25 MT	2001
12	M.B. SUHELI	NIL	60 MT	1987

B. Ship Currently Under Construction

Sl. No.	*Name of the Ship*	*Capacity*		*Building Yard*	*Date of Delivery*
		Passenger	*Cargo*		
1	M.V. Kavaratti	700	160 MT	HSL	-
2	Three 150 Pax Vessel	150	—	Penguin Shipyard Int, Singapore	07.02.2007
3	One 10 T Bullard Tug	—	—	Vipul Shipyard	04.03.2006
4	Three 50 Pax Vessel	50	—	NGV Tech Malaysia	03.11.2006
5	One 15 Pax Vessel	15	—	NGV Tech Malaysia	15.06.2006

C. Ships Approved for Acquisition* of the Following Ships

Sl.No.	*Type of Ship*	*Capacity*		*Cost (Rs. Crore)*
		Passenger	*Cargo*	
1	Acquisition of ONE Passenger-cum-Cargo Ship	250	100	45.00
2	Acquisition of ONE Oil Barge	NIL	100-150	5.20
3	Acquisition of ONE LPG Ship	NIL		2.50
	Total			**52.70**

Source: Dept. of Shipping & Transport, UT of Lakshadweep.

ANNEXURE A-16

Actual/Projected Annual Passenger Carrying Capacity (Mainland-Island Route) of the Ships Operated by Lakshadweep Administration

YEAR	M.V. TIPU SULTAN	M.V. BHARAT SEEMA	M.V. DWEEP SETU	M.V. AMDV.	M.V. MNCY	700 PAX	3*150 PAX	1st 250 PAX	2nd 250 PAX	400 PAX	Total Capacity
2003-04	53627	34532	8960	15000	15000	-	-		-	-	127119
2004-05	53627	34532	8960	15000	15000	-	-		-	-	127119
2005-06	53627	34532	8960	15000	15000	-	-		-	-	127119
2006-07	-	-	-	15000	15000	70000	-		-	-	100000
2007-08	-	-	-	15000	15000	70000	45000	25000	-	-	170000
2008-09	-	-	-	15000	15000	70000	45000	25000	25000	—	195000
2009-10	-	-	-	15000	15000	70000	45000	25000	25000	40000	235000
2010-11& beyond	-	-	-	15000	15000	70000	45000	25000	25000	40000	235000

Note: 1. 700 Pax vessel will be inducted by 2006-07
2. 1st 250 Pax vessel will be inducted by 2007-08.
3. 2nd 250 Pax vessel will be inducted by 2008-09.
4. 400 Pax vessel will be inducted by 2009-10.

Source: Same as Annexure A-15.

ANNEXURE A-17

Projections* for the Cargo Traffic

Year	*Cargo Traffic (in MT)*
2003-04	223030
2004-05	238182
2005-06	253333
2006-07	268485
2007-08	283636
2008-09	298788
2009-10	313939
2010-11	339091
2011-12	344242
2012-13	359394
2013-14	374545
2014-15	389697

Note: *: Based on Linear Extrapolation approach.

ANNEXURE A-18

A. Physical and Financial Targets for Construction of Rural Roads during the VIIIth to Xth Plans in Lakshadweep

Plan	*Road Length (Km)*		*Expenditure (in Lakh)*	
	Target	*Achievement*	*Target*	*Achievement*
1. VIIIth Plan (1992-1997)	30.36	34	316.25	429.13
2. IXth Plan (1997-2002)	64.45	40.163	834.33	759.88
3. Xth Plan (2002-2007) (P)	43.00		1268.00	

Source: Draft Ninth and Tenth Five Year Plans, UT of Lakshadweep and Department of PWD Kavaratti (for expenditure).

B. Road Construction in Lakshadweep Islands during the last 10 Years

(In Metres)

Island	*Year*									
	1994-95	*1995-96*	*1996-97*	*1997-98*	*1998-99*	*1999-2000*	*2000-01*	*2001-02*	*2002-03*	*2003-04*
1. Kavaratti	700	260	800	785	-	650	5170	770	110	-
2. Amini	1500	251	941	1105	640	-	300	200	313	-
3. Andrott	1000	-	-	-	980	-	1290	610	440	2285
4. Kadmat	700	1000	480	29	390	820	510	520	410	-
5. Kiltan	200	-	-	1526	310	910	400	-	85	-
6. Chetlat	300	-	27	175	-	400	-	-	112	-
7. Bitra	400	-	-	17	30	130	-	-	120	-
8. Minicoy	700	1664	1375	1688	920	1370	450	1300	1000	2930
9. Agatti	455	1850	1300	-	1500	600	-	530	—	321
10. Kalpeni	85	51	-	-	420	1540	-	550	1551	
Lakshadweep	**6040**	**5076**	**4923**	**5325**	**5190**	**6420**	**8120**	**4480**	**4141**	**5536**

Note: NA: Not Available; Figures within parenthesis are annual compound growth rate.
Source: Basic Statistics 2003-04, Table 2 (p.89), UT of Lakshadweep.

ANNEXURE A-19

Island-wise Area and Population during Various Census (1951-2001)

Sl. No.	*Name of Island*	*Area (sq km)*	*Population*					
			1951	*1961*	*1971*	*1981*	*1991*	*2001*
1.	Agatti	4.84	2029	2411	3155	4111	5670	7007
2.	Amini	2.59	3159	3530	5442	5367	6447	7340
3.	Andrott	4.84	3500	4183	5425	6812	9122	10720
4.	Bangaram	0.58	-	-	-	-	61	65
5.	Bitra	0.10	46	80	112	181	225	264
6.	Chetlat	1.04	948	953	1200	1484	2051	2289
7.	Kadmat	3.12	1641	1851	2416	3114	3985	5319
8.	Kalpeni	2.28	2269	2613	3152	3543	4084	4319
9.	Kavaratti	3.63	2390	2828	4420	6604	8677	10113
10.	Kiltan	1.63	1249	1520	2046	2375	3065	3666
11.	Minicoy	4.37	3804	4139	5342	6658	8320	9495
	Total	**29.02**	**21035**	**24108**	**32710**	**40249**	**51707**	**60595**

Source: Basic Statistics 2001-2002, UT of Lakshadweep.

ANNEXURE A-20

Male and Female Population in States and Union Territories

	States	1981		1991		2001	
		Male	*Female*	*Male*	*Female*	*Male*	*Female*
1	Andhra Pradesh	27.11	26.44	33.72	32.78	38.29	37.44
2	Arunachal Pradesh	0.34	0.29	0.47	0.40	0.57	0.52
3	Assam	10.47	9.43	11.66	10.76	13.79	12.85
4	Bihar	35.93	33.98	45.20	41.17	57.02	52.77
5	Chhattisgarh						
6	Goa	0.55	0.54	0.59	0.58	0.69	0.66
7	Gujarat	17.55	16.53	21.36	19.95	26.34	24.25
8	Haryana	6.91	6.01	8.83	7.64	11.33	9.76
9	Himachal Pradesh	2.17	2.11	2.62	2.55	3.09	2.99
10	Jammu & Kashmir	3.16	2.82	4.01	3.70	5.30	4.77
11	Jharkhand						
12	Karnataka	18.92	18.21	22.95	22.03	26.86	25.88
13	Kerala	12.53	12.93	14.29	14.81	15.47	16.37
14	Madhya Pradesh	26.89	25.29	34.27	31.91	41.91	39.27
15	Maharashtra	32.42	30.37	40.83	38.11	50.33	46.42
16	Manipur	0.72	0.70	0.94	0.90	1.21	1.18
17	Meghalaya	0.68	0.65	0.91	0.87	1.17	1.14
18	Mizoram	0.26	0.24	0.36	0.33	0.46	0.43
19	Nagaland	0.42	0.36	0.64	0.57	1.04	0.95
20	Orissa	13.31	13.06	16.06	15.60	18.61	18.09
21	Punjab	8.94	7.85	10.78	9.50	12.96	11.33
22	Rajasthan	17.85	16.41	23.04	20.96	29.38	27.09
23	Sikkim	0.17	0.14	0.22	0.19	0.29	0.25
24	Tamil Nadu	24.49	23.92	28.30	27.56	31.27	30.84
25	Tripura	1.05	1.00	1.42	1.34	1.64	1.56
26	Uttaranchal						
27	Uttar Pradesh	58.82	52.04	74.04	65.08	91.78	82.75
28	West Bengal	28.56	26.02	35.51	32.57	41.49	38.73
	Union Territories						
1	Andaman & Nicobar Is.	0.11	0.08	0.15	0.13	0.19	0.16
2	Chandigarh	0.26	0.20	0.36	0.28	0.51	0.39
3	Dadra & Nagar Haveli	0.05	0.05	0.07	0.07	0.12	0.10
4	Daman & Diu		0.05	0.05	0.09	0.07	
5	Delhi	3.44	2.78	5.16	4.27	7.57	6.21
6	Lakshadweep	0.20	0.20	0.27	0.25	0.03	0.03
7	Pondicherry	0.30	0.30	0.41	0.40	0.49	0.49
	All-India	**354.40**	**330.79**	**439.23**	**407.07**	**531.28**	**495.74**

Note: (1) Data has been taken at 2 digits after decimal.
(2) For 2001, data for Bihar, Madhya Pradesh and Uttar Pradesh includes those for Jharkhand, Chhattisgarh and Uttaranchal, respectively.
(3) 1981 Census data for Goa includes Daman & Diu.

Source: National Human Development Report 2001, Planning Commission (March 2002), Tables 5.45, 5.46 and 5.47.

ANNEXURE A-21

Gender Ratio in States and Union Territories

	States	*Female per 1000 Male*		
		1981	*1991*	*2001*
1	Andhra Pradesh	975	972	978
2	Arunachal Pradesh	862	859	901
3	Assam	910	923	932
4	Bihar	948	907	921
5	Chhattisgarh	996	985	990
6	Goa	975	967	960
7	Gujarat	942	934	921
8	Haryana	870	865	861
9	Himachal Pradesh	972	973	968
10	Jammu & Kashmir	892	896	900
11	Jharkhand	940	922	941
12	Karnataka	963	960	964
13	Kerala	1,032	1,036	1,058
14	Madhya Pradesh	921	912	920
15	Maharashtra	937	934	922
16	Manipur	971	958	978
17	Meghalaya	954	955	975
18	Mizoram	919	921	938
19	Nagaland	863	886	909
20	Orissa	981	971	972
21	Punjab	879	882	874
22	Rajasthan	919	910	922
23	Sikkim	835	878	875
24	Tamil Nadu	977	974	986
25	Tripura	946	945	960
26	Uttaranchal	936	936	964
27	Uttar Pradesh	882	876	898
28	West Bengal	911	917	934
	Union Territories			
1	Andaman & Nicobar Is.	760	818	846
2	Chandigarh	769	790	773
3	Dadra & Nagar Haveli	974	952	811
4	Daman & Diu	1,062	969	709
5	Delhi	808	827	821
6	Lakshadweep	975	943	948
7	Pondicherry	985	979	1,001
	All-India	**934**	**927**	**933**

Source: Census of India 2001, Provisional Population Totals Series 1, Table 10.

ANNEXURE A-22

Island-wise Literacy Rates during 1971 to 2001

Island	*Percentage of Literates to Total Population*			
	1971	*1981*	*1991*	*2001*
Kavaratti	44.37	60.22	72	88.6
Agatti	43.17	54.76	65	86.8
Amini	40.69	48.48	61	82.7
Kadmat	48.4	56.07	65	87.2
Kiltan	41.84	46.86	60	81.7
Chetlat	43.17	49.93	67	84.3
Bitra	42.86	46.96	64	84.4
Andrott	34.88	48.78	63	84.3
Kalpeni	47.56	55.88	66	84.4
Minicoy	51.03	65.29	75	93.0
Bangaram	—	—	97	98.3

Source: Basic Statistics 2003-04, Table 3 (p.42) of Lakshadweep.

ANNEXURE A-23

Ratio of Dropouts in Industrial Training Institute, Kavaratti, 1994-95 to 1998-99

Years	*Boys*	*Girls*	*Total*
1994-95	0	23.08	18.75
1995-96	2.94	13.64	7.14
1996-97	15.62	23.08	18.97
1997-98	28.95	4.00	19.05
1998-99	47.50	4.45	32.26

Source: Statistical Section, Education Department, Lakshadweep.

ANNEXURE A-24

Educational Wastage in Industrial Training Institute, Kavaratti

Year	*Number of Candidates Failed as Proportion of Number of Candidates Appeared*			
	Stenography	*Cutting and Tailoring*	*Carpentry*	*Diesel Mechanic*
1992-93	72.22	NA	NA	NA
1993-94	72.22	50.00	NA	NA
1994-95	40.00	00.00	33.33	NA
1995-96	77.78	00.00	NA	47.83
1996-97	41.18	00.00	25.00	68.75
1997-98	28.57	00.00	10.00	75.00
1998-99	28.57	00.00	10.00	75.00
1999-00	78.95	21.43	00.00	00.00
2000-01	20.00	00.00	00.00	Nil
2001-02	52.94	25.00	33.33	Nil

Source: Basic Statistics 2001-2002, Department of Planning & Statistics, Secretariat Lakshadweep, Kavaratti.

ANNEXURE A-25

Details of Water Supply Sources as on 1.10.1999

Sl. No.	Islands	Wells		Ponds		Hand Pumps		RWHT*	
		In Use	Abandoned	In Use	Abandoned	In Use	Abandoned	In Use	Abandoned
1.	Agatti	925	0	127	167	7	4	75	0
2.	Andrott	1609	0	399	0	48	8	0	0
3.	Amini	1002	103	137	7	49	2	98	0
4.	Bitra	62	300	10	0	0	0	52	0
5.	Chetlat	473	15	83	0	6	0	61	0
6.	Kadmat	922	26	168	99	4	1	5	0
7.	Kalpeni	711	0	456	0	18	23	61	0
8.	Kavaratti	1307	21	148	42	217	23	280	0
9.	Kiltan	683	103	127	7	4	0	47	0
10.	Minicoy	1365	0	76	48	279	0	230	0
	Total	**9059**	**268**	**1731**	**370**	**632**	**61**	**909**	**0**

Note: * Rain Water Harvesting Tanks. Source: Department of Public Works, Lakshadweep.

Source: Basic Statistics 2003–04, Table 6 (p.91), Lakshadweep Administration.

ANNEXURE A-26

Explanatory Note[1] on the Principles Adopted to Determine the Poverty Ratio in respect of Andaman & Nicobar Islands, Chandigarh, Dadra & Nagar Haveli, Daman & Diu, Pondicherry

In the estimation indicated above, the Poverty Ratios and Poverty Lines for the urban and rural areas of Tamil Nadu have been adopted for Andaman & Nicobar Islands and Pondicherry; the Poverty Ratio and Poverty Line of Punjab (Urban) have been adopted for Chandigarh; the Poverty Ratios and Poverty Lines for the urban and rural areas of Maharashtra and expenditure distribution of Dadra & Nagar Haveli are used to estimate the poverty ratio of Dadra & Nagar Haveli; the Poverty Ratios and Poverty Lines for the urban and rural areas of Goa are used to estimate the poverty ratio of Daman & Diu; and the Poverty Ratios and Poverty Lines for the urban and rural areas of Kerala are used to estimate the poverty ratio for Lakshadweep. These assumptions put certain limitations on the accuracy of these statistics in relation to the scenario actually prevailing. However, in the absence of a better set of data, these would need to be used.

Source: National Human Development Report 2001, Planning Commission, March 2002.

ANNEXURE A-27

Common Vegetation of the Lakshadweep Islands

Trees

Achras zapota, Adenanthera pavonina, Albizia lebbeck. Alstonia scholaris. Areca catechu, Artocarpus heterophylla. A. utilis, Azadirachta indica, Barringtonia asiatica, Bixa orellana, Calophyllum inophyllum, Casuarina equisetifolia, Ceriops tagal, Cordia subcordata, Delonix regia, Erythrina variegata, Ficus benghalensis, F. racemosa, F. religiosa, Guettarda speciosa, Gyrocarpus asiaticus, Hernandia peltata. Hibiscus tiliaceus, Leuceana latisiliqua, Mangifera indica. Messerschmidia argentea. Morinda citrifolia, Moringa oleifera, Muntingia calabura, Murraya koenigii, Ochrosia oppostifolia, Pemphis acidula. Pithecel1obium dulce, Polyalthia longifolia. Psidium guajava. Punica granatum, Suriana maritime, Syzygium cumini, Tamarindus indica, Terminalia catappa and Thespesia populnea.

Treelets/shrubs and Climbers

Abutilon indicum, Annona reticulata, A. squamosa, Averrhoa bilimbi. Caesalpinia crista, Calotropis gigantea, Clerodendrum inerme, Colubrina asiatica, Dodonaea viscose, Lantana camara, Lawsonia inermis. Leptadenia reticulata. Pavetta indica, Premna serratifolia, Ricinus comunis, Sesbania grandiflora and Tecoma stans.

Twiners and Herbaceous Plants

Acalypha indica, A. lanceolata, Acanthospermum hispidum, Achyranthes aspera, Adenostemma lavenia, Aerva lanata, Ageratum conyzoides. Al1mania nodiflora, Alternanthera sessilis, Alysicarpus bupleurifolius, A. vaginalis, Amaranthus spinosus, A. viridis. Ammannia baccifera, Anisomeles indica, Argemone mexicana, Asparagus racemosus, Bacopa monnieri. Bidens biternata, B, pilosa, Blumea mol1is, B. oblique, B. oxyodonta. B. virens, Boerhavia diffusa, B. chinensis, B. repens, Kalanchoe pinnata, Capsicum annuum, C. frutescens, Cardiospermum halicacabum, Cassia occidentalis, C. sophera, C. tora, Cassytha filiformis, Catharanthus roseus, Cayratia trifolia, Chrysopogon aciculatus, Cleome rutidosperma, C. viscosa, Clitoria ternatea, Coccinea grandis, Codium variegatum, Commelina diffusa, C. paludosa, Corchorus aestuans, C. capsularis, Crinum defixum, Crotalaria pallida var. obovata, C. retusa, C. verrucosa, Cucumis trigonus, Cucurbita maxima, C. moschata, Cymbopogon flexuosus, Cynanchum tunicatum, Cynodon dactylon, Cyanotis cristata, Cyperus compressus. C. pachyrrhizus, C. rotundus, Cyrtococcum trigonum. Dactyloctenium aegyptium, Desmodium gangeticum, D. triflorum, Digera muricata, Digitaria ciliaris. D. longiflora. Dipteracanthus prostratus, Echinochloa colona, Eclipta prostrata, Elaeocharis geniculata, Eleusine indica, Emilia sonchifolia. Eragrostis ciliaris, E. tenella. E, unioloides. Euphorbia articulata, E. heterophylla, E. hirta, E. indica, E. rosea, E. serpens, Evolvulus alsinoides, Fimbristylis cymosa, F. falcata, F. ferruginea, F. miliacea, Gloriosa superba, Hedyotis corymbosa, H. herbacea, H. puberula, Hyptis suaveolens, Impatiens balsamina, Indigofera cordifolia, I. tinctoria, Ipomoea alba, I. batatas, I. littoralis, I. pes-caprae, Ischaemum indicum. Laportea interrupta, Launaea sarmentosa, Leucas aspera, Malvastrum coromandelianum, Mariscus dubius, M. pedunculatus, Merremia vitifolia, Micrococa mercurialis, Mimosa pudica, Momordica charantia, Ocimum basilicum, Ophiuros exaltatus, Pancratium zeylanicum, Peperomia pel1ucida, P. tetraphyl1a, Peristrophe paniculata, Phyla nodiflora, Phyllanthus maderaspatensis, P. urinaria, Physalis minima, Piper betle, P. nigrum, Pistia stratiotes, Plumbago zeylanica, Polygala erioptera, Polycarpaea spicata, Polygonum barbatum, Portulaca oleracea, Pouzolzia zeylanica, Psilotum nudum,. Pycreus polystachyos, Rostllularia procumbens, Rungia parviflora, Sesuvium portulacastrum, Sida acuta, S. cordata, S. rhomboidea, Solanum melongena, S. nigrum, S. torvum, Spermacoce repens, Spilanthes calva, Sporobolus piliferus, Striga angustifolia, S. asiatica, Synedrel1a nodiflora, Tephrosia pumila, T. purpurea, T. strigosa, Teramnus labialis, Thecagonum biflorum, Thuarea involuta, Tragia involucrata, Trichosanthes anguina, Tridax procumbens, Tylophora indica, Vernonia cinerea and Wedelia biflora.

Food Plants Grown in the Lakshadweep Islands

Alocasia indica Schott, A.macrorrhiza Schott, Annona muricata L., A. squamosa L., Artocarpus altilis Fosberg, A. heterophyllus Lam., Carica papaya L., Citrullus lanatus (Thumb.) Mansf., Citrus medica L. Colocasia esculenta (L.) Schott, Cucumis sativus L., Cucurbita pepo DC., C. maxima Duch. Ex Lam., C. moschata Duch, Ipomea batatas (L.), Mangifera indica L., Manihot esculenta Crantz, Momordica charantia L., Moringa oleifera Lam., Musa sapientum L., Piper nigrum L., Psidium guajava L., Trichosanthes anguina L., Vigna unguiculata (L.) Walp., and Zea mays L. Avenue trees and ornamentals grown in these islands are Bougainvillea spectabilis Wild., Casuarina equisetifolia Forst., Catharanthus roseus(L.) G.Don, Codiaeum variegatum Bl., Cosmos sulphureus Cav., Delonix regia (Hook.) Raf., Hibiscus rosa-sinesis L., Nerium oleander L., and Pedilanthus tithymaloides (L.) Poit., Cocos nucifera, Areca catechu L., and Piper betle.

ANNEXURE A-28

Medicinal Plants of Lakshadweep

Sl.No.	Botanical Name	Family	Common/ Vernacular Name	Habit	Uses
1	*Abelmoschus esculentus*	Malvaceae	Lady-finger; *Vendakka (Mal)*	Herb	Leaf, fruit, root—treating venereal diseases, bronchitis, pneumonia, pulmonary tuberculosis
2	*Abrus precatorius*	Fabaceae	*Kakani (Mal)*	Climbing woody vine	Seed—treating sore throat, cough, chronic inflammation of mucus membrane of eyeball and eyelid
3	*Abutilon indicum*	Malvaceae	*Kanghi (H)*	Pubescent subshrub	Seed, roots—treating fevers, respiratory diseases, piles, skin diseases, threadworms Bark—astringent, diuretic
4	*Acalypha indica*	Euphorbiaceae	*Kuppamani (Mal)*	Herb	Plant—treating skin diseases, intestinal worms, constipation, earache, rheumatism, respiratory diseases Leaves—laxative, treating scabies, snake poison
5	*Achyranthes aspera*	Amaranthaceae	*Latjira (H); Nayurivi (Tam)*	Herb	Plant—treating renal dropsy, asthma, coughs, cholera, skin diseases, eye diseases
6	*Acorus calamus*	Araceae	Vayambu *(Mal)*	Rhizomatous herb	Rhizome—improves memory, digestion, clearing speech, piles, curing diarrhoea, dysentery, epilepsy, bronchitis.
7	*Adenanthera pavoniana*	Fabaceae	*Anaikundumani (Mal)*	Tree	Leaves—treating chronic rheumatism, gout. Seeds—treating boils and inflammation.
8	*Adhatoda vasica*	Acanthaceae	*Malabar nut; Adadodai (Tam)*	Shrub	Leaf, roots, flower—treating bronchitis, asthma, cough, tuberculosis, intestinal worms
9	*Aerva lanata*	Amaranthaceae	*Sirupulai (Tam)*	Branched herb	Plant—anthelmintic, diuretic. Root—demulscent, diuretic, treating headache.
10	*Ageratum conyzoides*	Asteraceae	*Pum-pillu (Tam)*	Herb	Leaves—styptic, treating cuts and sores.
11	*Albizia lebbeck*	Mimosaceae	*Shirish (H); Vagai (Tam)*	Tree	Plant—treating snake bite and scorpion sting. Bark and seeds—astringent, tonic, treating piles, diarrhoea. Leaves—treating night-blindness
12	*Allium cepa*	Liliaceae	Onion; *Ulli (Mal)*	Bulb	Bulb—treating earache, sunstroke, hypertension.
13	*Alternanthera sessilis*	Amaranthaceae	*Ponnanganni keeray (Mal. and Tam)*	Herb	Plant—galactogogue, febrifuge. Stem and leaves—treating snakebite
14	*Alstonia scholaris*	Apocynaceae	Devil's tree; *Pala (Mal)*	Tree	Leaf, bark, latex—skin disorders, treating diarrhoea, dysentery, vitamin-B deficiency, fevers, dyspepsia.
15	*Amaranthus spinosus*	Amaranthaceae	*Mulluk-kirai (Tam)*	Herb	Root—colic, galactogogue, treating menorrhagia, gonorrhea, eczema. Plant—treating snakebite
16	*Ammannia baccifera*	Lythraceae	*Jangli Mehandi (H); Nirumel-neruppu (Tam)*	Herb	Leaves—treating rheumatic pains, fevers, skin diseases.
17	*Annona squamosa*	Annonaceae	*Mullanjakka (Mal)*	Small tree	Leaves—hair care. Fruit—aphrodisiac, cardio-tonic.
18	*Areca catechu*	Arecaceae	*Supari (H); Adakka (Mal)*	Tree palm	Seeds—laxative, wormicidal, antiseptic, promotes menstrual flow
19	*Argemone mexicana*	Papaveraceae	*Ponnummattam (Mal)*	Prickly annual herb	Root—treating chronic skin diseases Seeds—laxative, emetic, expectorant, demulscent, antidote to snake poison. Plant juice—treating dropsy, jaundice.

20	*Artocarpus utilis*	Moraceae	Breadfruit	Tree	Latex—treating broken bones, sprains and bruises, fungal infections Leaves—treating high blood pressure, diabetes. Bark and roots—antimicrobial, anti-tumor activity.
21	*Azadirachta indica*	Meliaceae	*Neem; Vepa (Mal)*	Tree	Seed, leaf, bark—Hair care, Skin disorders, eczema, burn, worms, gingivitis, measles, diabetes, rheumatism, scrofula, teeth care. Berries—purgative, anthelmintic Flowers—tonic, stomachic. Root bark—tonic.
22	*Bacopa monnieri*	Scrophulariaceae	*Nirbrahmi (Mal)*	Branched creeper	Plant—hair nourisher, brain tonic, rejuvenator Stem and leaves—treating snake-bite
23	*Barleria prionitis*	Acanthaceae	*Shemmuli (Mal and Tam)*	Shrub	Leaves—treating fever and phlegm, toothache Bark—treating cough
24	*Bixa orellana*	Bixaceae	*Latkan (H); Japhara (Tam)*	Shrub	Fruit—astringent, purgative Root Bark—antipyretic Seed—aphrodisiac, natural color.
25	*Blumea lacera*	Asteraceae	*Narakkarandai* (Tam)	Annual herb	Plant—antipyretic Leaves—anthelmintic, astringent, diuretic, stimulant, febrifuge. Root—treating cholera.
26	*Boerhavia diffusa*	Nyctaginaceae	*Mukaratte-kirei*	Herb	Root—anti-infective, tonic, treating ascites, dropsy, asthma, fevers, stomach disorders, kidney stones, bladder stones, anaemia, respiratory diseases, liver disorders.
27	*Bombax cieba*	Bombacaceae	*Simul* (H); *Mocha* (Mal)	Tree	Root—stimulant, tonic, aphrodisiac Bark—emetic Gum—aphrodisiac, demulcent, haemostatic, astringent, treating diarrhoea, dysentry, menorrhagia. Flowers and fruits—treating snakebite
28	*Brassica juncea*	Brassicaceae	Mustard	Herb	Seed, oil—treating Rheumatism, sciatica.
29	*Caesalpinia bonduc*	Caesalpiniaceae	*Kalanji* (Mal)	Thorny shrub	Seed—antipyretic, treating asthma, inflammations
30	*Cajanus cajan*	Fabaceae	*Thuvara* (Mal)	Herb	Seeds and leaves—promotes milk secretion.
31	*Calophyllum inophyllum*	Clusiaceae	*Punna* (Mal)	Tree	Seed oil—treating skin diseases, rheumatism Bark—astringent Gum—emetic.
32	*Calotropis gigantea*	Asclepiadaceae	*Arka* (H); *Erikku* (Mal)	Shrub	Root, bark, leaf—tonic, expectorant, emetic, treating leg-ache, myalgia, dyspepsia, scabies, haemorrhage, rheumatism, dysentery.
33	*Capsicum annuum*	Solanaceae	*Lal Mirchi*(H); *Mulagay*	Herb	Fruit, leaf—blood-purifier, stimulant, carminative, counter-irritant, treating toothache, tonsillitis, throat diseases
34	*Cardiospermum halicacabum*	Sapindaceae	*Mudukottan* (Tam)	Herb	Plant, leaf, root—treating rheumatism, nervous disorders
35	*Carica papaya*	Caricaceae	*Pappayam* (Mal)	Herb	Leaf—digestive, treating dyspepsia, intestinal irritation. Flowers- treating respiratory disorders Seed—antidote for cancer
36	*Cassia fistula*	Caesalpiniaceae	*Konnai* (Tam)	Tree	Pod, leaf, root—fevers, constipation, skin disorders
37	*Cassia occidentalis*	Caesalpiniaceae	*Natram-takara* (Mal)	Branched annual herb	Leaf, seed, root—tonic purgative, diuretic.
38	*Cassia tora*	Caesalpiniaceae	*Tagarai* (Tam)	Annual herb Chakramandrakam (Mal)	Seed and leaf—treating skin disorders, fever, leprosy, ringworm, flatulence, colic, dyspepsia, bronchitis, constipation, cough, cardiac disorders.

39	*Cassytha filiformis*	Lauraceae	*Akasavalli (M)*	Parasitic leafless twiner	Plant—tonic, treating bilious affections, chronic dysentery, urethritis, skin diseases.
40	*Catharanthus roseus*	Apocynaceae	*Periwinkle; Sada bahar (H)*	Herb	Roots, leaf—anticancer, vermifuge, treating diabetes, diarrhoea, toothache.
41	*Ceratophyllum demersum*	Ceratophyllaceae	*Sivara (H)*	Rootless submerged perennial herb	Plant—cooling, treating biliousness, scorpion sting.
42	*Cissus quadrangularis*	Vitaceae	*Pirandai (Tam)*	Herb	Stem—treating fracture, asthma, scurvy. Leaves—treating digestive problems.
43	*Citrus medica*	Rutaceae	*Gilam (Mal)*	Thorny shrub	Rind, juice, oil—aromatic, astringent, digestive, refrigerant, stomachic, sedative Flowers and bud—astringent, stimulant Root—anthelmintic, treating constipation, vomiting, urinary calculus.
44	*Cleome viscosa*	Capparidaceae	*Hulhul (H); Ariavila (Mal)*	Herb	Leaves—treating wounds, ulcers, earache. Seeds—carminative, anthelmintic
45	*Clerodendrum inerme*	Verbanaceae	*Nirnochi (Mal)*	Sprawling shrub	Leaves—febrifuge Root—treating rheumatism
46	*Clitoria ternatea*	Fabaceae	*Aparajit (H)*	Climber	Plant—treating snake poisoning Root, seed—cathartic, intellect-promoting, refrigerant, diuretic, treating epilepsy
47	*Colocasia esculenta*	Araceae	*Shembu(Mal)*	Herb	Flowers—styptic, stimulant Corm—treating alopecia, scorpion sting
48	*Cymbopogon*	Poaceae	Lemon grass	Perennial aromatic herb	Oil—treating Athlete's foot, insect repellent, scabies, muscular aches, pains, fevers, insufficient milk in breast feeding mothers, indigestion, colitis, infections, illness, headaches, nervous exhaustion and other stress related disorders.
49	*Cynodon dactylon*	Poaceae	*Dhub (H); Arugampullu (Tam)*	Herb	Plant—diuretic, treating dropsy, secondary syphilis, conjunctivitis, piles, menorrhagia.
50	*Cyprus rotundus*	Cyperaceae	*Korai (Tam)*	Herb	Tubers—diuretic, emmenagogue, anthelmintic, astringent, treating stomach disorders and bowel irritation.
51	*Datura metel*	Solanaceae	*Vellummattai (Tam)*	Herb	Seed, leaves, root—antipyretic, strong analgesic, treating loose motions, cerebral complications.
52	*Desmodium gangeticum*	Fabaceae	*Pulladi (Tam)*	Woody perennial herb	Plant—analgesic, anti-inflammatory, curing fever. Root—astringent, tonic, treating chronic fever, biliousness, vomiting, asthma, snakebite.
53	*Desmodium triflorum*	Fabaceae	*Sirupulladi (Tam)*	Herb	Leaves—galactogogue treating diarrhoea, dysentery, abscess, convulsion, wounds.
54	*Eclipta prostrata*	Asteraceae	*Garuga (Tam)*	Herb	Plant—tonic, emetic, treating hepatic and spleen enlargement. Leaves—treating scorpion sting Root—emetic, purgative, antiseptic.
55	*Emilia sonchifolia*	Asteraceae	*Mulshevi (Mal)*	Herb	Plant—febrifuge, treating bowel complaints Leaves—treating eye inflammation, night blindness, sore ears. Root—treat diarrhoea.
56	*Erythrina variegata*	Fabaceae	*Kaliyanamurukku (Tam)*	Tree	Bark—astringent, anthelmintic, treating liver troubles, snakebite. Leaves—laxative, diuretic, anthelmintic, galactogogue, relieving joint pains.
57	*Euphorbia hirta*	Euphorbiaceae	*Nelapalai (Mal)*	Herb	Plant—treating bowel complaints, cough. Latex—treating warts

58	*Euphorbia tirucalli*	Euphorbiaceae	*Kalli (Tam)*	Herb	Latex—purgative, treating warts, rheumatism, asthma, neuralgia, toothache, cough, earache.
59	*Evolvulus alsinoides*	Convolvulaceae	*Vishnukarandi* (Tam) *Vistnaclandi (Mal)*	Hairy herb	Plant—tonic, febrifuge, vermifuge. Leaves—treating chronic bronchitis and asthma
60	*Ficus benghalensis*	Moraceae	Banyan; *Pudavam* (Tam)	Tree	Milky juice—relieving rheumatic pains Bark—astringent, tonic, treating diabetes. Seeds—cooling, tonic
61	*Ficus racemosa*	Moraceae	*Atti (Tamand Mal)*	Tree	Bark—galactagogue adenopathy, treating myalgia, hydrocele, epididymitis, scabies, boils, spermatorrhoea
62	*Ficus religiosa*	Moraceae	*Peepal; Arasu (Tam)*	Tree	Bark, leaf—laxative, astringent, cooling, treating scrofula, mumps, boils.
63	*Gloriosa superba*	Liliaceae	*Mentonni* (Mal)	Climber	Tubers—curing leprosy, debility inflammations, bleeding piles, skin diseases, ulcers, snakebites. Seeds—relieving rheumatic pain
64	*Gossypium herbaceum*	Malvaceae	*Karppasi* (M)	Shrub	Seed—Demulcent, laxative, diuretic, aphrodisiac, nervine tonic, expectorant, abortifacient.
65	*Hedyotis corymbosa*	Rubiaceae	*Daman papra* (H)	Herb	Plant—anthelmintic, treating jaundice and liver diseases
66	*Hibiscus rosa-sinensis*	Malvaceae	*Jasvand*	Shrub	Flower—demulcent, hair tonic, abortifacient, treating cough, urogenital, menorrhagia, bronchitis, skin diseases.
67	*Indigofera tinctoria*	Fabaceae	*Nilam* (Mal)	Subshrub	Plant—treating epilepsy, nervous diseases, old ulcers, bronchitis, haemorrhage, premature greying of hair. Root—treating hepatitis, scorpion sting.
68	*Ipomea batatas*	Convolvulaceae	Sweet potato; *Kapakalenga (Mal)*	Herb	Rhizome—laxative, nutritive, treating scorpion bite.
69	*Ipomea pes-caprae*	Convolvulaceae	*Atampa (Mal)*	Herb	Plant—laxative, astringent, stomachic Leaves—treating rheumatism.
70	*Ixora coccinea*	Rubiaceae	Techi (Mal)	Shrub	Flowers—treating dysentry and dysmenorrhea
71	*Kalanchoe pinnata*	Crassulaceae	Air plant; *Runakalli (Tam)*	Herb	Leaves—antibacterial, anti-inflammatory, antiviral, antitumorous, hypercholesterolemia treating bruises, wounds, boils and insect bites.
72	*Lantana camara var. aculeata*	Verbanaceae	*Arippu (Mal)*	Shrub	Plant—vulnerary, diaphoretic, antiseptic, carminative, treating tetanus, rheumatism, malaria, abdominal ataxy.
73	*Lawsonia inermis*	Lythraceae	*Henna; Mayilanji (Mal)*	Shrub	Bark—treating jaundice, spleen enlargement, calculus affections, skin diseases, leprosy. Leaves—relieving headache, burning of feet.
74	*Leea indica*	Leeaceae	*Manipiranta* (M)	Shrub	Root—cooling, treating diarrhoea, dysentery and relieves thirst.
75	*Leucas aspera*	Lamiaceae	*Tumbai (Tam)*	Herb	Plant—antipyretic, insecticide. Flowers—treating cold Leaves—treating chronic rheumatism, psoriasis, scabies, chronic skin eruptions.
76	*Lycopersicon esculentum*	Solanaceae	Tomato; *Thakkali (Tam)*	Herb	Fruits—rich in vitamin C and oxalic acid
77	*Mangifera indica*	Anacardiaceae	*Amram (Mal)*	Tree	Leaves—treating scorpion sting Fruits—laxative, diuretic, astringent. Fruit rind—treating stomach debility Bark—astringent, treating haemoptysis and melaena.

78	*Manihot esculenta*	Euphorbiaceae	*Sakarkanda (H)*	Herb	Rhizome—treating sores
79	*Mimosa pudica*	Fabaceae	*Tottavati (M)*	Herb	Leaves—treating piles and fistula
80	*Momordica charantia*	Cucurbitaceae	*Kappakka (Mal); Pavakkachedi (Tam)*	Climber	Fruits and leaves—anthelmintic, vermifuge, treating jaundice, leprosy, piles.
81	*Moringa oleifera*	Moringaceae	*Murungai (Tam) Sigru (Mal)*	Small tree	Root—treating hysteria, paralysis, intermittent fever, epilepsy, rheumatism, giddiness, nervous debility, flatulence. Bark—abortif. Fruit—treating liver diseases, articular pains, tetanus, paralysis Seed oil—treating rheumatism. Gum—treating dental caries. Flowers—stimulant, aphrodisiac.
82	*Morus alba*	Moraceae	*Pattupuchi-chedi (Tam)*	Small tree	Fruit—refrigerant in fever, treating sore throat, dyspepsia and melancholia. Bark—purgative, anthelmintic.
83	*Murraya koenigii*	Rutaceae	*Karivepu (Mal)*	Shrub	Plant—tonic, stomachic. Bark and root—stimulant, cure eruptions and poisonous animal bites. Leaves—curing dysentery, external eruptions.
84	*Musa paradisiaca*	Musaceae	*Kadali (Tam); Kadalam (Mal)*	Herb	Root and stem—tonic, antiscorbutic, treating blood and venereal diseases. Fruits—antiscorbutic, mild demulcent, astringent Sap—treating hysteria, epilepsy.
85	*Nerium oleander*	Apocynaceae	Rose bay	Shrub	Plant—poisonous
86	*Ocimum americanum*	Lamiaceae	*Katturamatulasi (Mal)*	Herb	Leaves—treating parasitical skin diseases fever.
87	*Ocimum basilicum*	Lamiaceae	*Tirunitru (Mal)*	Herb	Flowers—carminative, diuretic, demulscent. Seeds—treating gonorrhoea, dysentery, chronic diarrhoea. Root—treating bowel complaints
88	*Ocimum tenuiflorum*	Lamiaceae	*Tulasi (Mal* and *Tam)*	Herb	Leaves—expectorant, treating bronchitis Seeds—demulcent Root—diaphoretic Plant—treating snake and scorpion bite
89	*Operculina turpethum*	Convolvulaceae	*Rochani (Mal)*	Climber	Roots—treating obesity, bronchitis, ascites, skin diseases, tumours, jaundice, ophthalmia Leaves—Malarial fever
90	*Pandanus odoratissimus*	Pandanaceae	*Tala (Mal)*	Shrub	Leaves—treating leprosy, small-pox, syphilis, scabies and leucoderma.
91	*Phoenix pusilla*	Arecaceae	*Chittintal (Mal)*	Shrubby palm	Gum—treating diarrhoea and urinary disorders Sap—cooling and laxative Seeds—treating eye inflammation
92	*Phyla nodiflora*	Verbanaceae	Matgrass; *Kattuttippali (Mal)*	Herb	Plant—febrifuge, diuretic, treating boils, indigestion.
93	*Phyllanthus amarus*	Euphorbiaceae	Shatterstone	Herb	Plant—treating kidney and gallstones, hepatitis B, inflammation of the appendix, diabetes.
94	*Phyllanthus emblica*	Euphorbiaceae	*Nelli (Mal* and *Tam)*	Small tree	Fruit—cooling, refrigerant, diuretic, laxative, treating diarrhoea, dyspepsia, jaundice, anaemia. Root, Bark—astringent Flowers—cooling. Seeds—treating asthma, bronchitis, biliousness.
95	*Physalis minima*	Solanaceae	*Njodi njotta (Mal)*	Herb	Fruits—tonic, diuretic, purgative
96	*Piper betle*	Piperaceae	Betel; *Vettilai (Tam);*	Perennial creeper *Tambulam (Mal)*	Leaves—antioxidant, rich source of calcium Betel oil—treating respiratory diseases

97	*Plumeria rubra*	Apocynaceae	*Vellachampakam (Mal)*	Small tree	Bark—purgative, emmenagogue. Latex—purgative Flowers—expectorant
98	*Polyalthia longifolia*	Anonaceae	Cemetry tree; *Arana chorana (Mal)*	Tree	Bark—lowers blood pressure, stimulates respiration.
99	*Portulaca oleracea*	Portulacaceae	*Karie cheera (Mal)*	Succulent herb	Plant—refrigerant, anti-scorbutic, diuretic, blood purifier. Used in treating Scurvy. Leaves—treating spleen and cardio-vascular diseases, mouth ulcers, ear and toothache.
100	*Premna serratifolia*	Verbanaceae	*Munna (Mal); Munnai (Tam)*	Small tree	Plant—treating rheumatism, neuralgia Root—stomachic, treating liver problems Leaves—treating cold, fever, flatulence.
101	*Psidium guajava*	Myrtaceae	Guava; *Koyyaa* (Mal)	Shrub	Leaves—treating cholera, digestive problems, rheumatism, diarrhoea, epilepsy, bronchitis, toothache and gumboils. Flowers and fruits—antibacterial. Bark-treating diarrhoea, dysentry
102	*Punica granatum*	Punicaceae	Pomegranate; *Dadiman (Mal)*	Shrub	Fruits—coolant, treating dyspepsia. Seeds—stomachic Root/stem bark—astringent, anthelmintic.
103	*Rauvolfia serpentina*	Apocynaceae	*Chuvannavilpori (Mal)*	Undershrub	Plant—hypnotic, sedative Roots—treating high blood pressure, snake and rat bites, mental and abdominal disorders, corneal opacity.
104	*Ricinus communis*	Euphorbiaceae	Castor seed; *Avanakku (Mal)*	Shrub	Leaves—treating boils, sores, swellings, flatulence, lactagogue Root bark—purgative Castor oil—disinfectant, strong laxative, treating food poisoning.
105	*Saccharum officinarum*	Poaceae	Sugarcane; *Karimbu (Mal)*	Herb	Stem—source of sugar, laxative, diuretic, aphrodisiac Root—demulcent, cooling, diuretic.
106	*Sesbania grandiflora*	Fabaceae	*Swampea; Akatthi (Mal)*	Softwood tree	Leaves—tonic, diuretic, laxative. Root—expectorant. Bark—astringent, tonic, treating Scabies, tongue ulcers. Red gum-astringent.
107	*Sida acuta*	Malvaceae	*Vatta thirippi (Mal)*	Shrub	Leaves—demulcent, diuretic, anthelmintic, treating rheumatic problems, elephantiasis. Root—astringent, stomachic, anti-pyretic.
108	*Sida cordata*	Malvaceae	*Bariyara (H)*	Herb	Leaves—treating indigestion, cuts and wounds, bone fracture, scorpion sting. Root—treating tooth infection, rheumatism, indigestion. Plant—treating dropsy.
109	*Solanum melongena*	Solanaceae	*Valuthina (Mal)*	Perennial shrub	Plant—antiseptic, treating toothache, sore throat. Unripe berries—fish poison
110	*Solanum nigrum*	Solanaceae	Black night shade; *Manathakkali (Tam)*	Herb	Plant—antispasmodic, antiseptic, diuretic, laxative, treating liver cirrhosis, narcotic, opium poisoning. Leaves—treating sores and wounds Berries—treating fever, diarrhoea, ulcer
111	*Syzigium cumini*	Myrtaceae	*Naval* (Mal)	Tree	Bark—astringent Leaves—treating dysentery Fruit—stomachic, diuretic, carminative, treating bilious diarrhoea Seeds—treating diabetes
112	*Tamarindus indicus*	Caesalpiniaceae	Tamarind tree; *Amlam, Puli (Mal)*	Tree	Leaves—treating bilious fever Bark—astringent, asthma, amenorrhoea. Flowers—treating conjunctivitis Fruit pulp—laxative, carminative, antiseptic, treating bilious disorders

113	*Tephrosia purpurea*	Fabaceae	Wild Indigo; *Kozhenjil (Mal)*	Herb	Root—treating dyspepsia, diarrhoea, urinary disorders, elephantiasis Seed—inflammation, vomiting Seed oil—treating scabies, eczema, skin eruptions.
114	*Teramnus labialis*	Fabaceae	*Mashoni* (H)	Climbing or trailing herb	Fruit—treating paralysis, nervous diseases, rheumatism.
115	*Thespesia populnea*	Malvaceae	Portia tree; *Poovarasu (Tam)*; *Kallal (Mal)*	Tree	Plant—treating malaria Bark, leaves, flowers and Root-treating scabies, psoriasis, eczema. Fruit—treating herpetic diseases Bark oil—treating urethritis, gonorrhoea Seeds—treating skin disease
116	*Tinospora cordifolia*	Menispermaceae	*Sittamrytu (Mal)*	Climber	Stem—stomachic, antipyretic, aphrodisiac. Plant—diuretic, treating gonorrhoea.
117	*Tragia involucrata*	Euphorbiaceae	Indian stinging nettle; *Choriyanam (Mal)*	Perennial twiner	Leaves—treating headache Fruit—treating enlarged spleen. Root—blood purifier, diaphoretic, treating fever, cold, leg and arm pain, venereal complaints.
118	*Tylophora indica*	Asclepiadaceae	Emetic Swallow Wort; *Vallipala (Mal)*	Branching climber	Leaves—treating dermatitis, hydrophobia Roots—treating asthma, bronchitis, whooping cough, rheumatic pains
119	*Vernonia cinerea*	Asteraceae	*Puvankuruntal (Mal)*	Herb	Plant—treating malarial fever. Leaves—treating amoebiasis, elephantiasis. Flower—treat fever, conjunctivitis, rheumatism. Root—anthelmintic Seed—treat, psoriasis, flatulence, dysuria, leucoderma, cough.
120	*Vigna unguiculata ssp. cylindrica*	Fabaceae	Catjung pea; *Alasendi(Mal)*	Climber	Seed—antibilious, treating liver complaints, jaundice.
121	*Vitex negundo*	Verbanaceae	*Vellanocchi (Mal)*	Shrub	Leaves—insecticidal, anticancerous, treating headache, rheumatic problems. Root—treating piles, dyspepsia, rheumatism. Fruits—vermifuge.
122	*Ziziphus mauritiana*	Rhamnaceae	Indian jujube; *Elantha (Mal)*	Small tree	Fruits—source of Vitamin C, cooling, tonic, anodyne. Seed—treat diarrhoea. Leaves—treat typhoid.

ANNEXURE A-29

List of Corals Recorded from Lakshadweep Reefs

Family: **Acroporidae**

Acropora abrotanoides
Acropora aspera
Acropora corymbosa
Acropora nobilis
Acropora formosa
Acropora forskali
Acropora echinata
Acropora efflorescens
Acropora granulosa
Acropora hemprichii
Acropora humilis
Acropora hyacinthus
Acropora indica
Acropora irregularis
Acropora monticulosa
Acropora nasuta
Acropora palifera
Acropora robusta
Acropora squarrosa
Acropora teres
Astreopora listeri
Astreopora myriophthalma
Montipora explanata
Montipora foliosa
Montipora tuberculosa
Montipora turgescens
Montipora venosa
Montipora sp

Family: **Agariciidae**

Gardineroseris planulata
Pavona duerdeni
Pavona maldivensis
Pavona varians

Family: **Caryophylliidae**

Caryophyllia araucta
Caryophyllia clavus
Stephanocyathus nobilis

Family: **Dendrophylliidae**

Tubastrea aurea
Tubipora musica
Turbinaria crater
Turbinaria mesenterina
Turbinaria sp

Family: **Euphyllidae**

Diploastrea heliopra
Euphyllia glabrescens

Family: **Faviidae**

Cyphastrea microphthalma
Cyphastrea seralia
Echinopora lamellosa
Favia favus
Favia pallida
Favia speciosa
Favia stelligera
Favia valenciennesii
Favites abdita
Favites complanata
Favites flexuosa
Favites melicerum
Favites pentagona
Goniastrea australensis
Goniastrea pectinata
Goniastrea retiformis
Hydnophora microconos
Leptoria phrygia
Leptastrea bottae
Leptastrea purpurea
Leptastrea transversa
Platygyra daedalea
Platygyra sinesis
Plesiastrea versipora

Family: **Flabellidae**

Flabellum pavoninum

Family: **Fungiidae**

Cycloseris sp
Fungia danai
Fungia fungites
Fungia scutaria
Fungia somervillei
Podabacia crustacea
Polyphyllia talpina

Family: **Merulinidae**

Merulina ampliata

Family: **Mussidae**

Acanthastrea echinata
Lobophyllia corymbosa
Symphyllia radians

Family: **Oculinidae**

Galaxea fascicularis

Family: **Pocilloporidae**

Pocillopora damiconis
Pocillopora eydouxi
Pocillopora ligulata
Pocillopora meandrina
Pocillopora verrucosa
Stylophora pistillata

Family: **Poritidae**

Alveopora superficialis
Goniopora stokesi
Goniopora minor
Goniopora sp
Porites andrewsi
Porites convexa
Porites lobata
Porites lichen

Porites lutea
Porites minicoiensis
Porites solida
Porites sp

Family: **Siderasteridae**

Psammocora contigua
Psammocora digitata
Psammocora haimeana
Psammocora profundacella

Non Scleractinian Corals

Class: Hydrozoa

Order: Milliporina

Millepora exesa
Millepora dichotoma
Millepora platyphyllia

Class: Anthozoa

Order: Helioporacea

Heliopora coerulea

ANNEXURE A-30

Organisms Reported in the Lagoons of Lakshadweep Islands

Crustacea

The brachyuran crabs and lobsters of Lakshadweep have been studied by Alcock (1895, 1896, 1898, 1899 and 1900) and Borradaile (1903 and 1906). Alcock reported 41 species of crabs and Borradaile 52 species of crabs and 2 species of lobsters. Sankarankutty (1961) recorded 36 species of crabs from Lakshadweep out of these 27 were from Minicoy and the rest from Kavaratti, Aminidivi and Bitra islands. Kathirvel (MS) collected 28 species of brachyuran crabs and 1 species of Panulirid lobster from Kiltan atoll. Meiyappan and Kathirvel (1978) published records of the brachyuran crab *Grapsus albolineatus, Cardiosoma carnifex* and the lobsters *Parribacus antarcticus* and *Panulirus homarus* from Minicoy. Pillai *et al.* (1985) recorded *P. versicolor* mostly during the November-January period in Minicoy. *P. versicolor* is found to be the most common. The distribution pattern of the lobsters was found to be seasonal, more common on the reef flats during the November-January period. Meiyappan and Kathirvel (1978) found *P. penicillatus* to be the most common lobster in Minicoy in the late seventies while Pillai *et al.* (1984) found *P. versicolor* as the major lobster at Minicoy. This species is also recorded from Kiltan atoll (Kathirvel, MS).

Mollusca

Smith (1960) listed *Conus, Terebra, Sistrum, Purpura, Nassa, Oliva, Solarium* and *Trochus* as the common genera widely distributed in Maldives and Lakshadweep. Burton (1940) reported the common occurrence of the giant clam Tridacna over the reef of Chetlat Island when he visited the Lakshadweep in 1935. He recorded the shells of Pterocera from Bitra. Octopus was recorded from Chetlat and Bitra where they were found in plenty over the reef. In recent times on an average 20 tonnes of these are landed annually in the Lakshadweep islands. *Octopus macropus* and *O. vulgaris* are common in Minicoy, the former forming about 80 per cent of the catch. Both species inhabit crevices in the reef flat. The islanders use them as food and as bait for fishing.

Appukuttan (1973) observed nine species of coral boring bivalves causing destruction to the reefs of the Islands. Appukuttan and Pillai (MS) observed that the molluscan fauna of Lakshadweep are similar to those of other islands in the Indian Ocean. They have listed 48 gastropods and 12 bivalves and found an abundance of gastropods in number and species particularly in the littoral and eulittoral reef-flat habitats. Among the gastropods found in these islands, Top shells, Spider conch, Cone shells, Cowries and Helmet shells are commercially important. *Trochus radiatus, Lambis spp., Arabica arabica, Conus spp., Charonia tritonis* and *Cassis cornuta* are some of the beautiful shells available in good quantity in these islands. Giant clams *Tridacna maximum* is found in good numbers in all the islands in the lagoon. Till 1980 a sizeable population of the giant clam was observed in the lagoon of Minicoy but at present dead shells of this clam are found in large numbers along with corals. The probable reason for the large-scale mortality can be siltation due to the dredging operation done in the harbour area. There was also an incidence of aggregation of large spider shells (*Lambis truncata*) numbering 400-500 ranging 20-25 cm in length and weighing 1.15 kg in the lagoon during January 1984 when the water was calm. This species is not found very often in reef flat. It is understood from the older generation of fishermen of the islands that there was a good settlement of green mussel *Perna viridis* in Amini Island 20 years back and was used for edible purposes by the local people.

Sponges

Thomas (1973, 1979) mentions 41 species of sponges from Minicoy including typical coral and shell boring species such as *Spirastrella cuspidifera. S. inconsistence* and *Cliona spp.* The common Indian bath sponge, *Spongia officianalis* has been observed in Minicoy. Many sponges recorded from Minicoy are rich in Bromine and Iodine.

Echinodermata

Gardiner (1903) observed surface living holothurians very commonly in Minicoy. *Holothuria atra, H.seabra, Actinopyga mauritiana,* and *A. echinites* are the most abundant species in Minicoy. Ten species of echinoderms were recorded by James (MS) from Kiltan atoll of the northern part of the Lakshadweep. These include the *holothurians, Stichopus chloronotus, Bohadschina marmorata* and *ophiuroid* were the other echinoderms collected around Kiltan.

Turtles

Bhaskar (1984) reports four species of turtles which occur and nest in Lakshadweep. They are the Hawksbill

(*Erethmochelys imbricata*), the Olive-Ridley (*Lepidochelys olivacea*), the Green Turtle (*Chelonia mydas*) and the Leather-back (*Dermochelys coriacea*). The last one is reportedly rare.

The green turtles nest mainly during the southwest monsoon (June-September) on the Suheli, Valiakara, Suheli Cheriakara, Tinnakara, Bangaram and Parali. A feeding and nesting population of green turtles are observed in Minicoy. A few hawksbill and Olive-Ridleys also nest on Andrott, Kadmat and Agatti islands. Trading in hawksbill scutes through Mangalore existed in earlier years. Turtle fat especially that of the green, Olive-Ridley and the leatherback is used by islanders for waterproofing the wooden boats.

ANNEXURE A-31

Laws Applicable to Land Regulation and Biodiversity in Lakshadweep

Year	*Laws*
1959	1. Laccadive Islands and Minicoy Regulation and Rules.
	2. Survey and Boundary Regulations—this was modified in 1976 and 1979, supplementary rules were published.
1965	The Laccadive, Minicoy and Amindivi Islands Land Revenue and Tenancy Regulations. To provide for the settlement and assessment of land revenue rights relating to land in the UT of Lakshadweep. By Ministry of Law (Legislative Department), New Delhi–15th July 1965.
1968	The Laccadive, Minicoy and Amindivi Islands Land Revenue and Tenancy Regulation Rules.
1973	Laccadive Minicoy and Amindivi Islands (Alternation of Name) Act—Renamed as Lakshadweep by Ministry of Home Affairs, GoI, New Delhi–15th October 1973.
1979	Survey and Boundary Regulations Supplementary Rules.
	Biodiversity/Coast Management
1972	Wild Life Protection Act.
1973	1. Wild Life (Transactions and Taxidency) Lakshadweep Rules 2. Lakshadweep Wild Life (Stock Declaration) Rules. By Ministry of Agriculture, GoI, New Delhi, November 1973.
1991	Coastal Zone Regulations, Ministry of Environment and Forests, New Delhi, 19 February 1991.This regulation framed under section– 3(1) and section–3(2) of the Environment (Protection) Act 1986 and Rule-5(3) of DoE(Protection) Rules, 1986 declaring coastal stretches as Coastal Regulation Zone (CRZ) and regulating activities in the CRZ.
1996	Coastal Zone Management Plan for UT of Lakshadweep by DSTE, Kavaratti November 20, 1996.
1998	Lakshadweep Protection of Corals By-laws. Published by the UT of Lakshadweep Administration (DST&E), Kavaratti 4th August 1998. For protection of the coral to preserve the environment of Lakshadweep Island. This law is framed on basis of the regulation 82(1)(g) of Lakshadweep Panchayat Regulations, 1994. Lakshadweep Protection of Corals (Amendments) Bye-laws. Regarding collection of coral shingle, boulder and sands, etc. and declaring coastal stretches as coastal regulation zone (CRZ) and regulation of activities within the CRZ. Lakshadweep Sanitation Conservancy Bye-law. Prohibiting the use of non-biodegradable wastes hazardous to the Islands.
2000	The Lakshadweep Marine Fishing Regulation No. 3 of 2000 published by the Ministry of Law Justice and Company Affairs (Legislative Department), New Delhi, 21st September, 2000. This regulation provides for the regulation of fishing and fishing vessels in the lagoon and sea around the UT of Lakshadweep.
2001	The Lakshadweep Marine Fishing Regulation and Rules by Lakshadweep Administration (Department of Fisheries) Kavaratti–24th February 2001. According to this, fishing by a ship or boat fitted with mechanical means of propulsion may be regulated, restricted or prohibited in any specified area under clause (b) of the sub-section (1) of section 4. Notification by the Ministry of Environment and Forests banning collection of corals and molluscs, Vol. No. 53, December 21, 2001

ANNEXURE A-32

Revenue Receipts of Lakshadweep Administration from 1984-85 to 2002-03 (R.E.)

Year	*Revenue Receipts-Actuals# ('000 Rs.)*	*Annual Growth over Previous Year (%)*	*Annual Growth Rate (AGR) %*	
			1984-85 to 1992-93	*1993-94 to 2002-03 (R.E.)*
1984-85	11740			
1985-86	12812	9.13	Compound AGR=	
1986-87	13530	5.60	12.89	20.68
1987-88	18469	36.50		
1988-89	21563	16.75		
1989-90	10115	-53.09	Trend Growth Rate=	
1990-91	15842	56.62	10.78	23.23
1991-92	29947	89.04		
1992-93	30967	3.41		
1993-94	33744	8.97		
1994-95	34151	1.21		
1995-96	50268	47.19		
1996-97	54843	9.10		
1997-98	66850	21.89		
1998-99	85379	27.72		
1999-00	116345	36.27		
2000-01	144612	24.30		
2001-02	175313	21.23		
2002-03 (R.E.)@	183185	4.49		

Source: #: Dept of Planning & Statistics, Lakshadweep Administration.
@: Detailed Demand for Grants for the year 2003-04, Ministry of Home Affairs.

ANNEXURE A-33

Revenue Receipts of Lakshadweep by Detailed Heads of Account

('000 Rs.)

Head of Account	*2000-01 (R.E.)*	*2001-02 (R.E.)*	*2002-03 (R.E.)*	*2003-04 (B.E.)*
A. Tax Revenue				
0014- Administration of Justice	200	0	0	0
0021- Tax other than Corporation Taxes	6570	7500	8000	8050
0029- Land Revenue	670	696	670	700
0030- Stamp & Registration	1455	1665	1810	1820
0040- Sales Tax	0	0	0	0
Total- Tax Revenue	8895	9861	10480	10570
B. Non-Tax Revenue				
0049- Interest Receipts	1600	2800	4200	4300
0050- Dividends & Profits	0	0	0	0
0055- Police	1325	180	210	230
0058- Stationery & Printing	7800	4100	4900	5000
0059- Public Works	3200	4300	6000	6100
0070- Other Administrative Services	232	465	450	475
0071- Contribution & Recoveries Towards Pension & Other Retirement Benefits	470	280	800	850
0075- Miscellaneous General Services	2	5	10	10
0202- Education, Sports, Arts & Culture	290	300	280	300
0210- Medical & Public Health	350	280	250	275
0216- Housing	1000	900	1000	1050
0220- Information & Publicity	65	200	150	150
0230- Labour & Employment	25	30	5	10
0235- Social Security & Welfare	110	200	220	230
0401- Crop Husbandry	550	1400	1400	1450
0403- Animal Husbandry	9700	15000	14000	14500
0405- Fisheries	5968	15000	19000	19000
0425- Cooperation	1612	1300	150	150
0435- Other Agri. Programme	1700	1600	1900	1900
0801- Power	40925	63000	75700	78000
0810- Power & Non-conv. Energy	4500	400	950	950
0851- Village & Small Industries	1350	1012	1100	1200
1051- Ports & Light Houses	200	0	300	300
1052- Shipping	14000	27500	31000	31000
1053- Civil Aviation	6500	7500	7000	7500
1055- Road Transport	280	0	600	600
1056- Inland Water Transport	750	600	770	800
1075- Other Transport Services	750	300	0	0
1425- Other Scientific Research	55	0	10	10
1452- Tourism	615	0	300	300
1475- Other General Economic Services	11	90	50	50
Total: Non-Tax Revenue	105935	148742	172705	176690
Total Revenue: Tax + Non-tax	**114830**	**158603**	**183185**	**187260**

Note: In the Detailed Demands for Grants Documents for 2001-02 to 2003-04, sales tax is shown under non-tax revenue.

Source: Detailed Demand for Grants for the years 2000-01 to 2003-04, Ministry of Home Affairs.

ANNEXURE A-34

Tax and Non-Tax Revenue Receipts of Lakshadweep and Other Union Territories (without Legislature) for 2002-03 (R.E.)

	Unit	*A & N Islands*	*Chandigarh*	*Dadra & Nagar Haveli*	*Daman & Diu*	*Lakshadweep*
A. Tax revenue	(Rs. in '000)	126000	4067010	523150	617400	10480
B. Non-Tax revenue	(Rs. in '000)	751370	3099490	800234	407400	172705
C. Total revenue (A+B)	(Rs. in '000)	877370	7166500	1323384	1024800	183185
D. Population	2001 Census	356265	900914	220451	158059	60595
E. Per capita Tax revenue	(Rs.)	354	4514	2373	3906	173
F. Per capita Non-Tax revenue	(Rs.)	2109	3440	3630	2578	2850
G. Per capita Total Rev. (E+F)	(Rs.)	2463	7955	6003	6484	3023

Source: Budget Documents of MHA.

ANNEXURE A-35

Tax and Non-Tax Revenue Receipts of Lakshadweep and other Union Territories (without Legislature) under Various Heads of Account for 2002-03 (R.E.)

(Rs. in Thousands)

Head of Account	*A & N Islands*	*Chandigarh*	*Dadra & Nag. Haveli*	*Daman & Diu*	*Lakshadweep*
A. Tax Revenue					
0014- Administration of Justice	—	—	—	—	0
0021- Tax other than Corporation Taxes	—	—	—	—	8000
0029- Land Revenue	8400	10	2350	7000	670
0030- Stamp & Registration	9000	190000	14800	30000	1810
0039- State Excise	105000	810000	6000	130200	—
0040- Sales Tax	—	2800000	450000	400000	0
0041- Taxes on Motor Vehicles	3200	140000	50000	40000	—
0042- Taxes on Goods & Passengers	—	32000	—	10000	—
0043- Taxes and Duties on Electricity	—	70000	—	—	—
0045- Other Taxes on Commodities and Services	400	25000	—	200	—
TOTAL-TAX REVENUE	**126000**	**4067010**	**523150**	**617400**	**10480**
B. NON-TAX REVENUE					
0049- Interest Receipts	—	—	—	1500	4200
0050- Dividends & Profits	1200	—	600	—	0
0055- Police	4000	22500	1400	—	210
0056- Jails	100	600	—	—	—
0058- Stationery & Printing	5500	60000	15	200	4900
0059- Public Works	30000	6000	600	2500	6000
0070- Other Administrative Services	8270	25000	458	1000	450
0071- Contribution & Recoveries Towards Pension & Other Retirement Benefits	—	—	—	700	800
0075- Miscellaneous General Services	—	—	—	800	10
0202- Education, Sports, Arts & Culture	1800	39000	200	700	280
0210- Medical & Public Health	1500	65000	208	500	250
0215- Water supply & Sanitation	8000	—	580	3000	—
0216- Housing	2000	22000	360	900	1000
0217- Urban Development	—	100	—	—	—
0220- Information & Publicity	100	100	30		150
0230- Labour & Employment	50	2520	225	900	5
0235- Social Security & Welfare	50	500	20	100	220
0401- Crop Husbandry	4000	150	600	800	1400
0403- Animal Husbandry	1900	250	102	400	14000
0404- Dairy Development	500	—	650	—	—
0405- Fisheries	4000	10	5	500	19000
0406- Forestry and Wildlife	65000	300	1100	—	—
0425- Cooperation	50	2500	50	100	150
0435- Other Agri. Programmes	20	—	50	—	1900
0515- Other Rural Development Programmes	30	1405	31	—	—
0702- Minor Irrigation	—	—	3600	—	—
0801- Power	250000	2250000	781300	380000	75700
0810- Non-conventional sources of energy	700	—	—	—	950
0851- Village & Small Industries	3500	900	2500	—	1100
0852- Industries	—	—	0	4300	—
1051- Ports & Light Houses	125400	—	—	800	300
1052- Shipping	195000	—	—	—	31000

1053- Civil Aviation	0	—	—	—	7000
1054- Roads & Bridges	—	—	1200	100	
1055- Road Transport	22600	600000	—	—	600
1056- Inland Water Transport	3700	—	—	—	770
1075- Other Transport Services	—	—	—	—	0
1452- Tourism	12000	5	3950	7000	300
1475- Other General Economic Services	400	650	400	600	50
1425- Other Scientific Research	—	—	—	—	10
Total-Non-Tax Revenue	751370	3099490	800234	407400	172705
Total Revenue-Tax + Non-tax	**877370**	**7166500**	**1323384**	**1024800**	**183185**

Source: Budget Documents of MHA.

ANNEXURE A-36

Revenue Receipts and Total Expenditure of Lakshadweep Administration from 1984-85 to 2002-03 (R.E.)

Year	*Revenue Receipts-Actuals#* *('000 Rs.)*	*Total Expenditure (Revenue+ Capital, Plan+Non-Plan)-Actuals#* *('000 Rs.)*	*Excess of Expenditure over Receipts* *('000 Rs.)*	*Total Expenditure as percentage of Revenue Receipts* *(in Per Cent)*
1984-85	11740	195273	183533	1663
1985-86	12812	228366	215554	1782
1986-87	13530	253091	239561	1871
1987-88	18469	337151	318682	1825
1988-89	21563	395072	373509	1832
1989-90	10115	334707	324592	3309
1990-91	15842	385594	369752	2434
1991-92	29947	419779	389832	1402
1992-93	30967	610000	579033	1970
1993-94	33744	826000	792256	2448
1994-95	34151	873601	839450	2558
1995-96	50268	1309800	1259532	2606
1996-97	54843	1323588	1268745	2413
1997-98	66850	1439217	1372367	2153
1998-99	85379	1720734	1635355	2015
1999-00	116345	2092549	1976204	1799
2000-01	144612	2983391	2838779	2063
2001-02	175313	2846783	2671470	1624
2002-03 (R.E.)@	183185	2784000	2600815	1520

Source: #: Department of Planning & Statistics, Lakshadweep Administration.

@: Detailed Demand for Grants for the year 2003-04, Ministry of Home Affairs, Lakshadweep Administration.

ANNEXURE A-37

Sectoral Distribution of Eighth and Ninth Plan Expenditure and Tenth Plan Outlay for Lakshadweep

Major/Minor Heads of Development	*Eighth Plan Expenditure**		*Ninth Plan Expenditure***		*Tenth Plan Outlay#*	
	Rs. in Lakh	*% to Total*	*Rs. in Lakh*	*% to Total*	*Rs. in Lakh*	*% to Total*
1	*2*	*3*	*4*	*5*	*6*	*7*
I. Agriculture & Allied Activities						
Crop Husbandry & Horticulture	863.10	6.17	883.17	2.50	860.79	1.97
Soil and Water Conservation	152.28	1.09	165.46	0.47	81.51	0.19
Animal Husbandry	669.41	4.78	1099.42	3.11	929.47	2.13
Fisheries	788.95	5.64	1101.58	3.12	5989.26	13.71
Forestry & Wild Life (incl. social forestry)	152.51	1.09	132.70	0.38	92.30	0.21
Other Agricultural Programmes:						
Cooperation	140.76	1.01	395.71	1.12	2730.27	6.25
Total - (I)	2767.01	19.78	3778.04	10.70	10683.60	24.45
II. Rural Development						
Special Programmes for Rural Dev.						
Integrated Rural Energy Programme (IREP)	38.39	0.27	92.31	0.26	0.00	0.00
Rural Employment						
Land Reforms	42.52	0.30	45.59	0.13	0.00	0.00
Other Rural Development Programmes (incl. Community Devt. and Panchayats)	207.92	1.49	554.16	1.57	559.61	1.28
Total - (II)	288.83	2.06	692.06	1.96	559.61	1.28
III. Special Area Programmes	0.00	0.00	0.00	0.00	0.00	0.00
IV. Irrigation & Flood Control						
Flood Control (incl. anti-sea erosion, etc.)	988.44	7.07	1700.08	4.82	1733.85	3.97
Total - (IV)	988.44	7.07	1700.08	4.82	1733.85	3.97
V. Energy						
Power	609.60	4.36	1282.61	3.63	1388.96	3.18
Non-conventional Sources of Energy	669.78	4.79	1327.83	3.76	648.76	1.48
Total - (V)	1279.38	9.15	2610.44	7.39	2037.72	4.66
VI. Industry & Minerals						
Village & Small Industries	676.33	4.83	816.40	2.31	506.23	1.16
Total - (VI)	676.33	4.83	816.40	2.31	506.23	1.16
VII. Transport						
Ports and Light Houses	364.38	2.60	711.57	2.02	7705.94	17.63
Shipping	2506.19	17.91	14552.22	41.22	4305.89	9.85
Civil Aviation	0.00	0.00	66.00	0.19	1113.35	2.55
Roads and Bridges	435.00	3.11	721.26	2.04	657.14	1.50
Road Transport	3.59	0.03	2.13	0.01	0.00	0.00
Inland Water Transport	315.23	2.25	263.11	0.75	833.06	1.91
Total - (VII)	3624.39	25.90	16316.29	46.23	14615.38	33.44
VIII. Communications	129.50	0.93	69.58	0.20	0.00	0.00
IX. Science, Technology & Environment						
Scientific Research (incl. S&T)	100.83	0.72	172.20	0.49	307.64	0.70
Ecology & Environment	63.60	0.45	212.18	0.60	400.30	0.92
Total - (IX)	164.43	1.17	384.38	1.09	707.94	1.62
X. General Economic Services						
Secretariat Economic Services	44.07	0.32	79.58	0.23	19.03	0.04
Tourism	303.03	2.17	260.42	0.74	5015.45	11.48
Census, Surveys & Statistics	2.03	0.01	23.68	0.07	29.70	0.07
Civil Supplies	179.60	1.28	587.45	1.66	0.00	0.00

Other General Economic Services:						
Weights & Measures, etc.	55.84	0.40	78.43	0.22	54.75	0.13
Total - (X)	584.57	4.18	1029.56	2.92	5118.93	11.71
XI. Social Services						
Education						
General Education	732.95	5.24	1796.49	5.09	1221.82	2.80
Sports & Youth Services	114.97	0.82	465.00	1.32	361.53	0.83
Art & Culture	191.63	1.37	166.57	0.47	241.56	0.55
Sub-Total (Education)	1039.55	7.43	2428.06	6.88	1824.91	4.18
Medical & Public Health	576.59	4.12	1225.24	3.47	901.30	2.06
Water Supply & Sanitation	508.05	3.63	1014.33	2.87	904.33	2.07
Housing (incl. Police Housing)	498.02	3.56	1050.63	2.98	1271.83	2.91
Urban Development (incl. State Capital Proj.)	8.94	0.06	467.45	1.32	225.96	0.52
Information & Publicity	106.45	0.76	96.66	0.27	160.99	0.37
Labour & Employment						
Labour & Labour Welfare	88.36	0.63	117.01	0.33	7.51	0.02
Social Security & Social Welfare	131.83	0.94	126.48	0.36	112.73	0.26
Nutrition	80.72	0.58	140.90	0.40	74.56	0.17
Total - (XI)	3038.51	21.71	6666.76	18.88	5484.12	12.55
XII. General Services						
Jails	24.36	0.17	0.00	0.00	0.00	0.00
Stationery & Printing	325.42	2.33	247.43	0.70	139.87	0.32
Other Administrative Services$	98.94	0.71	994.32	2.82	2112.75	4.83
Total - (XII)	448.72	3.21	1241.75	3.52	2252.62	5.15
Grand Total	**13990.11**	**100.00**	**35305.34**	**100.00**	**43700.00**	**100.00**

Note: *: Based upon actual expenditure for 1992-93 to 1995-96 and anticipated expenditure for 1996-97, as reported in the *Draft Ninth Plan Document of Lakshadweep* brought out by Lakshadweep Administration.

**: Based upon actual expenditure figures for 1997-99 to 2000-01 and anticipated expenditure figures for 2001-02 at 1996-97 prices. Source for Ninth Plan data, *Draft Tenth FYP Document of Lakshadweep*.

#: Source for Tenth Plan data, *Tenth FYP Document* (Vol. III), Planning Commission.

$: Includes, for Eighth Plan, Fire Protection and for Ninth Plan, Fire Protection (186.11), District Police (76.80), Information Technology (111.61), Rural Shelter (119.8) and Major Works- PMSGY (500).

ANNEXURE A-38

Composition of the Village (*Dweep*) and the District *Panchayats* in Lakshadweep

Village (Dweep) Panchayats

No. of Village (*Dweep*) *Panchayats*:	10
Total No. of Members in the Village (*Dweep*) *Panchayats*:	79
No. of Women in the Village (*Dweep*) *Panchayats*:	30
No. of Women as Chairperson in the Village (*Dweep*) *Panchayats*:	4
No. of Members in VDP Amini:	10 (4 women)
No. of Members in VDP Andrott:	10 (4 women)
No. of Members in VDP Agatti:	8 (3 women)
No. of Members in VDP Bitra:	3 (1 women)
No. of Members in VDP Chetlat:	6 (2 women)
No. of Members in VDP Kavaratti:	10 (4 women)
No. of Members in VDP Kalpeni:	8 (3 women)
No. of Members in VDP Kadmat:	8 (3 women)
No. of Members in VDP Kiltan:	6 (2 women)
No. of Members in VDP Minicoy:	10 (4 women)
Total No. of Members in the Village (*Dweep*) *Panchayats*	**79 (30 women)**

Constituencies Reserved in Village (*Dweep*) *Panchayats*

Sl. No.	*Reserved For*	*No. of Constituency*
1.	Scheduled Tribe	49
2.	Scheduled Tribe – Women	27
3.	General Women	3
	Total	**79**

Reservation in the Office of Chairperson of Village (*Dweep*) *Panchayats*

Sl. No.	*Name of the VDPs*	*Reserved for*
1.	Minicoy	Scheduled Tribe
2.	Kavaratti	Scheduled Tribe
3.	Kalpeni	Scheduled Tribe – Women
4.	Agatti	Scheduled Tribe
5.	Amini	Scheduled Tribe
6.	Kadmat	Scheduled Tribe – Women
7.	Kiltan	Scheduled Tribe
8.	Bitra	Scheduled Tribe – Women
9.	Chetlat	Scheduled Tribe – Women

District *Panchayat*

No. of District Panchayats:	1
Total No. of members in the District Panchayats:	33 (12 women)
No. of directly elected members:	22 (8 women)
No. of Chairpersons of VDPs:	10 (4 women)
Member of Parliament representing Lakshadweep:	1

Constituencies Reserved in the District *Panchayats*

Sl. No.	*Reserved for*	*No. of Constituency*
1.	Scheduled Tribe	13
2.	Scheduled Tribe – Women	7
3.	General Women	1
4.	Unreserved	1
	Total	22

Women Participation in the Panchayati Raj Institution in Lakshadweep

No. of women members in the Village (*Dweep*) *Panchayats*:	30
No. of women chairpersons in the Village (*Dweep*) *Panchayats*:	4
No. of women members in the District *Panchayat*:	12

Source: Lakshadweep Administration.

ANNEXURE A-39

Schemes Transferred to the Panchayats

Schemes Transferred to the District *Panchayat*

Agriculture

Coconut development programme

Soil and water conservation

Social and agro-forestry

Fisheries

Maintenance and repair of boats

Industries

Prime Ministers Rozgar Yojana

Promotion of traditional handicrafts and setting up handicraft training cum production centre

Financial assistance to the local entrepreneurs/transport subsidy to SSI Units

Human resource development plan

Social Welfare

Arts and culture

Special Nutrition Programme

Education

Primary education

Labour and Employment

Pre–recruitment training to the local Scheduled Tribes

Co-operation and Civil Supplies

Development of other types of cooperative societies

Schemes Transferred to Village (*Dweep*) *Panchayats*

Medical and Health Service

Registration of births and deaths

Animal Husbandry

Fashioning of goat rearing system to suit the ecosystem

Cattle/Buffalo development (Integrated Cattle Development)

Agriculture

Horticulture development

Olericulture development

Manure and fertilisers

Integrated plant protection

Agriculture extension service and strengthening department activities

Floriculture and orchid development

Agricultural marketing and processing

Department of Environment and Forests

Scientific management of biodegradable and non-biodegradable wastes

Social Justice Empowerment and Culture

Social security and welfare

Aid to women welfare organisations

Fisheries

Deep sea fisheries and development of shark fishing

Mechanisation and improvement of fishing crafts

Public Works

Water supply programme

Labour and Employment

Imparting training in typewriting

Incentive aid to local ST candidates seeking employment

Source: Lakshadweep Administration.

ANNEXURE A-40

A. Staff (Functionaries) Transferred to the District *Panchayat*

Agriculture	28
Fisheries	13
Animal Husbandry	2
Industries	5
Social Justice Empowerment and Culture	35
DOP & RD	18
Education	698
Total	**799**

B. Staff (Functionaries) Transferred to the Village (*Dweep*) *Panchayat*

Medical & Health	35
Animal Husbandry	30
Agriculture	133
Fisheries	42
Labour and Employment	9
Total	**249**

Source: Lakshadweep Administration.

ANNEXURE A-41

History of Disasters in Lakshadweep

One of the earliest natural disasters recorded was the storm that struck the islands in April 1847. It commenced in Kalpeni, passed on to Andrott and finally reached Kiltan after devastating these two islands. All the houses in Kalpeni were damaged or washed away. Out of the population of 1,682, 246 were drowned or washed away in Kalpeni. In 1891, a violent storm burst upon Kavaratti Island causing considerable damage to coconut trees. The storm caused damage in Agatti and Amindivi group of islands also. Kalpeni Island was hit by a severe cyclone in December 1922. The waves washed completely over the narrow northern end and the sea poured across the island into the lagoon. There was no loss of life. The cyclone was felt in other islands also. Another major storm that struck the islands occurred in 1941. In 1963 and 1965 also major calamities occurred causing considerable loss of properties in Andrott, Kalpeni, Agatti and Kiltan. There was no loss of life. A cyclone occurred in 1977 in Kalpeni and Andrott without causing any loss of life. The last cyclone occurred in May 2004 in Lakshadweep. Though no human or animal life was lost, a large number of coconut trees were uprooted and some houses were also damaged. High density of population, poor sanitation, and greater exposure to the external world also pose threat of disease epidemics.

Disaster type	*Year*	*Loss of life—Island wise*	*Severely Affected Islands*	*Other Affected Islands*
Storm	1847	Kalpeni–246 drowned out of a total population of 1682.	Kalpeni, Andrott	Kiltan
	1891	-	Andrott	Kavaratti, Agatti, Amini and Kalpeni
	1922	No loss of life.	Kalpeni	
	1963	No loss of life.	Andrott, Kalpeni	Agatti, Kiltan
	1965	No loss of life.	Andrott, Kalpeni	Andrott, Kalpeni, Agatti, Kiltan
	1977	No loss of life.	Kalpeni	Andrott
	2004	No loss of life.	Amini, Kadmat, Chetlat	Kiltan, Bitra
Sea ingress	1847	Kalpeni–246 drowned out of a total population of 1682.	Kalpeni	-
	1977	-	Kalpeni	-
Epidemics				
Malaria	1974	780 cases of *Plasmodium vivax* malaria detected and treated.	Minicoy, Chetlat, and Bitra	-
Gastroenteritis	1994	126 cases of Gastroenteritis treated. 4 deaths.	Agatti	Amini
Diarrhoea	1997	738 cases of Diarrhoea reported and treated. Later on Cholera was isolated from few cases. 5 deaths.	Kalpeni	Kavaratti

Source: Lakshadweep Administration

ANNEXURE A-42

List of the R&D Organisations and other Central Government Institutions that are Mandated to Work on Issues that Relate Directly or Indirectly to Natural and other Disasters

Soil Resources

Central Soil and Water Conservation Research and Training Institute, Dehradun

Controlling degradation of soil through erosion and rehabilitation of degraded lands.

The National Bureau of Soil Survey and Land Use Planning (NBSS and LUP), Nagpur

Inventorise and upgrade scientific information on the nature, extent and distribution of soils and associated climatic features.

Central Soil Salinity Research Institute (CSSRI), Karnal

Development of strategies for salinity control and management of salt affected soils and use of poor quality water.

Forestry Sector

A network of research institutions under the Indian Council of Forestry Research and Education (ICFRE), Dehradun is addressing problems related to the development of suitable technologies for afforestation and improving forest productivity. These include the Forest Research Institute, Dehradun

Institute of Forest Genetics and Tree Breeding, Coimbatore

Shelterbelt plantations of tree species and agroforestry options can play a crucial role in disaster mitigation efforts of Lakshadweep.

Water Resources

Central Ground Water Board (CGWB) under the Ministry of Water Resources is responsible for carrying out surveys and assessment of ground water resources and guiding in scientific and technical matters relating to ground water survey, monitoring and assessment.

The National Bureau of Soil Survey and Land Use Planning (NBSS & LUP), Nagpur

Inventorise and upgrade scientific information on the nature, extent and distribution of soils and associated climatic features.

India Soil and Land Use Survey (AISLUS)

Indian Space Research Organisation (ISRO)

National Remote Sensing Agency (NRSA)

Department of Space (DOS) Centres, such as the *Space Application Centre* (SAC)

India Meteorological Department is engaged in prediction and monitoring of natural disasters such as droughts and floods using long series of meteorological data and for the study of district level droughts.

National Medium Range Weather Forecasting Centre (NMRWFC)

Energy

Tata Energy Research Institute (TERI)

Council for People's Action and Rural Technology (CAPART)

Indian Renewable Energy Development Agency (IREDA)

Rural Development

National Institute of Rural Development (NIRD)

State Institutes of Rural Development (SIRDs)

Council for Advancement of People's Action & Rural Technology (CAPART)

National Bank for Agriculture and Rural Development (NABARD)

Coral Reef Protection

Central Pollution Control Board

Department of Ocean Development

Central Marine Fisheries Research Institute

Institutes on Disaster Management

Central Disaster Management Authority (Government of India, Ministry of Agriculture, Department of Agriculture & Cooperation, Natural Disaster) is the apex body for natural disaster management and mitigation.

National Centre for Disaster Management (NCDM) set up by the Indian Institute of Public Administration.

NCDM is the nodal agency for coordinating relief and rehabilitation work during natural calamities and for human resource development in the area of disaster management.

Centre for Disaster Management set up by the Y S Chavan Academy of Development Administration, Pune, conducts workshops and seminars for civil servants and government officials.

Disaster Management Institute, Bhopal set up after the gas tragedy, conducts awareness programmes for NGOs and the public at large.

Disaster Mitigation Institute, Ahmadabad, Gujarat.